D0456151

Imperial Germany and the Great War, 1914–1918

This important contribution to the successful textbook series New Approaches to European History explores the comprehensive impact of the First World War on Imperial Germany. It examines military aspects of the conflict, as well as the diplomacy, government, politics, and industrial mobilization of wartime Germany. Unlike other existing surveys, however, Roger Chickering's also offers a rich portrait of life on the home front: the pervasive effects of "total war" on wealthy and poor, men and women, young and old, farmers and city-dwellers, Protestants, Catholics, and Jews. At the same time, Roger Chickering analyzes the growing burdens of war and discusses the translation of the hardship of war into political opposition. This excellent, well-illustrated study of the military, political, and socio-economic effects of the First World War is essential reading for all students of German and European history, as well as for those interested in the history of war and society. Now appearing in a second edition, this accessible book reflects important new scholarship in the field and boasts an expanded and revised bibliography.

ROGER CHICKERING is Professor of History in the BMW Center for German and European Studies, Georgetown University. He is an established scholar of modern Germany and is the author of *Das Deutsche Reich und der Erste Weltkrieg* (2002); *Karl Lamprecht: A German Academic Life, 1856–1915* (1993); *We Men Who Feel Most German: A Cultural Study of the Pan-German League, 1886–1914* (1984); and *Imperial Germany and a World Without War: The Peace Movement and German Society 1892–1914* (1975).

NEW APPROACHES TO EUROPEAN HISTORY

Series editors
WILLIAM BEIK *Emory University*
T. C. W. BLANNING *Sidney Sussex College, Cambridge*

New Approaches to European History is an important textbook series, which provides concise but authoritative surveys of major themes and problems in European history since the Renaissance. Written at a level and length accessible to advanced school students and undergraduates, each book in the series addresses topics or themes that students of European history encounter daily: the series embraces both some of the more traditional subjects of study, and those cultural and social issues to which increasing numbers of school and college courses are devoted. A particular effort made to consider the wider international implications of the subject under scrutiny.

To aid the student reader, scholarly apparatus and annotation is light, but each work has full supplementary bibliographies and notes for further reading: where appropriate chronologies, maps, diagrams, and other illustrative material are also provided.

For a list of titles published in the series, please see end of book.

Imperial Germany and the Great War, 1914–1918

Second Edition

ROGER CHICKERING

CAMBRIDGE
UNIVERSITY PRESS

PUBLISHED BY THE PRESS SYNDICATE OF THE UNIVERSITY OF CAMBRIDGE
The Pitt Building, Trumpington Street, Cambridge, United Kingdom

CAMBRIDGE UNIVERSITY PRESS
The Edinburgh Building, Cambridge, CB2 2RU, UK
40 West 20th Street, New York, NY 10011–4211, USA
477 Williamstown Road, Port Melbourne, VIC 3207, Australia
Ruiz de Alarcón 13, 28014 Madrid, Spain
Dock House, The Waterfront, Cape Town 8001, South Africa

http://www.cambridge.org

First published 1998

Second edition 2004

Printed in the United Kingdom at the University Press, Cambridge

Typeface Plantin 10/12 pt.   *System* LATEX 2$_\varepsilon$ [TB]

A catalogue record for this book is available from the British Library

ISBN 0 521 83908 4 hardback
ISBN 0 521 54780 6 paperback

For Kyle

When I view the radiant valleys of our fatherland which spread out here at our feet, I can only wish: May the day never come when the hordes of war rage through them. And may the day also never come when we are forced to carry war to the valleys of a foreign people.

Gustav Wyneken
October 1913

Contents

Plates

Figures

Maps

Tables

Preface

This book originated in another project, which is at once broader in scope and much narrower in focus. In deference to the principle that total war requires total history, I have been studying the comprehensive impact of the First World War in a single mid-sized German city. In conjunction with this project, I decided several years ago to explore the history of the war and German society with a class of undergraduate students at the University of Oregon. I discovered that there was no suitable text for such a course. The present volume grew directly out of discussions with students in that class. It is conceived in the first instance for readers like them, but it is also intended for others who are interested in the modern history of Germany and Europe, as well as the history of war and society. The scholarly apparatus is designed for those whom the text entices into further reading.

It is now a pleasure to repay my many intellectual debts with public gratitude. My thanks go first to my students in Oregon, my former home, for contributions that pervade the volume. In addition, I owe great thanks to a number of scholars who have offered comments on the manuscript as it progressed. They include Gerald Feldman, Wilhelm Deist, Belinda Davis, Stig Förster, and Richard Stites, who is now my colleague at Georgetown. My friend Bruce Wonder, who counts himself in the category of "informed general reader," has also offered invaluable suggestions for the manuscript's improvement. My research assistant, David Freudenwald, provided much-needed help in my dealings with a number of libraries. Several institutions have also supported the manuscript in various stage of its gestation. My gratitude goes to the Gerda Henkel Foundation, which supported a year's research in Europe in 1991–92, the Graduate School at Georgetown University, which made possible several subsequent trips to Europe, and to the Woodrow Wilson International Center for Scholars in Washington DC, which provided me with the opportunity to complete the work in a stimulating atmosphere of intellectual exchange.

Abbreviations

SPD   Social Democratic party
KRA   War Raw Materials Section
OHL   Supreme Command of the Army
USPD   Independent German Social Democratic party
MSPD   Majority Social Democratic party

Prologue: Imperial Germany

"What a paradise this land is! What clean clothes, what good faces, what tranquil contentment, what prosperity, what genuine freedom, what superb government!"[1] Mark Twain's exclamations in 1878 to his friend and editor, William Dean Howells, sounded a theme that echoed in the judgments of countless visitors who followed the American writer to Germany. Indeed, the German empire's renown as a dynamic and prosperous land, whose accomplishments were the envy of the modern world, only grew during the next decades, as evidence accumulated of breathtaking change.

By the turn of the twentieth century, Germany had become Europe's foremost industrial power. In the production of steel and chemicals and in electrical engineering, the sectors that drove the so-called "second industrial revolution," Germany's accomplishments were rivaled only in the United States. German engineers were pioneers of the new industrial technologies. Mammoth firms like Krupp, Siemens, and Bayer spearheaded the growth of the German economy. Coal production in Germany increased more than seven times between 1870 and 1913, steel production fifteen times.[2] Gross national product multiplied six times in the same era. In a manner that belied Mark Twain's picture of "tranquil contentment," German society was transformed within a generation. The population exploded by nearly 60 percent between 1871 and 1910. Half of it farmed in 1875; less than one-third did in 1913. During the same interval, the number of Germans doubled whose primary occupations were in industry, and in 1913 they outnumbered Germans who worked in agriculture. In the wake of torrid industrial growth, Germany became one of the world's most urban societies. The capital city, Berlin, grew

---

[1] Samuel Clemens to William D. Howells, Frankfurt am Main, 4 May 1878, in *Mark Twain–Howells Letters: The Correspondence of Samuel L. Clemens and William D. Howells 1872–1910* (2 vols., Cambridge, MA, 1960), vol. I, 227.

[2] For a convenient survey of the pertinent statistics, as well as an accessible introduction to the German empire, see Volker R. Berghahn, *Imperial Germany, 1871–1914: Economy, Society, Culture, and Politics* (Providence and Oxford, 1994).

1

by nearly five times between 1871 and 1910, to more than 2,000,000 inhabitants; six other German cities counted over 500,000 inhabitants in 1910.

Other features of the German empire impressed contemporary observers no less. Germany's claim to "superb government" reflected the reputation of its bureaucracies for efficiency and incorruptibility. German trains ran on time; and the streets were clean. Defenders of Germany's constitution could likewise appeal to standards of efficiency in order to justify vesting the monarch with substantial authority and, conversely, limiting the powers of parliament. In an era when – in Germany and elsewhere – democratic government carried the taint of corruption and fecklessness, Germany's more authoritarian system could plausibly claim to embody "true freedom." In all events, it spawned the most progressive system of social insurance in the world, which offered entitlements that industrial workers do not to this day enjoy in the United States. In the eyes of most observers, however, the greatest emblem of bureaucratic authoritarianism was Germany's cultural achievement. The German public school system was reputed to be the finest and most comprehensive in the world. It banished illiteracy. Germany's public universities served as models throughout the world. Whether in medicine, the natural sciences, the social sciences, or the humanistic disciplines, German scholarship was preeminent. Between 1900 and 1925, over one-third of the Nobel prizes in chemistry and physics went to Germans. German was the international language of scientific discourse.

There was a darker side to this spectacle. The German empire was born on the battlefield; and the legacy of its birth had a profound and enduring impact on society and politics in the new state. The German army was the mightiest in the world, the model for military reformers everywhere. Soldiers enjoyed enormous influence and respect in Germany. The authoritarian features of the German constitution were designed in the first instance to isolate the army from civilian control. The views of the generals figured significantly in councils of state, while deference to martial virtues permeated institutions of civil society, from student fraternities to corporate board rooms. German nationalism, the civic religion of the new state, reflected the centrality of military values, as well as an aggressive confidence in Germany's growing industrial power and the conviction that German influence in the world ought to correspond to the country's economic might. Germany's participation in overseas colonialism began late, in the middle of the 1880s, but it became as loud and provocative as its most public champion, the emperor William II. It also accompanied the relentless construction of a battle fleet, which made Germany a naval power second only to Great Britain. In the early

years of the twentieth century, as a series of diplomatic crises in North
Africa and the Balkans raised the prospect of European war, the accents
in contemporary fascination with Imperial Germany changed, and admi-
ration for its industrial and cultural accomplishments ceded to apprehension over the combination of German military power and an erratic
foreign policy. "The ultimate aims of Germany surely are, without doubt,
to obtain the preponderance on the continent of Europe," read a bleak
British analysis in 1909, which concluded that Germany would then
"enter on a contest with us for maritime supremacy."[3]

After two great European wars had lent plausibility to this British judgment of German intentions, fascination with Imperial Germany migrated
to the historians.[4] The decisive moment in the recent historiography
of the German empire was in 1961, when the German historian Fritz
Fischer charged not only that the Imperial German government launched
the great European war in 1914, but also that Germany's leaders were
guided in this decision by ambitions that bore a chilling resemblance to
Hitler's hegemonic designs during the Second World War.[5] In the furious
debate that attended Fischer's provocation, the principal issue became the
German empire's location in a story that reached its terrible conclusion
in the Third Reich. Particularly among a younger generation of West
German historians, it became common to portray the history of Imperial
Germany as a critical juncture along a *Sonderweg*, a special German path
of social and political development. In this reading, the German route to
the modern world was plagued by the survival of "pre-industrial elites"
in positions of social and political power, notably in large-scale farming,
the upper echelons of the civil bureaucracies, and in the army, whose officer corps remained the preserve of the aristocracy.[6] The power of these
elites then served to frustrate the development of modern institutions
and attitudes conducive to democratic government. Because this view
clashed, however, with contemporary impressions of Imperial Germany's
vibrant modernity and industrial power, it came under attack itself.[7] In

---

[3] A. Nicolson to Edward Grey, St. Petersburg, 24 March 1909, in G. P. Gooch and Harold
Temperley (eds.), *British Documents on the Origins of the War* (11 vols., London, 1926–38),
vol. V, 737.
[4] For a survey of the literature, see Roger Chickering (ed.), *Imperial Germany: A Historiographical Companion* (Westport, CT, 1996); *cf.* James Retallack, *Germany in the Age of
Kaiser Wilhelm II* (New York, 1996).
[5] Fritz Fischer, *Griff nach der Weltmacht: Die Kriegszielpolitik des kaiserlichen Deutschland
1914–1918* (Düsseldorf, 1961); in English as *Germany's Aims in the First World War*
(New York, 1967).
[6] Hans-Ulrich Wehler, *The German Empire, 1871–1918* (Leamington Spa, 1985).
[7] David Blackbourn and Geoff Eley, *The Peculiarities of German History: Bourgeois Society
and Politics in Nineteenth-Century Germany* (Oxford and New York, 1984).

an alternative reading, the problems of Germany's long-term development towards Nazism, and hence the pathologies of Imperial Germany, inhered in the social pressures and disruptions of modernity itself.

The immediate issue in the present volume is not the place of Imperial Germany in the incubation of National Socialism. It is instead the death of Imperial Germany at war. This focus makes it possible to skirt the now tired debate over the modernity of the *Kaiserreich*. The recent discussions have, however, isolated aspects of the German empire's prewar history that are relevant to its wartime ordeal. The most pertinent feature of this history was the persistence of deep internal divisions in the state that emerged in 1871. These divisions were of several orders, and they raised difficult questions about the sources of the new state's integration, legitimacy, and cohesion.

One order of division was immediately obvious, for it was written into the constitution of 1871. The German empire was a federation of twenty-five constituent states. By the terms of the constitution, the states retained many of the attributes of sovereignty, including their dynasties, the bulk of their institutional apparatus, and most of the powers that these semi-authoritarian regimes had traditionally exercised over their subjects. The purview of the federal executive in Berlin was limited to matters of common concern, such as national defense, foreign affairs, and aspects of commercial policy, like tariffs, while the powers of the federal legislature were restricted still further, in the first instance to budgetary questions. The lower house of the federal parliament, the Reichstag, was democratically elected (by adult males); and for just this reason, it was largely excluded from deliberations on basic matters of state, such as foreign and military policy.

The result of these arrangements was the fragmentation of Germany's basic political and administrative structures. The public institutions that most immediately affected the lives of Germans were not national in scope. They fell instead into the jurisdictions of the states or municipal governments, which themselves remained autonomous in significant respects. The federal government neither legislated nor administered policies that related to police and criminal-justice systems, transportation and communication, poor-relief, public health, or education (at all levels). State and local government also levied and collected the direct taxes on property and income.

Germany's constituent states were not, however, equal. They ranged in size and importance from the dwarf principality of Schwarzburg-Sondershausen to the kingdom of Prussia, which sprawled over two-thirds of the empire's land area and encompassed about 60 percent of its population. Prussia predominated in Imperial Germany. The Prussian king was the German Kaiser, or emperor; the Prussian prime minister was normally the federal chancellor, and his Prussian ministerial colleagues normally doubled as the top officials in the federal government. None of these officials was responsible, however, to parliament for their power; they served instead at the pleasure of their monarch. In the upper house of the federal legislature, which was called the Bundesrat (or Federal Council) and comprised fifty-eight members selected by the governments of the German states, the Prussian vote was usually sufficient to determine the agenda and always sufficient to block constitutional change. The powers of the federal parliament were much less extensive than those of the Prussian parliament, which was not democratically elected. The franchise in Prussia, as in most of the other states (and municipalities), was restricted in ways calculated to ensure the power of the wealthy and educated. In the Prussian case, the suffrage system also preserved a disproportionate voice for the Junker nobility, the class whose great estates dominated the lands where grain was grown east of the Elbe River.

Institutional fragmentation overlay other cleavages. The areas that were forged together in 1871 were confessionally mixed, and these divisions remained pervasive and deep-seated. They originated in the Protestant Reformation of the sixteenth century. That they continued to inspire intense loyalties in the early twentieth century was due in large measure to the *Kulturkampf*, the bitter conflict that marked Imperial Germany's first decades, when the Protestant rulers of the new state undertook a campaign to reduce the autonomy of the Catholic church in the German territories. Among other things, legislation passed during the 1870s in Prussia and other states extended controls over the training and appointment of the Catholic clergy, regulated parochial education, and banned the Jesuits and a number of other religious orders from German soil. The campaign fed on the belief, which was popular among German Protestants, that Catholics owed their ultimate loyalties to the Pope and hence could not be true Germans. Before it abated in the 1880s, the *Kulturkampf* mobilized German Catholics in defense of their own interests; and it left a legacy of mistrust and suspicion that had by no means disappeared in 1914.

The Catholic minority counted about 40 percent of the German population. The German church comprised five archbishoprics and twenty-five bishoprics. The flock was concentrated in the south and west – in Bavaria, southern Baden and Württemberg, and in the Prussian provinces of Westphalia and the Rhineland, as well as in Prussian Poland and Silesia to the east. Although it encompassed a full social spectrum, from peasants and landed aristocrats to businessmen, professionals, and workers in the cities, Catholic Germany tended to be more agrarian and less

industrial or commercial, than Protestant Germany, so confessional segregation reinforced popular Protestant images of backward and supersti-
tious Catholics. The gulf was emphasized, in all events, by the systematic
underprivileging of Catholics in public bureaucracies, the officer corps,
the professions, and in higher education.

The Protestant majority in Germany was organized in thirty-nine separate churches. Most of these churches were Lutheran in their doctrinal
and liturgical coloration. All of them were state institutions. Their heads
were Germany's secular rulers, from the Hamburg senate to the grand
duke of Baden or the Prussian king, who oversaw ecclesiastical administration, dogma, and discipline, and appointed the Protestant clergy.
While it was the principal confession in the northern and eastern parts of
the country, Protestantism also predominated in the country as a whole.
Nearly all the dynasties were Protestant, as were most of the elite groups
that dominated Germany's public bureaucracies, both military and civilian. In addition, Germany's civic religion carried clear Protestant overtones; and Martin Luther was a national symbol in a way that no German
Catholic church figure could be.

Patterns of confessional distribution reinforced regional divisions in
Imperial Germany, and they, too, survived well into the twentieth century. Compulsory elementary schooling eliminated illiteracy, but it did
not erase regional patterns of speech, which were sufficient to block oral
communication between Bavarian and Frisian peasants – or, for that matter, between Bavarian peasants and middle-class residents of the Bavarian
capital city, Munich. The vitality of local dialects fed on regional tensions.
Anti-Prussian sentiment was common; and it fostered local patriotism in
other states, like Bavaria, as well as within Prussia itself – in regions such
as the Rhineland, where local traditions and confessional practices kept
uneasy company with rule from Berlin.

These antagonisms were particularly marked in regions that were
inhabited by groups whose first language was not German. Imperial
Germany's principal ethnic minorities included Danes in the north,
French-speaking people in the western territories annexed in 1871, and
several million Poles in the eastern provinces of Prussia. All of these
groups had to contend with official policies of "Germanization," whose
object was, among other things, to compel them to use the German language in schools and public business. None of these minorities was happy
under German rule, but the Catholic Poles were the largest and best
organized for resistance, and hence the most persistent source of ethnic
conflict.

The real template of domestic tension in Imperial Germany lay elsewhere, however. Class conflict was the product of prodigious economic

development and social change at the end of the nineteenth century. These processes generated a huge industrial workforce. While working-class organizations of several confessional and political colorations took shape, the mobilization of the German proletariat transpired principally under the militant banner of Marxism. By the beginning of the twentieth century, the Social Democratic Party of Germany (SPD) was the largest and best organized socialist party in the world. Its program envisaged the revolutionary overthrow of Germany's basic social and political institutions, the replacement of capitalism and private property with socialism, and the establishment of democratic government in place of Germany's system of semi-authoritarian rule.

This agenda looked anything but idle, as the growth of the Socialist party registered in the relentless increase of its vote in successive elections to the Reichstag. The government responded to this specter with a broad array of countermeasures, which included the outlawing of the SPD between 1878 and 1890, persecution of the party thereafter by the police and in the courts, and, for the last resort, plans for a counterrevolutionary *coup d'état* against the Reichstag. Imperial Germany was also the site of bitter industrial strife. With the support and encouragement of the state, employers contested the organization of the labor force at every juncture. Despite all these efforts, over 2,000,000 workers belonged to Socialist trade unions in 1912, while the SPD itself counted 1,000,000 members. When, in the federal parliamentary elections of the same year, the Socialists registered a spectacular victory, winning one-third of the popular vote and returning as the largest party in the Reichstag, their success provoked consternation and alarm outside the working class, as well as the prospect of constitutional crisis. Although signs abounded by the turn of the century that the revolutionary energy of the party was moderating amid the material gains that organized labor had achieved, the Socialists' success symbolized powerful resentments against the manifold sources of social and political inequality in the German empire.

Regional, confessional, ethnic, and social conflict was thus rife. It focused on the very structures of German politics. Parliamentary rule on the basis of democratic suffrage was virtually nowhere in place – neither in federal, state, nor local deliberative bodies. The desirability of democratic rule was, however, a principal issue at all levels of government, advocated foremost by the Socialists and Progressive liberals, resisted tenaciously by the Conservatives and other groups on the political right.

The ubiquity of domestic conflict lent issues of legitimacy and national integration a special urgency in Imperial Germany. From the beginning, the effort to cultivate a popular sense of national unity in Imperial Germany featured an emphasis on enemies, both domestic and foreign.

The demonization of Catholics and Socialists, branding them as *Reichs-feinde* ("enemies of the fatherland") was one facet of this effort, which was calculated to justify their persecution while it unified the rest of the population in opposition to them. The campaign found expression not only in exclusionary legislation and the courts, but also in schoolbooks, the sermons of Protestant clergymen, and patriotic oratory. A variation on this theme provided a degree of ideological coherence to the German conduct of foreign affairs. The slogan "*Feinde ringsum!*" ("enemies on all sides of us") enjoined national solidarity and the suspension of domestic conflict in the face of a hostile world. Bismarck and those who succeeded him atop the national government were alive to the domestic implications of international rivalries. The German decisions to establish overseas colonies and then to construct a battlefleet were due in part to considerations of domestic policy – to the calculation that colonial empire and a navy would become proud symbols of national power, around which much of the population, even Catholics and industrial workers, might rally in support of established institutions. The pursuit of "active" policies towards the country's diplomatic rivals was designed to achieve the same ends.

The deterioration of European international relations after the turn of the twentieth century owed a great deal to these German calculations. It also led to Germany's growing isolation among the European powers and placed the country's leaders under additional duress, lest the appearance of diplomatic weakness further threaten their domestic position. At home, a "national opposition" deployed in loud nationalist associations, such as the Pan-German League and the German Army League, to assail the government in the name of patriotism for its feeble defense of German interests at home and abroad. The victory of the Socialists in the elections of 1912 fueled this attack and lent plausibility to visions of the nation's doom. The sense of apprehension and beleaguerment lingered into the summer of 1914, when another diplomatic crisis intruded.

In 1871, German national unification came in the wake of foreign war. The transcendence of domestic divisions in a great moment of international crisis was thus a defining motif in the history of Imperial Germany. As conflict continued to plague domestic politics in the new German empire, the motif endured as an enticement to statesmen and nationalist politicians. Like the preoccupation with enemies, competition for colonies and naval power gestured to its logic. Decisions made in the summer of 1914 capitulated to the same logic. "Let us regard war as holy, like the purifying force of fate," proclaimed one nationalist leader in 1913, "for it will awaken in our people all that is great and ready for selfless sacrifice, while it cleanses our soul of the mire of petty egotistical concerns."[8] The patriotic enthusiasm that swept the country in the summer of the next year suggested that this sentiment was broadly shared, that a great many people hoped that war would banish "petty egotistical concerns" and bring Germans of all classes and confessions together in a great common experience.

The great war that followed did indeed provide a common national experience. It affected profoundly the lives of every German man, woman, and child who endured it. After the initial enthusiasm had passed, however, the common experience of war not only exacerbated old domestic conflicts; it bred new ones. As the war's ramifications seeped into every aspect of life in Germany, they eroded the legitimacy of a government that had embarked upon the conflict with little anticipation of the dreadful costs. Imperial Germany thus died as it had been born, in war. This is the story.

[8] Quoted in Roger Chickering, "Die Alldeutschen erwarten den Krieg," in Jost Dülffer and Karl Holl (eds.), *Bereit zum Krieg: Kriegsmentalität im wilhelminischen Deutschland 1890–1914* (Göttingen, 1986), 25.

1 The war begins

It began, to use the formula familiar in today's newspapers, with an "act of state-sponsored terrorism." The archduke Francis Ferdinand was the heir-apparent to the Habsburg throne of Austria–Hungary; and when, on 28 June 1914, a Serbian student shot him and his wife to death in Sarajevo, the capital of the Austrian province of Bosnia, the act provoked astonishment and outrage throughout Europe. Public excitement quickly receded, however, despite lingering rumors in the newspapers – subsequently substantiated – that officials of the Serbian government had been complicit in the assassination. In Germany and elsewhere the summer season had begun. The onset of warm weather signaled travel for those who could afford it; and for those who could not, it brought less idle adjustments in the annual rhythms of life in town and countryside.

In Berlin, the events in Sarajevo provoked a series of fateful deliberations during the first weeks of July. The German leadership concluded that the assassination carried far-reaching implications for German security. Austria-Hungary was Germany's principal ally. The Serbian affront promised to encourage discontent not only among the South Slav inhabitants of Austria-Hungary, but also among the other ethnic groups that made up the Habsburg monarchy. In the eyes of the German leaders, the logic of this process boded the dissolution of the monarchy and ultimately Germany's full diplomatic and military isolation in Europe.

This alarming prospect loomed over the consultations in the German capital. The decisions that emerged out of these deliberations have themselves given rise to a bitter dispute among professional historians.[1] At the center of the dispute stands the German chancellor, Theobald von Bethmann Hollweg, the civilian head of the German federal government. Some historians, with Fritz Fischer in the lead, have argued that Bethmann seized upon the assassination as the pretext to launch a long-planned war of aggression, whose goal was German hegemony on the

---

[1] John A. Moses, *The Politics of Illusion: The Fischer Controversy in German Historiography* (New York, 1975).

Plate 1   Theobald von Bethmann Hollweg (reproduced courtesy of the Hulton Getty Picture Collection Limited)

European continent. The preponderance of evidence, however, now suggests instead that the chancellor pursued a somewhat more cautious policy, which grew out of his anxiety over the future of the Austrian monarchy, whose survival, he believed, did justify the risk of a European war. Bethmann was strengthened in this belief by the country's leading soldier, the chief of the army's General Staff, Helmuth von Moltke. Moltke's calculations were technical. They originated in his fear that military reforms already underway in France and Russia, Germany's principal continental antagonists, would reach completion in 1917 and render the alliance of these two powers invincible thereafter. With this date in mind, Moltke recommended risking a general war, which he believed would be fought "the sooner the better."

The thinking of both Bethmann and Moltke betrayed as well the malaise that was rife among Germany's political and social elites over the country's domestic future – particularly over the dramatic growth of the world's most formidable Socialist party. Domestic concerns figured in the German calculations. A diplomatic triumph promised to rally public opinion – at least non-Socialist opinion – in favor of the established order; on the other hand, Germany's numerous patriotic organizations would as surely mobilize public anger if the government failed to act vigorously in response to the new challenge.

Debates in Vienna had meanwhile also produced a decision to "settle accounts" with Serbia, and when an Austrian emissary arrived in Berlin in early July 1914 to seek German help, he received the famous "blank check" – the assurance of full German support – along with German pleas to move swiftly, lest public sympathy for the Austrian position dissipate along with international outrage over the assassination.[2] During the next weeks, the German leaders thus prodded their allies into an option – war with Serbia – that the Austrians themselves had originally defined. The Germans did so in full view of the possible consequences, chief among them the intrusion of Russia into the dispute; and their decision was tempered only in the hope that the military conflict could be localized between the two immediate antagonists. The ultimatum that the Austrians thereupon delivered to the Serbs on 23 July was the product of this policy; the demands it made on the Serbian government were calculated to be unacceptable. In all events, the document provoked a diplomatic crisis that, within little more than a week, activated Europe's alliance network and brought Russian military intervention on Serbia's behalf,

[2] Samuel R. Williamson, Jr., *Austria–Hungary and the Origins of the First World War* (London, 1991); Manfried Rauchensteiner, *Der Tod des Doppeladlers: Österreich-Ungarn und der Erste Weltkrieg* (Graz, 1993).

Germany's on Austria's behalf, France's on Russia's, and Great Britain's on France's.

The "spirit of 1914"

The announcement of the Austrian ultimatum on 24 July (a Friday) electrified public discourse in Germany. The principal media of local communication in 1914 were the newspaper and the public placard; and the points where they were displayed became the nodes of public excitement in the final week of July, as the crisis unfolded. In towns throughout the land, crowds gathered at newsstands, the windows of buildings where newspapers were published, public houses, and at kiosks, in order to learn of the most recent announcements – and to embellish the bulletins with all manner of rumor. As the crisis intensified, the crowds grew; and in many places the mood became euphoric to the accompaniment of military and civilian bands, the singing of patriotic songs, the waving of flags, and spontaneous processions through the centers of cities, particularly in university towns, where students provided the lead.

The spectacle had already taken on the air of a public festival when, on 31 July (another Friday), the big news broke. The kiosks and newspapers now announced that the Russian armies were in general mobilization. The German proclamation of a state of imminent war with Russia followed immediately. The headlines of the first four days in August then registered the inexorable march of events towards general war – the declaration of a state of national emergency in Germany and the mobilization of the German armies, the German declaration of war on Russia, the mobilization of the French army, the German declaration of war on that country, and the British intervention against Germany. The public festivals in Germany kept pace with the escalating drama, but their focus shifted to the barracks that housed the local regiments. Armed young men in uniform now took over the processions through town, as they began to make their way to the front, towards an adventure that most Germans thought would be over by Christmas.

The exhilaration of early August was captured in innumerable scenes – many of them photographed – of flag-bedecked public squares, like the Marktplatz in Darmstadt, where crowds gathered in increasing numbers as the crisis reached its climax. The most famous scenes took place in Berlin. There, at the royal palace, the Kaiser proclaimed on 4 August that the war had suspended domestic strife and that henceforth he "recognized no parties, only Germans." Several blocks away, the Reichstag gave formal expression to the same sentiments, when – to the enormous relief of the government – the Socialists joined the other parties in a unanimous vote in favor of the credits necessary to finance the war.

These were heady days. Testimony abounds from those who participated in these festive scenes and were captured in the conviction that a new era in German history had begun. A historian in Leipzig testified to "a single great feeling of moral elevation, a soaring of religious sentiment, in short, the ascent of a whole people to the heights. . . ."[3] "I have experienced such a physical and moral condition of luminosity and euphoria two or three times since," recalled the writer Carl Zuckmayer, who witnessed the events in Berlin, "but never with that sharpness and intensity."[4] And a restless young man in Munich, who appeared in one of the photographs amid the multitudes at the Odeonsplatz, found the experience "like a release from the painful feelings of my youth." "Overpowered by stormy enthusiasm," he wrote later, "I fell down on my knees and thanked heaven from an overflowing heart for granting me the good fortune of being permitted to live at this time."[5]

These statements reflected what might be called an initial "reading" of the war, a rendering of events that quickly became known variously as the "ideas of 1914" or the "spirit of 1914."[6] Countless documents of the summer of 1914 – speeches, newspaper articles, letters, and diary entries, as well as photographs – spoke to a spontaneous and overpowering sense of national unity, a unanimity of views about the origins and meaning of the conflict that was beginning. This consensus was, to be sure, inchoate and vaguely formulated; it nonetheless framed the public understanding of the war, and in some circles it proved remarkably durable.

Its foundation was the proposition that Germany had been attacked. Whatever the truth of this proposition, the German government had managed by its skillful manipulation of the news during the crisis, and then by the selective release of diplomatic documents, to convey the impression that Germany's mobilization was only a response to the aggression of Russia and its western allies. The motto *"Feinde ringsum"* now became the moral foundation of the war effort, which, in the eyes of most Germans who experienced it, remained for the duration a defensive struggle.

---

[3] Quoted in Roger Chickering, *Karl Lamprecht: A German Academic Life (1856–1915)* (Atlantic Heights, NJ, 1993), 433.

[4] Quoted in Eric Leed, *No Man's Land: Combat and Identity in World War I* (Cambridge and New York, 1979), 39.

[5] Adolf Hitler, *Mein Kampf* (translated by Ralph Mannheim, Boston, 1943), 161.

[6] Wolfgang Kruse, "Die Kriegsbegeisterung im Deutschen Reich zu Beginn des Ersten Weltkrieges: Entstehungszusammenhänge, Grenzen und ideologische Strukturen," in Marcel van der Linden and Gottfried Mergner (eds.), *Kriegsbegeisterung und mentale Kriegsvorbereitung: Interdisziplinäre Studien* (Berlin, 1991), 73–87; Jeffrey Verhey, *The Spirit of 1914: Militarism, Myth and Mobilization in Germany* (Cambridge, 2000).

This conviction could not alone engender the feelings that emerged in the summer of 1914. The public celebrations testified as well to the belief that the transition from peace to war had produced a dramatic break, a fundamental transformation in German society and politics, and that the forces that would galvanize the new Germany were nothing like those that had plagued the old one. The contrasts that informed this thinking reflected many of the issues that had long polarized German politics. They were captured in the dichotomy, made famous at the end of the previous century by the German sociologist Ferdinand Tönnies, between "society" (*Gesellschaft*) and "community" (*Gemeinschaft*). The one suggested a social system ridden by materialism, artificiality, and the selfish and calculated pursuit of individual interest; the other implied a community bound organically by patriotic idealism and selfless determination to achieve common goals. "One perceived in all camps that it was not a matter merely of the unity of a gain-seeking partnership, but that an inner renovation of our whole state was needed." These were the terms in which the historian Friedrich Meinecke, who had just arrived at the university in Berlin as the war broke out, recorded the German transition from peace to war. "We generally believed," he continued, "that this [renovation] had already commenced and that it would progress further in the common experiences of war."[7] Meinecke's expectation was widely shared. The common experience of war promised the transformation of basic relationships among Germans – the suspension, if not the transcendence of narrow loyalties of class, confession, and party. When the Kaiser announced that he only recognized Germans, he gave expression to the same belief, as did the theologian who wrote that "my first impression was that war changed men, and it also changed the relationship between men."[8]

The drama and extravagant expectations of war lent almost mystical status to the "spirit of 1914," and not a little of this mysticism has colored subsequent historical writings on the subject. It soon became an article of faith that Germans had entered the war in euphoric unanimity. In their search for the roots of these emotions, commentators have written of a general flight from (or into) modernity, the longing to escape from the boredom of civilian life, or the venting of primitive drives.[9] Much of the commentary is speculation; and even basic generalizations about the unanimity of enthusiasm require qualification. The evidence on

---

[7] Friedrich Meinecke, *The German Catastrophe: Reflections and Recollections* (Boston, 1950), 25.

[8] Quoted in Leed, *No Man's Land*, 42.

[9] Modris Eksteins, *Rites of Spring: The Great War and the Birth of the Modern Age* (Boston, 1989).

which these generalizations rest is drawn largely from urban Germany. The attitudes of women and men in the countryside and small towns await the attention they deserve. Nor did the euphoria over war extend to all of urban Germany. "There was no unified 'August experience,'" writes a historian who has examined this phenomenon in Darmstadt, "rather there were many different August experiences."[10] In Darmstadt and elsewhere, anxiety was as widespread as jubilation. The leaders of the German Socialist party and trade unions endorsed the war, but this step marked a rupture with the pacifism and internationalism that had long animated the German labor movement; and many in this movement – and elsewhere – accepted the war with reluctance and fatalism, but with little enthusiasm. Finally, generalizations about the German "spirit of 1914" must accommodate evidence that the public reception of war was similar in other countries, and that the scenes in Berlin and Munich were indistinguishable from those in London, Paris, and St. Petersburg.

Nonetheless, in its German context the "spirit of 1914" was of vital importance to the history of the war that was now beginning. It massively informed the reaction of the most powerful, influential, and articulate people in the country – the men of property, education, and high birth, whose military, economic, political, and cultural power put them in positions to represent the experience of war to Germans of all stations. The incantations of community spoke foremost to anxieties that had long been resident in these elite circles; in fact, the *Gemeinschaft* that they invoked in the summer of 1914 represented a mirror image of the society over which they actually presided. On the eve of war, Imperial Germany was not united. Its society, culture, and political system were characterized by all manner of discord. Virtually no issue debated in the German houses of parliament – whether it had to do with taxes, tariffs, canal-building, schools, welfare, or defense policy – failed to stir these tensions. Well might political life in Germany have conveyed the impression of narrowness and the pursuit of self-interest, for the parties were wedded to parochial constituencies, divided by basic differences and suspicions, and they found it difficult to act durably in concert.

The "spirit of 1914" implied the definitive end of all these divisions in the face of the external threat. Germans of all stations were to be bound in a great common experience, which would recast fundamentally the dynamics of national life. The difficulty was that this rhapsody on national unity offered no realistic formula for solving the problems that beset Germany in 1914, to say nothing of problems in the offing. The

---

[10] Michael Stöcker, *"Augusterlebnis 1914" in Darmstadt: Legende und Wirklichkeit* (Darmstadt, 1994), 9.

"spirit of 1914" was bound instead to raise expectations that the pressures of industrial warfare were calculated to frustrate. Compelling practical questions remained unaddressed. How was the country to be governed, particularly once the consensus of the early days receded? Who was to make the painful decisions about allocating the burdens of war? How in fact were these growing burdens to be allocated? The initial elation suggested that they would be equitably distributed, but was this expectation consistent with the mechanisms of capitalism, which preserved fundamental inequalities of wealth and access to goods and services? How far was the transformation of human relationships to extend? Were German women, who constituted roughly half of the adult population but were everywhere excluded from politics, to be accorded full membership in the new national community?

The "spirit of 1914" offered little practical guidance for negotiating the unimagined strains of war in the twentieth century. It also brought to the fore basic issues of social and political equity, which had long plagued the country. Its premise was the involvement of all Germans in a great national exertion. It implied as well, however, an equitable sharing of both the burdens and rewards of this endeavor. Once these expectations were shown to be empty, the "spirit of 1914" took on the aura of an elusive fantasy, a painful reminder of the idealism that had reigned in the first hour. While some circles henceforth attempted to manipulate it for their own ends, the expectations that it raised became the object of growing popular discontent. The "spirit of 1914" framed the war in terms that could only nourish disillusionment, which commenced almost the moment the German armies encountered the dreadful new realities of combat.

The plan

The armies of the European powers had not clashed in almost a half century. Nonetheless, memories of the last of these conflicts, which resulted in the crushing defeat of France by the armies of Prussia and its German allies in 1870–71, dominated the thinking of every professional soldier who, during the ensuing era, was called upon to forecast the next European war. Among military planners from Paris to St. Petersburg, agreement reigned in retrospect that the German victory over France had been due, above all, to the superiority of military institutions that the Prussians had introduced in the 1860s. A series of reforms turned the Prussian army into a body of short-term conscripts and reserves, who were initially mobilized in the localities where they were recruited; from here they were then deployed, combat-ready, to the front. As a

consequence, Prussian troops arrived in greater numbers and better prepared to fight the decisive early battles that settled the outcome of the
whole campaign. The other German states had already begun to reorga-
nize their armies on this pattern in the 1860s. Then, in 1870–71, the
numerical superiority, mobility, and coordination of these formations
brought the humiliation of both the professional army of Imperial France
and the militias raised by the new government of republican France.

In the aftermath of the Franco-Prussian War, the armies of every
continental power underwent restructuring on the Prussian model. The
specifics varied, but all armies instituted a combination of conscription
and reserve levies, into which conscripts passed after several years of active
service. The continental armies also emulated the Prussians in establishing the corps as the central administrative and operational unit and in
anchoring each of these bodies in a home-district in peacetime, where
it recruited and barracked its own constituent combat units, drew its
supplies, and underwent its initial mobilization. Finally, in order to coordinate the movements of these units onto and about the field of battle,
European armies established – again on the Prussian model – centralized
general-staff organizations, which linked planning agencies in the capital
through a network of staff officers to the headquarters of the combat units.
Conscription guaranteed that the size of European armies increased in
pace with the growth of population, so that the armies that clashed in a
future war would dwarf those that had met in 1870.[11] Nonetheless, military planning everywhere remained wedded to the idea that the dynamics
of combat had not changed since 1870, that the first encounters between
armies would prove decisive in any future campaign, and that victory
therefore awaited the side that best organized its forces for rapid mobilization and initial deployment. These calculations put a premium on the
management and planning of military forces, for they suggested that the
issue in any future struggle would be all but settled before the first shots
were exchanged.

The army in the German empire represented the epitome of these
principles, while its development after 1871 reflected both the demographic and technological transformations of the late nineteenth century.
Technically, there was no single "German army."[12] Its great core was the

[11] See David Stevenson, *Armaments and the Coming of War: Europe, 1904–1914* (Oxford, 1996); David G. Herrmann, *The Arming of Europe and the Making of the First World War* (Princeton, 1996).

[12] Stig Förster, "The Armed Forces and Military Planning," in Roger Chickering (ed.), *Imperial Germany: A Historiographical Companion* (Westport, CT, 1996), 454–88; Martin Kitchen, *The German Officer Corps, 1890–1914* (Oxford, 1968); Herbert Rosinski, *The German Army* (New York, 1966), 76–130.

army of the state of Prussia, which had absorbed the armies of most of the smaller German states after unification in 1871. Several of the larger German states – the kingdoms of Saxony, Württemberg, and Bavaria – retained degrees of administrative control over their own units in peacetime, including the powers of promotion within their officer corps. Upon declaration of war, however, the constitution provided that all German contingents come under the command of the German emperor. The effect of this provision was to place all German units under the operational control of the Prussian General Staff.

The pattern of military administration was nonetheless uniform throughout the German empire. On the eve of war in 1914, German land forces were organized into 217 infantry regiments distributed into twenty-five corps, which were in turn based in "home" military districts, called *Wehrkreise*. The peacetime strength of the army numbered about 800,000 soldiers of all arms, who had been called up at the age of twenty. Upon completion of a two-year term of service, these young men passed for five years into a first levy of reserves, where they remained available for action alongside the active troops, and then into the *Landwehr*, or second levy of reserves, in which they served until they were nearly forty years old. The active peacetime army thus remained small, but combining the active troops with the first-levy reserves made it possible within a matter of days to mobilize a well-trained combat force nearly three times as large.

The soldiers who were the objects of these maneuvers were supplied with the military fruits of industrial advance. In Germany and elsewhere, combining technologies of steel and nitrate explosives had led to the introduction of rapid-firing weapons that were vastly more durable, long-ranged, accurate, and destructive than those of the Franco-Prussian war. The standard infantry weapon in the German army was a bolt-action magazine rifle, which fired 7.65mm shells. Its effective range was two kilometers. The heavier weapons were more fearsome still. To every infantry regiment was attached a machine-gun company, each of which tended six weapons that fired up to 500 rounds per minute at a range of four kilometers. The standard artillery piece was a breach-loading 77mm field gun, which had a range of 8.4 kilometers; this weapon, which represented the foundation of the artillery arm, was distributed in 633 batteries throughout the army. It was supplemented by an array of heavier guns and howitzers, most of which were designed to accompany the movements of footsoldiers and cavalry.

The dramatic increase in the size of European armies and the sophistication of the tools that they employed portended far-reaching changes in the face of warfare; but their impact was difficult for planners to gauge. Most indications suggested the growing difficulty of mobile, offensive operations by mass armies in the face of entrenched defenses and the intense fire-power of these new weapons. For the German planners, these prospects presented special strategic problems. The great challenge in Berlin was to devise an effective way to fight on two fronts against the allied armies of France and Russia, both of which offered formidable obstacles to offensive operations. If the sheer size of the Russian army militated against a rapid victory in this theater, the construction of a string of redoubtable fortresses in eastern France, from Belfort to Verdun, dimmed German hopes for a reprise of the triumphs of 1870 in the west.

German planners had designed a succession of unpalatable solutions to these strategic problems before Alfred von Schlieffen became Chief of the General Staff in 1891.[13] Schlieffen embodied – to the point of caricature – the German conviction that planning represented the key to success in modern warfare. He was more alive than most of his contemporaries to the difficulties of mounting offensive operations against well-established defensive positions; and he had a dread of frontal offensives at all levels of combat. He was also convinced that his forces could not prevail in a long war against the combined resources of Germany's likely antagonists. If he believed nonetheless that the country could win a two-front war, his confidence resided above all in the organization and managerial efficiency of the German army – the virtues required to mobilize a force that would be initially so superior in numbers and mobility as to inflict decisive defeats on its enemies.

Schlieffen's tenure in office was devoted to planning a war that Germany could win against both France and Russia. He concluded that German forces would have to engage these antagonists one at a time and that the anticipated sluggishness of the Russian mobilization recommended an initial campaign in the west, against the French. The specifics of this campaign, which was to culminate in the destruction of the French armies, then became Schlieffen's obsession. The general envisaged a colossal strategic envelopment, a twentieth-century reprise of Cannae, the great battle in which the Carthaginian warrior Hannibal had destroyed an entire Roman army in 216 BC. Schlieffen's vision featured the outflanking of the French fortress system by means of a grandiose wheeling movement through Belgium and into France from the north. That this scenario meant the violation of a sovereign state's neutrality, hence the addition of Belgium and probably Britain to the roster of

---

[13] Arden Bucholz, *Moltke, Schlieffen, and Prussian War Planning* (Providence and Oxford, 1991); Helmut Otto, *Schlieffen und der Generalstab: Der preussisch-deutsche Generalstab unter der Leitung des Generals von Schlieffen 1891–1905* (East Berlin, 1966); Jehuda Wallach, *The Dogma of the Battle of Annihilation: The Theories of Clausewitz and Schlieffen and Their Impact on the German Conduct of Two World Wars* (Westport, CT, 1986).

Germany's enemies, weighed little on Schlieffen, for whom diplomatic considerations (and their long-term military implications) were in all events of less moment than the immediate calculations of war. The contours of his vast design were already in evidence in the first drafts of the plan that bore his name.[14] In subsequent revisions, it became bolder still (see map 1). The arc of the German pivot broadened, and the route of its forward elements extended northward into Holland and westward to the English Channel. The advance of the German armies into France from the north was to complement the retreat of German forces in the south, so that the French would be lured into a breathtaking "reversal of fronts," a strategic "revolving-door," in which the French armies would find the bulk of the German forces in their rear.

The plan was a tribute not only to Schlieffen's fantasy but also to his passion for detail. It represented the apotheosis of the idea that planning reigned supreme in modern war. It scripted the entire campaign. It prescribed movements down to the level of individual corps during the projected forty-two days of the apocalypse. But in its sovereign inflexibility, its disregard for what the great military philosopher Karl von Clausewitz had called the "frictions" of warfare, and in its inattention to the manpower and logistical requirements of the massive armies on which it imposed such titanic expectations, Schlieffen's plan defied a lot of professional wisdom and created perplexing problems for the man who succeeded him in 1906.

This was Moltke, the nephew of the great soldier who had led the Prussian armies to victory in the mid-century wars of unification.[15] The younger Moltke's legacy was thus difficult in more than one respect; and his caution reflected a deep sense of personal insecurity, as well as his professional doubts about the military plan that he had inherited. Many of the adjustments that he wrote into Schlieffen's plan addressed its logistical deficiencies, but his critics later charged that his alterations also sapped the plan of its basic conception and brilliance. In the calculation that Germany could ill afford another enemy in the field, he decided not to invade Holland – a step that also reduced the arc of the German wheeling motion and shortened the supply lines of its vanguard units. More controversial was another decision, which followed from his reluctance to allow French forces onto German territory. Moltke strengthened the left wing of his forces, the southern sector along the French border,

---

[14] Gerhard Ritter, *The Schlieffen Plan: Critique of a Myth* (New York, 1958). The plan is currently the object of an intense dispute: see Terence Zuber, *Inventing the Schlieffen Plan: German War Planning, 1871–1914* (Oxford, 2002).

[15] Annika Mombauer, *Helmuth von Moltke and the Origins of the First World War* (Cambridge, 2001).

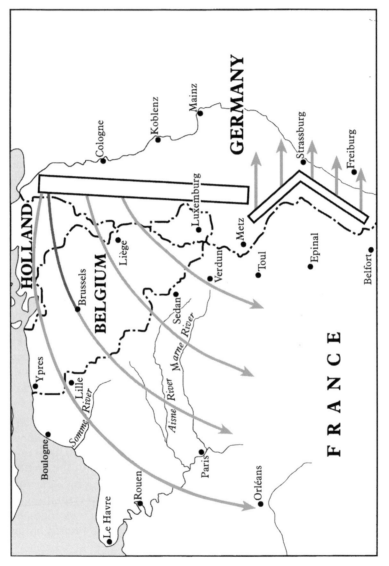

Map 1   Schlieffen's Plan

at the expense his right wing, which comprised the armies that were to undertake the invasion of Belgium. Not only did this decision weaken the spearhead of the great flanking movement, but it also robbed the plan of its revolving-door effect, which was, in Schlieffen's thinking, the key to the annihilation of the French forces.

The modified Schlieffen Plan was nonetheless the basic operational plan with which the German army entered the war. Whether or not it was conceived as a panacea or a "recipe for victory," it provided German military leaders with cautious confidence in the face of the impending uncertainties of war. Armed with the plan, most soldiers – and civilians – expected a campaign on the model of 1870, in which a victory over the major elements of the French forces would eventuate within the first months of hostilities, reducing the western campaign to minor operations as the bulk of German forces redeployed in the east.[16] The absence of plans or stockpiles for a war of more than several months was not due to frivolity or incompetence; it bespoke the widely shared assumption that the conflict would end within a year. In the event, the defeat of these expectations was the defining moment of the First World War.

Tannenberg and the Marne

It started well. The German troops who had departed amid the public celebrations of early August were dispatched with remarkably little confusion by train to the east and west, where their corps were amalgamated, in keeping with the priorities of the Schlieffen Plan, into eight armies. Seven of them, which together comprised 1,600,000 men, accordingly deployed in the west; five of these, which represented two-thirds of the German forces in the west, were concentrated in the northern sector.

The initial action appeared to reward the care with which the German planners had prepared for it. On 4 August, the day after the declaration of war on France – and, more pertinently, day 3 of the great plan – German forces were in Belgium in order to attack the fortress of Liège, whose position athwart the designated marching routes of the northernmost German armies made it a strategic objective of the utmost urgency. After a brief battle, which exhibited the destructive power of the German heavy guns, the fortress fell, allowing the German armies to begin their march through Belgium on schedule. This march commenced on 16 August

---

[16] L. L. Farrar, *The Short-War Illusion: German Policy, Strategy and Domestic Affairs, August–December 1914* (Santa Barbara, CA, 1974). This point is now, however, a matter of controversy. See Stig Förster, "Der deutsche Generalstab und die Illusion des kurzen Krieges 1871–1914: Metakritik eines Mythos," *Militärgeschichtliche Mitteilungen* 54 (1995), 61–95.

and made spectacular progress against light resistance – but with frightful brutality toward civilians who were caught in the path (see map 2).[17] The Belgian capital fell four days later, as German armies to the southeast entered France. The magnitude, speed, and scope of the German advance surprised alike the Belgians, the French, and the British, whose Expeditionary Force arrived on the continent in time to engage the lead German army in southern Belgium on 23 August before falling back, like the French, in general retreat. By 25 August predictions of a brilliant German triumph, a repeat of 1870, began to look sober.

The confidence was premature. It disguised difficulties that were basic to the German campaign and could only accumulate with the continuation of operations. The rapidity and expanse of the German advance required enormous, prolonged exertions of armies that did not yet enjoy the support of motorized vehicles. To the dictates of the schedule, soldiers in the lead armies marched up to twenty-five miles a day. Problems of provisioning these men – and their horses – grew with each day's advance beyond assigned railheads. Roads that were jammed with thousands of horse-drawn wagons made the supply and reinforcement of the units increasingly difficult. Resistance from the Belgian army remained an annoyance. Meanwhile, unforeseen developments threatened the strategic conception of the campaign. To the south, in Lorraine, initial German successes in action against the French tempted Moltke to seek a decision in this theater and to launch an offensive on 25 August, for which he drew reserves that might otherwise have gone to his northern wing.

The news from the east threatened the German plan more profoundly.[18] The Russian mobilization was swifter than the Germans had planned; and by mid-August two massive Russian armies, which together numbered 650,000 men, were preparing to march from the south and east onto German soil in East Prussia, a province that was screened, in keeping with Schlieffen's projections, by a single German army of about 135,000 men. An initial encounter with the eastern Russian army on 20 August resulted in a German defeat and a panicky decision by the German commander in the theater to order a general withdrawal westward. When reports of these developments reached Moltke at his headquarters in Luxembourg, he himself made several momentous decisions. He first called Paul von Hindenburg out of retirement to replace the German commander in the east; and he named Erich Ludendorff, who had led the German attack on Liège a few days earlier, to be Hindenburg's

[17] John Horne and Alan Kramer, *German Atrocities, 1914: A History of Denial* (New Haven and London, 2001).

[18] Dennis Showalter, *Tannenberg: Clash of Empires* (Hamden, CT, 1991).

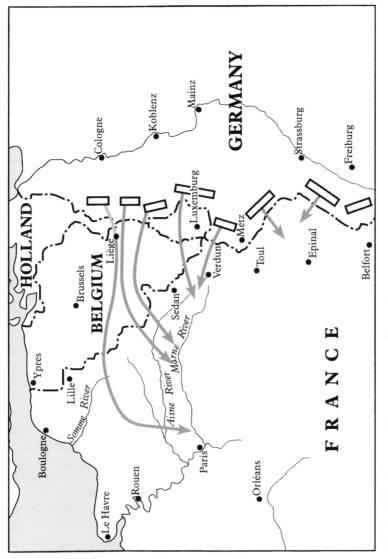

Map 2   The German Advance, August–September 1914

chief of staff. Then, on 25 August, in a sign of his confidence in the outcome of the western campaign, Moltke decided to remove two corps from Belgium in order to reinforce the forces in the east.

The situation in the east, however, had already turned significantly for the better. When Hindenburg and Ludendorff arrived in East Prussia, they discovered that the staff of the eastern command had already reversed the decision to withdraw and had ordered a general redeployment, which the new commanders endorsed. Capitalizing on the failure of all coordination between the two Russian armies, as well as on the availability of a modern rail system in East Prussia, the bulk of the German armies moved rapidly from the eastern part of the province to converge opposite the southern Russian army, which they surrounded on three sides (see map 3). The encounter that followed was one of the great strategic achievements of the war. In a maneuver that would have made Schlieffen proud, the German forces in the center withdrew, luring the Russians into a pocket where they found themselves nearly surrounded. In three days of fighting, between 27 and 30 August, the Germans compensated in their mobility and weaponry – particularly their artillery – for their great inferiority in numbers. The Battle of Tannenberg, as it quickly became known, resulted in Russian losses of 120,000, most of whom were taken prisoner. The Germans, joined only now by the reinforcements from the west, thereupon turned eastward, where, in a series of encounters in early September known as the Battle of the Masurian Lakes, they pushed the eastern Russian army out of Germany and took an additional 125,000 Russian prisoners.

There was no little irony in these developments. The Germans had exploited their mobility and planning to defeat two superior enemy armies in succession, in a campaign whose high point was a strategic envelopment reminiscent of Cannae. Schlieffen's vision had materialized in the wrong theater.

In the right theater, circumstances were meanwhile conspiring to defeat this vision. In the east the Germans had enjoyed a clear superiority in the coordination of their forces. In the west they faced much greater challenges in harmonizing the movements of the five armies that were wheeling though Belgium and northern France. The plan demanded that the flanks of these huge moving bodies remain in contact – an undertaking that grew more difficult as each day's march broadened the gaps to be spanned. The technologies that linked the advancing armies to Moltke's headquarters, and to one another, were inadequate to the challenge. Wireless telegraphy was in its infancy and easily jammed, while wires strung through hostile rear areas were easily cut. As a result, vital

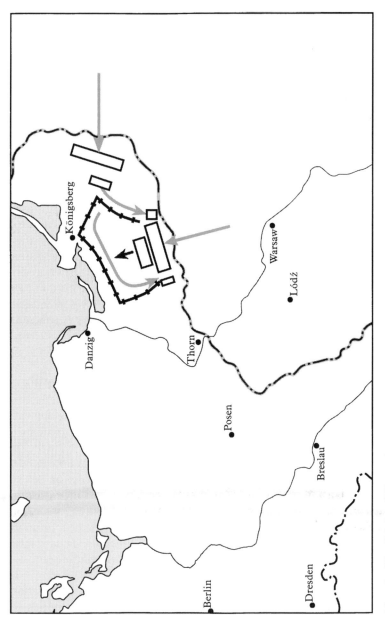

Map 3 The Battle of Tannenberg

information traveled the crowded roads, via couriers on horseback or in motor vehicles, along the German lines.

The hope of reducing these difficulties of communication figured in the controversial German decision of 30 August. The commander of the lead German army resolved to swing to the southeast in pursuit of retreating French and British forces, rather than continuing to the southwest, as planned, to encircle Paris. Moltke, who still awaited a German breakthrough in Lorraine and welcomed the convergence of his own forces, concurred. The decision meant, however, the abandonment of the Schlieffen Plan and whatever basis the German commanders had had for anticipating one another's moves. Contact between the two westernmost German armies thereupon broke down as they advanced in early September towards the Marne River, where, to the east of Paris, the French and British forces were regrouping.

The furious hostilities that raged in the vicinity of this stream in the first half of September became known as the First Battle of the Marne.[19] It represented a decisive moment in the war. The position of the three German armies in action became precarious. The British drove into the gap between the two western armies, while a French army, newly assembled in Paris out of units brought in from the southeast, threatened the German position from the west. The German decision on 9 September to retreat belonged to a lieutenant-colonel, who was Moltke's only contact to the scene of battle; the decision of needs applied to all three German armies, which began a concerted withdrawal to a more secure line to the north, along the Aisne River, where they dug in.

The aftermath of this battle witnessed a desperate German attempt to salvage the remnants of Schlieffen's plan by means of a renewed flanking movement, this time to the north. For the next two months the opposing armies were in constant contact, as they sought, as if in a clinch, to maneuver around one another towards the coast of the English Channel. This action culminated in late October and early November, in an extended battle around the city of Ypres in the southwestern corner of Belgian Flanders. The failure of either side to break through the other's position cast the final piece into the impenetrable wall known henceforth as the Western Front (see map 4). There were no more flanks to turn. From the Flemish coast to the Swiss border, the armies of Imperial Germany faced those of the allied western powers along a continuous front of some 450 miles.

The results of the fighting in 1914 vindicated the expectations of no one. To the Germans, the situation offered little grounds for

---

[19] Robert Asprey, *The First Battle of the Marne* (Westport, CT, 1979).

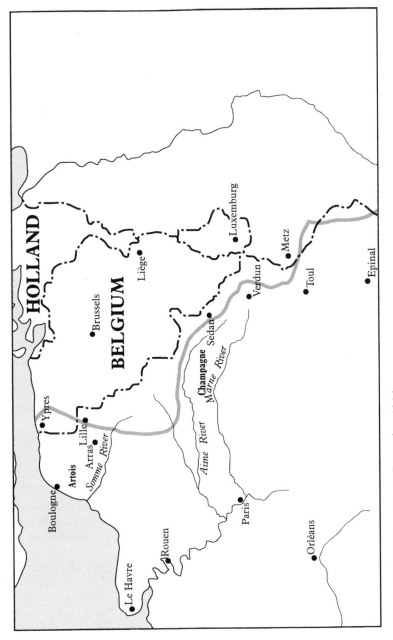

Map 4   The Western Front, December 1914

optimism – least of all to Moltke, who suffered a nervous breakdown in the aftermath of the Marne and had to be replaced. German armies had, to be sure, won a spectacular victory in the east, in which the Russians had lost more men than the French had lost at the decisive Battle of Sedan in 1870. Yet despite their frightful losses, huge Russian armies remained in the field, their spirits buoyed shortly thereafter by significant gains in Galicia against Austrian forces, whose strategic value to the Germans already appeared dubious. To the west, the failure of the German grand design could not be disguised. Despite the brilliant strokes of the first hour, which brought large expanses of Belgian and French territory under German control, enemy armies remained in the field, in positions that could henceforth only be attacked frontally.

The campaigns of 1914 suggested that the Schlieffen Plan had been geared to the wrong century, that the model of 1870 had lost its validity to the demographic and technological transformations of the intervening era. The failure of the Schlieffen Plan was due in no small part to the difficulties of moving vast bodies of footsoldiers, while combat in both theaters revealed that the machines of war – artillery and machine guns – had become the dominant elements of the modern battlefield, where they posed prohibitive disadvantages to forces on the attack. The costs of learning these lessons were staggering. The Germans lost more than 500,000 casualties in action on the western front and perhaps one-third as many in the east. To the human costs were added the enormous expenditures in weapons, munitions, and supplies needed to support the soldiers in combat. The campaigns of 1914 exhausted nearly all the available German stocks of war material. It was of little comfort that Germany's antagonists had endured still higher costs and losses, for these countries commanded resources that were vastly superior.

Schlieffen's plan was in ruins, and the debate over the blame began almost immediately. Moltke was long assigned the principal responsibility, because of the adjustments that he made to the plan's original conception and for his deviations during the battle itself – particularly for weakening the attacking flank at the crucial moment.[20] The weight of evidence has since turned, however, in the direction of Schlieffen himself, the man who devised a plan that – for all its brilliance – lay beyond the capacities of the armies of his day to execute.

Regardless of the culpability, the year 1914 ended in Schlieffen's nightmare. Imperial Germany faced a long war that the country's military

---

[20] This view informs the official German history of the war and most of the accounts composed between the two world wars: Reichsarchiv, *Der Weltkrieg 1914 bis 1918* (14 vols., Berlin, 1925–44). Professor Ritter's *Schlieffen Plan* offers the most powerful retort.

leaders had gambled desperately to avoid. Germany now faced a new kind of warfare, for which there were no plans whatsoever. The new dynamics of combat defied a rapid decision at arms, and they suggested a ghastly possibility. The fighting front threatened to become a peripheral arena, where armies were locked in strategic paralysis, occupied in destroying the prodigious human and material resources that belligerent societies had mobilized for military use. In this scenario, the war was to be won elsewhere than on the field of battle.

2   The war continues

The military failure to resolve the war in 1914 surprised soldiers in Germany and everywhere else. It also surprised civilian leaders in all the belligerent countries, who now confronted unanticipated and unprecedented challenges. They had to redirect the productive energies of society towards the massive demands of industrial warfare. The first year and a half of the war established the framework of mobilization in all these lands. Public institutions invaded economies and societies, as vast material and moral resources were channeled to military ends.

The transition to new modes of organization for war took place everywhere by improvisation during the first months of the conflict, but some of the belligerent powers were better able than others to adjust. Imperial Germany, which in 1914 was reputed to be the most efficiently organized society on earth, faced major impediments to meeting the challenges. Deficiencies in the organization of mobilization contributed to the mounting burdens of war on the homefront. They also fed the political controversies that attended the prolongation of the war.

Bureaucratic foundations

Institutions were a fundamental problem. Germany's reputation for bureaucratic efficiency was deceptive, for the country's basic administrative structures were fragmented among federal, state, and local institutions. Administrative particularism had its champions, but it posed grave obstacles to the execution of common policies in a national emergency.

The institutions of military administration, which were conceived with national emergency in mind, only compounded the difficulties.[1] These institutions were as much geared to the wrong century as was Schlieffen's

---

[1] Wilhelm Deist (ed.), *Militär und Innenpolitik im Weltkrieg 1914–1918* (2 vols., Düsseldorf, 1970) covers all aspects of the institutional problem. The introductory essay to this collection of documents, "Voraussetzungen innenpolitischen Handelns des Militärs im Ersten Weltkrieg," is republished in Deist, *Militär, Staat und Gesellschaft: Studien zur preussisch-deutschen Militärgeschichte* (Munich, 1991), 103–52.

plan. They were designed to mobilize forces rapidly in the event of war (or revolution) and to provide basic services and security at home during a limited period of crisis, as they had in 1870–71. Their legal foundation was the Prussian Law of Siege, which was first promulgated in 1851 and then taken over into the Imperial constitution in 1871. Upon declaration of national emergency, this law specified that executive power passed into the hands of the corps commander in each of the country's twenty-four military districts. However, because these commanders accompanied their corps into battle, their executive powers devolved to their deputies, the so-called Deputy Commanding Generals. These soldiers then enjoyed almost unlimited powers over a broad range of public affairs in their respective districts, including censorship, transportation, and the preservation of public order in the civilian sector, as well as ensuring the recruitment, training, supply, and deployment of additional troops for combat.

Several features of this system made it ill suited to the demands of the war that broke out in 1914. In the first place, the military districts were superimposed onto the civilian bureaucratic structure with little heed to the jurisdictions of these other public agencies. Boundaries did not coincide. Fifteen of the military districts severed the geographical bounds of state or regional governments, while others encompassed parts of two or more different states. The district of the eleventh army corps sprawled over the boundaries of eight small Thuringian states in central Germany. Civilian officials at all levels were legally subordinate to the Deputy Commanding Generals, but the soldiers could not govern without the cooperation of the civilians. The proliferation of jurisdictions complicated the already daunting difficulties of bureaucratic coordination, particularly as the lengthening war brought ever broader facets of civilian life into the purview of military administration.

A second feature of German military administration was more perverse. Each Deputy Commanding General was responsible only to his commander-in-chief, the German emperor. This arrangement need not have been an impediment had the commander-in-chief been a stabilizing force, capable of lending coherent direction to the policies of his military subordinates. Instead, the commander-in-chief was William II, whose erratic thinking and impulsive behavior were legendary.[2] These traits had already eroded his effective power before the war. As the conflict continued, he became an increasingly peripheral figure, closeted among his warriors at military headquarters near the front – as remote from

---

[2] See now Lamar Cecil, *Wilhelm II: Emperor and Exile* (Chapel Hill, NC, 1996); Christopher Clark, *Kaiser Wilhelm II* (Harlow, 2000), 225–45.

the Deputy Commanding Generals as he was from policy discussions in Berlin. However, because he was determined to guard his powers of command, his inclinations could never be ignored, and he was a factor in repeated intrigues at the centers of power. In these circumstances, the Deputy Commanding Generals remained autonomous for much of the war; they were like rulers of independent satrapies, and they could – to the extent they wished – resist attempts from above, from civilian or military agencies, to impose common policies or institutional constraints on them.

The most serious consequence of this bureaucratic maze was to impede the execution of legislation designed in Berlin to coordinate economic mobilization throughout the country. Fashioning the central legislative procedures themselves was, by contrast, swift and smooth. On 4 August 1914, the same day as it authorized funding for the war, the Reichstag, in a demonstration of national unity, passed a special enabling act, which became known immediately as the *Burgfrieden* – an allusion to the peace that was supposed to reign in a medieval fortress when it was attacked. For the duration of the war, the Reichstag, the most democratic body in the country and hitherto the focus of partisan conflict in Germany, delegated its legislative powers to the Bundesrat. This body was now empowered to issue emergency legislation, which was binding on all levels of civil government. Although the Reichstag was entitled to review the laws so decreed, it vetoed none of the more than 800 orders that emerged out of the upper house during the war. Instead, it became a peripheral arena during the first half of the conflict; and its principal charge was to convene at six-month intervals in order to authorize the continued funding of the war.

Most of the Bundesrat's decrees related to questions of mobilizing the economy for military purposes. The administrative agency most directly concerned with these questions was the Ministry of War in Berlin. Although this was technically a Prussian institution – the counterpart of similar agencies in the states of Bavaria, Saxony, and Württemberg – its responsibilities for supplying the army had made it effectively a national institution before the war broke out. During the war, its competence and powers grew rapidly, as many of the agencies created by the Bundesrat to oversee the mobilization of production found a bureaucratic home here. This arrangement appeared logical, but it had an astonishing defect. The Minister of War, who was a political figure insofar as he represented the army's affairs in the Reichstag, remained for this very reason outside the chain of military command. He did not have the power to discipline the Deputy Commanding Generals. Nor did the Bundesrat. Each new agency that was rooted in the War Ministry accordingly multiplied the bureaucratic friction between the officials who formulated policies and those who, in a myriad of jurisdictions, were supposed to enforce them.

Imperial Germany was already a bureaucratic wonderland before the war. Existing institutions remained in place during the war on all levels, where they provided the basis of most day-to-day administration. But the bureaucratic network now became a nightmare, first in the super-imposition of autonomous military institutions and then in the prolifera-tion of new civilian and military offices to oversee the reorganization of the economy. The result was disorder so imposing that it initially disguised a number of important truths. Governmental power remained in the hands of the men who had traditionally exercised it in Imperial Germany. How-ever, their position was now more exposed and vulnerable than before, for they faced a situation that offered neither precedents nor reliable rules of procedure. The intrusion of public power into private life was massive; but in no small part as a consequence of bureaucratic chaos, it was also unplanned, unsystematic, and in significant ways unfair. These features were bound to nurture popular discontents, which attached eas-ily onto the officials who embodied public authority in all its clutter. This proposition reigned even in the areas where mobilization was most effective.

Mobilizing industrial resources

During the Battle of the Marne, German armies expended more muni-tions daily than they had during the entire Franco-Prussian War. Stock-piles were exhausted by the conclusion of the same battle, so waging war during the remainder of the year was possible only on the strength of current German industrial production. The expenditure of munitions was merely the most direct and dramatic sign of the vast demands that combat in the new mode was placing on the economies that supplied it.

Several preliminary questions suggest the dimensions of the prob-lem. What, in the first place, was the "war economy"? The march of German armies westward into Belgium and France, and later eastward into Russian Poland, was like the export of a population as large as a small state's. Several million men, whose principal occupation was fight-ing, had to be supported abroad. To a degree, they could "live off the land," although obstruction from the inhabitants of occupied territories and the destruction wrought in frontline areas limited sources of sup-ply in these places. Much of the burden of equipping, clothing, healing, feeding, and transporting these men to and from the front fell accord-ingly onto the home economy. In principle, every phase of production that was involved, however remotely, in supporting the German armies abroad – and their replacements at home – represented a facet of the "war economy." The description was comprehensive. It included not only the immediate manufacture of arms and munitions, but the goods and services necessary for the employment of arms and munitions – such things as wooden boxes for cartridges, hemp for sandbags, rubber for tires, and nails for myriad uses. Even the watchmakers of the Black Forest discovered that one of their special wares, the small mechanisms in cuckoo clocks, were essential to the manufacture of time-fuses. With the inclusion of other sectors whose support for the soldiers was less immediate though hardly less essential, the list became almost endless. It included firms that produced or processed food, textiles and leather goods, reading materials, medicines, transport vehicles (including horses), as well as those that provided all these firms with the materials, equipment, and services that they required.

A second question pertains to mechanisms by which goods and services were to be marshaled to support the armies in the field. The German economy in 1914 was capitalist, in the basic sense that most of the means of production were in the hands of private entrepreneurs, whose decisions were governed by market forces and the expectation of profit. The outbreak of war brought a sudden and seismic shift in the market mechanism. It conjured up a voracious new consumer of goods and services, for the demands of the armed forces now enjoyed absolute priority. Other massive disruptions accompanied the departure of workers of all descriptions for the front, while the Royal Navy's blockade of the German coast soon cut the country off from nearly all overseas supplies. These extraordinary circumstances required major modifications of the market mechanism, whose workings were too slow to adjust to the military emergency. Quite apart from the thought that the "spirit of 1914" implied fundamental economic reform (a proposition embraced by few people other than the Socialists), the immediate pressures of the war made some form of "collectivistic" intervention – the kind of public planning and compulsion suggested by the term "command economy" – seem inescapable.

Nowhere were these pressures more urgent than in the core sectors of the war economy, the manufacture of the weapons and munitions without which the war would have come quickly to an end. At the outbreak of war, about 40 percent of this manufacture took place in state-run factories, while a number of private firms – notably the Krupp Works in Essen – produced the remainder under contracts let by the Ministry of War. The technologies of production required wood and steel for weapons and – for munitions – a combination of nitrates (usually in the form of saltpeter or sodium nitrate), sulfur, and a cotton base. Although the country was well endowed with many of these staple resources, the prodigious expenditures during the initial campaigns of 1914 far overtaxed the capacity of the state firms to produce sufficient quantities of munitions. As the War Ministry struggled to recruit additional private firms, it discovered that many were reluctant to retool for what they thought would be a short war, while the blockade and the enormous demand for the necessary raw materials further jeopardized the whole undertaking.

That the munitions shortage did not result in a terminal crisis was due to the initiative of one of the country's leading industrialists. Walter Rathenau was president of the German General Electric Company (AEG), a firm whose growth before the war into one of the country's most far-flung, technologically advanced conglomerates had already demonstrated the indispensability of comprehensive planning and coordination.[3] Within days of the war's outbreak, Rathenau had persuaded officials in the War Ministry that the conflict demanded centralized control over the procurement and distribution of all war-related raw materials. Rathenau's overture led immediately to the creation of the "War Materials Section" (*Kriegsrohstoffabteilung*, or KRA) of the War Ministry. The new agency was staffed by Rathenau himself and a team of business leaders, who were charged with steering adequate supplies of raw materials to the firms that accepted the contracts to produce the weapons of war.

This effort quickly produced a remarkable marriage of public and private power.[4] The institutional network that soon radiated out of the KRA comprised a series of "war raw-materials corporations" (*Kriegsrohstoffgesellschaften*), which loomed over every critical sector of the economy. The corporations were organized as joint-stock companies, in which the state participated as an investor while the leading firms in each sector put up the bulk of the capital. The corporations were empowered to buy up – if necessary, by means of requisition or confiscation – all available stocks of the materials in question and then to distribute these materials to the firms that held the military contracts. The first corporation to be set up, "War Metals, Inc." set the pattern. Founded on 2 September 1914, it combined twenty-two leading metal-processing firms. The corporation was empowered to corner the supplies of all critical non-ferrous metals, such as copper and nickel. It then let out these materials to firms that processed them for military use – those that undertook, for example, the extraction of metals from the ores or the manufacture of copper wiring.

---

[3] Lothar Burchardt, "Walther Rathenau und die Anfänge der deutschen Rohstoffbewirtschaftung im ersten Weltkrieg," *Tradition: Zeitschrift für Firmengeschichte und Unternehmerbiographie* 15 (1970), 169–96; Gerhard Hecker, *Walther Rathenau und sein Verhältnis zu Militär und Krieg* (Boppard, 1983).

[4] Hans Gotthard Ehlert, *Die wirtschaftliche Zentralbehörde des Deutschen Reiches 1914 bis 1919: Das Problem der "Gemeinwirtschaft" in Krieg und Frieden* (Wiesbaden, 1982).

But the processing firms were in most cases the same ones that constituted the war corporation. The practical enticement of the arrangement was thus to enable the participating firms to distribute the contracts among themselves, so that (to continue with the same example) Rathenau's own AEG manufactured the copper wiring. To sweeten the enticement, the war corporations bought up the materials at legally fixed prices, while the lucrative terms of the military contracts set no limits on costs and guaranteed a 5 percent profit to the participating firms. The same institutional arrangements operated elsewhere – in chemicals, ferrous metals, cotton and other textiles, leather, and rubber, and other sectors. By early 1915, twenty-five war materials corporations encompassed the sectors of the economy that were immediately involved in military production. Without exception, the corporations were dominated by the largest, most powerful firms in each sector.

The final element in the constellation that formed in the summer of 1914 was the "War Committee for German Industry." This body emerged from the marriage of the two leading industrial federations, which were in turn dominated by the same large and powerful firms that populated the war corporations. The committee advised the War Ministry on industrial policy, a role that gave this body vast influence not only over the general design and administration of policy, but also over the distribution of war contracts.

The effectiveness of this hastily improvised effort stood out in the annals of Germany's economic mobilization for war. Despite the anxieties of the War Ministry, the German armies did not collapse in late 1914 for want of weapons or munitions; and in this respect at least, German soldiers were well supplied for the duration of the conflict. There was no munitions crisis in Germany. A number of other developments contributed to this state of affairs. The War Chemicals Corporation would have been a pointless undertaking had not the chemists Fritz Haber and Robert Bosch worked out a practical process for nitrogen fixation, which liberated German munitions production from a dependence on imported nitrates. Another triumph of German chemistry, the development of synthetic cellulose, likewise compensated for the loss of imported cotton for use in munitions. These technological advances came in response to pressures that the British blockade had made critical. The same pressures encouraged the merciless exploitation of industrial resources in areas that fell under German control in the fall of 1914.

These corporations were the central feature of Germany's industrial mobilization, and they made it clear that the war would bring no tampering with the foundations of German capitalism. The state's cooperation with the private sector was a retort to those who had called for public ownership of war industries. In war, as in peace, the allocation of resources was ultimately to be guided by considerations of profit. Administrative *fiat* did not supplant market forces; rather, it mediated these forces, for capitalists themselves controlled the administrative apparatus. Consensus prevailed that profit was the surest prop of the war effort. As a leading official in the War Ministry explained, "Exploiting the national emergency to promote private interests does not mean that capitalism is decadent; rather [this policy] is the logical outcome of capitalism's basic philosophy and a fruitful field for the employment of capitalist expertise."[5]

This thinking underlay industrial mobilization in other belligerent countries as well. Businessmen oversaw the business of war almost everywhere. Germany represented a special case nonetheless. Before the war, cartelization had proceeded here to an extreme unmatched elsewhere in the industrial world. Concentration reigned particularly in those sectors of German heavy industry that were central to war production, and the dynamics of mobilization provided massive encouragement to this trend. A telling sign was that no war corporation with the title "War Coal, Inc." had to be created. The War Ministry simply turned to the existing coal syndicate, which already functioned as a trust for the entire sector. By war's end, other basic sectors such as chemicals, iron and steel, and electricity, were likewise in the consolidated control of a few monster concerns, like Rathenau's AEG and the chemical companies that several years later merged into I. G. Farben. The industrial barons who presided over these combines were among the wealthiest men in the land, as well as the mightiest. The generals and statesmen who dealt with Emil Kirdorf, who ran the coal syndicate, or with the steel baron August Thyssen, or Hugo Stinnes (who seemed at times intent on bringing the whole economy under his control) did so, with good reason, in a spirit of deference.

The enterprise of war in Germany thus unfolded in a hybrid institutional framework. In a series of semi-public war corporations, which eventually numbered almost 200, industrialists operated with both the capital and the official sanction of the government. Public agencies were the principal consumers of industry's produce, as well as the guarantors of industry's profits. Industrialists in turn served as agents and advisors of these same agencies. Some observers, Rathenau among them, suggested that this condominium represented the basis for a unique "German" or "national socialism," a new system of industrial relations that would

---

[5] Otto Goebel, *Deutsche Rohstoffwirtschaft im Weltkrieg einschliesslich des Hindenburg-Programms* (Stuttgart, Berlin, and Leipzig, 1930), 175.

ultimately supplant the market mechanism with intelligent public planning and allocation, if not public ownership.

Most of the businessmen who sold their services to the public agencies that oversaw industrial mobilization were not interested in socialism of any description. These were hard-headed capitalists, for whom the war represented a very "fruitful field" indeed, with scarcely limited profits and opportunities for growth. Other entrepreneurs, however, found the prospects of war more uncertain. These businessmen were situated further to the peripheries of the war economy and had to supplicate among the powerful for contracts and allocations of vital raw materials – notably for coal, without which virtually no industry could survive. Particularly vulnerable were those firms that produced "civilian goods" and could not credibly or profitably retool for military purposes. Vulnerable, too, were the civilians themselves. Their needs for basic goods and services remained a pressing concern, but administrative improvisation did not serve these needs well.

Feeding soldiers and civilians

While the Germans averted a munitions crisis, they were less fortunate in another crucial area. Food was no less essential than weapons to the war effort, for undernourishment threatened both the fighting strength of the armed forces and the physical capacity of civilians at home to support them. Yet the food supply proved intractable to administrative control. While no one died directly of starvation in Germany during the war, undernourishment became a mass phenomenon, a festering source of demoralization, discontent, and domestic strife.[6]

Food was more difficult than weapons to mobilize. The reasons for this state of affairs had nothing to do with priorities inspired by German militarism. It was due instead to basic differences of market structure in the two sectors of the economy, as well as to the differential impact of the blockade. The public officials and business leaders who mobilized the armaments sector confronted a small population of well-organized producers, processors, and consumers. The number of mines and other sources of raw materials was no greater than several hundred, while the cartelization of German heavy industry had reduced the major processors to a comparable number of large firms. The army, the near-exclusive consumer of these products, was itself well set up to distribute them to their ultimate users, who fought in the field.

---

[6] Avner Offer, *The First World War: An Agrarian Interpretation* (Oxford, 1989), 21–78; Friedrich Aereboe, *Der Einfluss des Krieges auf die landwirtschaftliche Produktion in Deutschland* (Stuttgart, Berlin, and Leipzig, 1927).

German agriculture was organized in no such fashion. About 30 percent of the population, in excess of 5,000,000 German families, were engaged in agriculture on the eve of the war. Most farming was small scale, as was the processing of farm products. There were, for example, 341 plants that processed sugar beets in Germany in 1914, while butchers, millers, bakers, and agricultural wholesalers were too numerous for anyone but the census-takers to count. There were also more than 65,000,000 German consumers of farm products. Patterns of fragmentation and dispersion made the challenge of regulating agriculture prodigious from the start, as did the mass and variety of the products to be regulated.

But the problem was more complicated. In 1914, Germany was anything but self-sufficient in agriculture. In addition to several hundred thousand farmworkers, who migrated annually from Russian Poland to the grain-growing estates of eastern Germany, the country imported about 25 percent of its food – particularly eggs, dairy products, vegetable oils, fish, and meat. Moreover, much of the fodder consumed by German farm animals came in the form of barley and clover from Russia, maize from Argentina, and oil cake from the United States. Finally, Chilean nitrates provided a significant part of the fertilizers that sustained the high yields of German fields.

The outbreak of war introduced a basic new calculus into the production and consumption of food in Germany. The British blockade soon led to a drop of about 25 percent in German agricultural production. Some consumers, however, continued to claim a full share of their prewar allotments. First in this category were the more than 8,000,000 adult males who were under arms by 1915. A comparable number of Germans – most of them women, children, and older men – continued to farm in the fields, where they enjoyed immediate access to the products of their own labor. Together, these two groups, whose consumption claims remained at prewar levels, constituted roughly one-quarter of the population. The remaining 75 percent of the population thus contended for the remaining half of the prewar farm production. The dynamics implied in this equation set in immediately. As the army's procurement officers purchased massive stocks of food for military use, and as troop movements blocked the delivery by rail of agricultural goods, civilian consumers panicked. Runs on stores in the summer of 1914 resulted in price increases across the board on staples like bread, meat, and milk.

Some economists argued that this phenomenon represented but a temporary dislocation, which market forces would eventually repair. Political considerations, however, made the consequences of inaction unacceptable. While Germans of means could in fact find abundant supplies of most foodstuffs, the census-takers could estimate that at least half of the urban population lacked the means to do so. These were lower-class families whose budgets were devoted primarily to food and whose health was immediately imperiled by the sudden rise of prices. Loud protests from these consumers and their political representatives quickly prompted a series of responses.

Like the measures undertaken to mobilize industry, these responses were improvised, but they had unanticipated results. They encountered a complex, fragmented, yet interdependent market. Within weeks of the war's beginning, city governments and other local authorities began independently to impose price ceilings on bread, milk, potatoes, and other staples that were sold within their jurisdictions. Farmers needed no coaxing to exploit the resulting price differentials and to remove their goods to local markets that offered higher prices. In an effort to repair the chaos of this competition, the Bundesrat empowered the federal Ministry of the Interior in October to fix general price levels for the same staples. In response to these prices, which the government set low in order to pacify consumers, farmers turned their attentions to products that remained unregulated. Capping the price of milk, for example, resulted quickly in a milk shortage, as farmers either switched to producing butter and cheese, whose prices were not regulated (yet), or they slaughtered their livestock for sale. Price controls on bread likewise produced shortages, as farmers withheld grains to use as fodder for livestock.

If this hapless intervention suggested administrative incomprehension of the problem, the events of the first three months of 1915 stand as a monument of bureaucratic clumsiness. It is not clear which agency concluded that pigs represented "co-eaters," whose appetites for fodder grains threatened the supply of bread for humans. In all events, the government thereupon decreed the great "pig massacre" (*Schweinemord*), which claimed over 9,000,000 victims. The slaughter produced a momentary glut of pork on the market, but it did nothing to relieve the grain shortage. The gravest failing of the *Schweinemord* was to ignore the delicate ecology that bound humans and animals in a community of production. Pigs were not only consumers of fodder but producers of fertilizer; and their departure from the fields had dire long-term consequences.

Similar miscalculations plagued early efforts to regulate the food supply in every sector. Price controls were fixed haphazardly but at ever higher levels. Their immediate impact was to drive foodstuffs from the market, for farmers, too, were hard-headed capitalists who responded to demand as it registered in ever higher prices – whether for meats, potatoes, vegetables, or fruits. A general increase in food prices was the

Table 1 *Food prices in Karlsruhe, 1914–1915*

	Price in marks		
	June 1914	December 1914	June 1915
Bread (per kg)	0.27	0.34	0.42
Pork (per kg)	1.60	1.84	3.10
Butter (per kg)	2.40	3.00	3.20
Milk (per liter)	0.22	0.24	0.26
Potatoes (per 100 kg)	6.38	7.00	11.50

Source: Statistische Mitteilungen über das Grossherzogtum Baden (Neue Folge, Karlsruhe, 1914–15), vol. VII, 95, 192; vol. VIII, 106

natural consequence, as price ceilings rose to lure out supplies. Nor did demand abate, as agencies of local government joined the army's procurement officers in buying up large stocks of food for their constituents. The rise of prices in the city of Karlsruhe betokened the strains that these pressures put on consumers throughout the country (see table 1).

By the end of 1914 it was clear that price controls were merely distorting the operation of market forces and that these controls alone could not regulate the food supply. The only alternative appeared to be the suspension of the market mechanism altogether and the regulation of the entire agricultural cycle, from production to consumption. Rationing was the device. From the start, however, it took shape haphazardly, too. It began with bread. In January 1915, the Bundesrat established the Imperial Grain Corporation within the federal Ministry of the Interior. This body resembled the industrial corporations that inhabited the War Ministry, insofar as it was composed of the sector's leading capitalists, the grain farmers and wholesalers who were empowered to buy up the entire grain crop at controlled prices. This corporation then rationed grain, via an assortment of state and provincial bureaus, to local governments throughout the land, which in turn rationed it out to their citizens at prices that climbed perhaps a little less rapidly for being controlled.

The Grain Corporation provided the model for the administration of rationing in virtually all sectors of German agriculture during the next two years. By 1916 there was even a War Corporation for Sauerkraut. The process of control was painful and reluctant, and it came in response to crises that descended serially on the supply of meats, vegetables, fruits, oils, and potatoes. In hopes of bringing a measure of oversight and control to the whole system of regulation, the Federal Council established an independent War Food Office (*Kriegsernährungsamt*) in 1916. The lawmakers failed, however, to appoint this office with effective powers of compulsion over either the military or civilian agencies, so the Food Office became "a blunt sword" – yet another, albeit central, factor in a bureaucratic morass.[7] In the end, the administrative network that regulated the German food supply was populated by interested federal and state ministries, forty different imperial food corporations and their attendant bureaus, offices of military procurement, and thousands of municipal and communal governments, which bought, stored, processed, and distributed scarce food supplies to their beleaguered populations.[8]

In the distribution of food – and many other essential household items likewise in short supply – Germany was thus transformed into a command economy, in which market forces yielded, at least in theory, to the rule of law. Farmers and other producers had to frame basic economic decisions on the basis of legal constraints. The moral basis of this system was never made explicit, but it inhered in the "spirit of 1914," the proposition that the burdens of the conflict ought to be equitably shared – as well as in the calculation that a major portion of the population would otherwise starve.

It did not work well. While the system nourished a maze of bureaucratic regulations, the food supply itself was an enduring nightmare, the principal object of domestic discontent among hungry and frustrated consumers. Popular cynicism about regulations was widespread. It surfaced in the joke, heard in Berlin later in the war, that the best way to ensure the removal of snow from the city's streets was to establish an "Imperial Snow Corporation," which would, like nothing else, ensure the disappearance of the snow supply. Not all of the difficulty was due to administrative confusion, however. Local systems of distribution were generally effective; and towns that enjoyed local access to farm products fared better than did larger cities, which relied on long-distance transport for much of their food. Crippling bottlenecks, which accompanied the strains of war on the country's rail system, constricted the flow of foodstuffs towards local points of distribution. The impact of the blockade is difficult to overstate.[9] It produced critical shortages in basic areas,

[7] Martin Schumacher, *Land und Politik: Eine Untersuchung über politische Parteien und agrarische Interessen 1914–1923* (Düsseldorf, 1978), 60–62.

[8] Anne Roerkohl, *Hungerblockade und Heimatfront: Die kommunale Lebensmittelversorgung in Westfalen während des Ersten Weltkrieges* (Stuttgart, 1991); George L. Yaney, *The World of the Manager: Food Administration in Berlin during World War I* (New York, 1994); August Skalweit, *Die deutsche Kriegsernährungswirtschaft* (Stuttgart, Berlin, and Leipzig, 1927).

[9] C. Paul Vincent, *The Politics of Hunger: The Allied Blockade of Germany, 1915–1919* (Athens, OH, 1985); Marion C. Siney, *The Allied Blockade of Germany, 1914–1916* (Ann Arbor, MI, 1957).

particularly in fertilizers and fats, which translated into diminished or erratic supplies of many staple commodities.

In these circumstances, official rations soon ceased to describe what Germans could in fact purchase. The nutrient quality of food also declined, to say nothing of its palatability. The search for alternatives to foods in short supply lent a new, pejorative meaning to the German words "*Ersatz*" (substitute) and "*strecken*" (stretch). Coffee made of tree bark became a familiar item on German tables, as did milk and beer that were "stretched" with water. So did bread that was made from coarsely milled grains or laced with potato flour. By the war's end, some 11,000 different ersatz products – including over 800 varieties of meatless sausage – had found their way into general circulation.

All of these vexations bore witness to the structural difficulties of regimenting the food supply. The suppliers were too numerous and savvy. Peasants greeted the incursions of regulators into their lives with an arsenal of evasions, which ranged from simple hoarding to elaborate schemes to misrepresent the size of their crop yields. This behavior was not, as some critics charged, a sign of want of patriotism among the rural folk. Farmers were responding rationally to a simple fact: the market for agricultural produce had not disappeared. Rationing had merely driven the free market underground and colored it black.

The black market survived as the competitor to the administered food supply. The forces of supply and demand thrived here, and practically any foodstuff could be found – for a price. The prolongation of the conflict fed the black market to the point that it became far more just a supplement; in the estimation of the authorities, Germans were purchasing fully one-third of all food on the black market by war's end. The twin of the black market was the so-called *Hamsterfahrt*. Despite the persistent efforts of the police and army to suppress it, this "foraging jaunt" occupied multitudes of Germans in visits to relatives, acquaintances, or anyone else in the countryside who might be persuaded – for a price – to part with some of their produce.

These alternatives to the official food supply were not available to all Germans. They were expensive, and hence less accessible to the poor. The *Hamsterfahrt* required proximity to farmland. The logic of this situation assembled the problems of food shortage above all in Germany's large cities, particularly those in the west, which were dependent on long-distance transport to feed large populations of poor people, who had little opportunity to supplement their rations. Because these cities were also the centers of Germany's armaments industry, they became neuralgic points as the war dragged on.

The food supply was a source of grave concern for the duration of the war. Because every German experienced it on a daily basis, it was an immediate source of discontent. During the first two years of the conflict, however, the problem remained within bounds better described as vexing than critical. Good harvests in the late summer of 1914 and in 1915 relieved the pressure, while the initial enthusiasm and the attendant hopes of a short war survived to ease material burdens.

The mobilization of morale

The mobilization of society for war was not limited to regimenting material resources. It extended to the hearts and minds of Germans on the homefront, most of whom experienced the war as growing sacrifice and material hardship. The effort to maintain their moral support for the war demanded the rationing of information, the administration of the war's meaning.

The language of patriotism governed the official reading of the war. Its terms prescribed the meaning of the war effort in a way that comported with the "spirit of 1914" – that the conflict was necessary, just, destined for vindication, and that, whatever the sacrifices it required, opposition to it was unthinkable. This reading was organized in the national symbolism. These symbols had carried heavy military implications before the war, and they now became as omnipresent as the uniforms worn by an ever growing segment of the population. An essential additional component of this symbolism emerged in the first days of fighting, in the form of a powerful countersymbol. This was not Russia, whose specter had haunted the final diplomatic crisis. It was England.[10] Anti-English feeling had a long tradition in Imperial German politics, and it had been fueled by colonial and naval rivalry. With the outbreak of war it became a passion. "Now that England has showed its cards," proclaimed the semi-official *Kölnische Zeitung* on 7 August, "everyone can see what is at stake: the most powerful conspiracy in the history of the world."[11] This belief directed the military crusade foremost against a sinister power, which – for reasons of envy and greed – loomed as the driving force behind the hostile coalition against Germany. "May God punish England!" – a motto that became almost a form of address in 1914 – captured the enduring intensity of this sentiment, as well as the compelling sense of moral orientation that it provided.

[10] Matthew Stibbe, *German Anglophobia and the Great War, 1914–1918* (Cambridge, 2001).
[11] Quoted in Wolfgang J. Mommsen, *Bürgerstolz und Weltmachtstreben: Deutschland unter Wilhelm II, 1890 bis 1918* (Berlin, 1995), 563.

The initial mobilization of German opinion came spontaneously in August 1914, and it required neither official encouragement nor compulsion. Thereafter, the great challenge became to sustain this mood of commitment, if not euphoria, in the much more trying circumstances that followed the failure of the German armies to win the war in 1914. The principal responsibilities for this undertaking fell onto official and semi-official agencies of communication and opinion-formation, which enjoyed an interpretive monopoly in representing the war to a broad popular audience.

Newspapers remained the principal medium of communication on the homefront, so they occupied a central place in the calculations of the country's leadership.[12] While it was possible for Germans to purchase newspapers from abroad via the neutral lands, particularly through Holland and Switzerland, most people learned about the war from newspapers published in their own country. The importance of managing news about the war was transparent, in the interests of security as well as public morale. Through neutral countries, enemy agents, or German soldiers captured in battle, information published in Germany could easily find its way into the wrong hands. From the start, this truth governed the way troop movements were reported in the press; and it extended quickly to obituary notices, which were purged of information about the fallen soldier's unit or the locale where he met his end.

While foreign military reports were regularly published in the German press, the German news from the front was thus censored from the first day of the war. Reports from units in the field proceeded first to staff headquarters in the eastern and western theaters, and from there to central staff headquarters in Berlin, where the army's press department digested them. Only then was the news made public. Most of the news releases were distributed nationwide via the national wire service (called the WTB) or representatives of the major papers in Berlin. The result was to produce identical reports of battlefield operations in local papers throughout the land. The Battle of the Marne was in this respect an exemplary occasion.[13] During the last week of August, the press reports sang vaguely but in unison of a general German advance and the retreat of French and Belgian armies. On 5 September, the reports at once became more fragmentary; accounts of German advances were punctuated with ambiguous reports of enemy attacks (successfully repelled) and German "repositionings." The real news lay in the orchestrated silence of the

[12] Kurt Koszyk, *Deutsche Pressepolitik im Ersten Weltkrieg* (Düsseldorf, 1968).
[13] Karl Lange, *Marneschlacht und deutsche Öffentlichkeit 1914–1939: Eine verdrängte Niederlage und ihre Folgen* (Düsseldorf, 1974).

reports, which failed to bring the eagerly awaited announcement of a breakthrough in the west; instead, they turned with more enthusiasm in mid-September to developments on the eastern front.

Reporting the "facts" of military operations represented but a minor facet of censorship. Placing these facts in a broader context – endowing them with interpretive coherence and meaning – was a more sensitive problem. The fact that masses of young men were being killed could not be concealed, and its interpretive implications were dangerous. So this information was kept incoherent. Local papers were allowed to report only local casualties, unaccompanied by statistics or cumulative lists. The operational reports from the front never once mentioned a German defeat until the fall of 1918, when the whole propaganda campaign collapsed along with the army. Other agencies found it more difficult, but no less necessary, to disguise the fact that the war was not going well. Many of these agencies, such as the Foreign Office, the Naval Office, and the Ministry of the Interior (which oversaw the food supply), ran their own press offices or otherwise managed what the public learned about their endeavors.[14] In hopes of coordinating the distribution of information, the government began late in 1914 to stage regular press conferences in the capital. Here the Berlin correspondents of major newspapers congregated for briefings (both on and off the record) by representatives of the army and navy, as well as the principal civilian offices. Once they had cleared the censor, reports filed from these conferences found their way into the local press.

Despite the hopes of the officials who fed the press in this fashion, the newspapers that served thousands of localities in Germany were not the pliant vessels of news managed in Berlin. The government's claims to interpret the war did not go uncontested. The local press was in the hands of local editors, who themselves attempted to make sense of the reports they received. Their power resided in the editorial commentary with which they garnished the official reports, as well as in their control over the content of their papers. In a large majority of cases, these editors remained sympathetic to the official reading of the war; but the prolongation of the conflict and the injection of contentious issues of domestic and foreign policy nourished interpretive dissension.

The government attempted early in the conflict to define the limits of permissible dissent. In October 1914, in the aftermath of the Marne, a central office of censorship was set up in Berlin, for whose guidance

---

[14] Wilhelm Deist, "Zensur und Propaganda in Deutschland während des Ersten Weltkrieges," in Deist, *Militär, Staat und Gesellschaft*, 153–64; Heinz-Dietrich Fischer (ed.), *Pressekonzentration und Zensurpraxis im Ersten Weltkrieg: Texte und Quellen* (Berlin, 1973).

the chancellor promulgated a number of propositions.[15] These directed that nothing was to challenge the impression of German domestic unity and resolve, while in the official reading German troops remained in the field in order to defeat Russian despotism and British designs on world hegemony. Criticism of high policy was proscribed, as was discussion of war aims. These guidelines suggested that tensions had already begun to build on some scores, but they also allowed the venting of criticism on a range of other matters, particularly when these were of local concern. The officials who oversaw municipal rationing procedures were hence more vulnerable to criticism in the local papers than were military and civilian leaders in Berlin.

The obstacles to the public expression of dissent of any kind were nevertheless high. Institutions of censorship permeated the country. At the most basic level, in the communities where local editors had to submit copy before they published it, responsibility for managing information lay in the hands of the army, specifically in local censors' offices, which were manned by military officers or civilian policemen. These officials were in turn responsible to the Deputy Commanding General in each corps district. Despite the creation of the central office of censorship and, in October 1915, of a War Press Office within the War Ministry, attempts by military and civilian agencies alike to enforce common guidelines for censorship foundered on the autonomy of the Deputy Commanding Generals. Standards of tolerance varied accordingly throughout the country. Censorship was particularly tight in Berlin and its environs – the domain of the Third Army Corps – and in the working-class centers of the Rhineland and Westphalia, which lay within the realm of the Seventh Corps, while regulations tended to be more permissive in Bavaria. However, the hand of the military censor was heavy everywhere. It registered with increasing frequency in the columns of local newspapers, where empty white spaces announced editorial transgressions, the specific character of which was left to conjecture.

Censorship represented the negative facet of rationing information. The term "propaganda" suggests another, more proactive side – the systematic attempt to read the war in an optimistic light and to encourage the patriotic resolve of those whose enthusiasm had begun to wane in the face of food shortages, high prices, and the deaths of loved ones. In addition to commanding a monopoly on the news of events from the front, the government could mobilize an extended network of civilian public agencies whose impact on opinion was direct. The public display

---

[15] Wolfgang J. Mommsen, "Die Regierung Bethmann Hollweg und die öffentliche Meinung 1914–1917," *Vierteljahrshefte für Zeitgeschichte* 17 (1969), 117–55.

of flags and the staging of parades to celebrate happy occasions, like the Battle of Tannenberg, were not spontaneous. The corps of available public employees comprised school teachers at all levels, who interpreted the war for their charges. The same principle applied to the Protestant clergy, whose enthusiasm for the war was both uncritical and unrivaled. The Catholic clergy operated in a more complex relationship with state power, but Catholic pulpits likewise functioned for most of the war as centers of moral mobilization.

Public employees also managed the secular rites of patriotism in localities throughout the land. City fathers and other local notables – such as prominent businessmen, professors, and leading officials in local bureaus of state and federal agencies – presided over patriotic festivals, which convened regularly in public halls or (in the summer) in the open air. These were elaborate affairs, staged amid the heavy national symbolism of flags and depictions of monarchs and war heroes. The liturgy featured patriotic speeches punctuated with presentations of music, poetry, and drama (all of which were remarkable for the absence of British, French, or Russian pieces). The function of these festivals was demonstrative. They were scripted to create – both in Germany and the enemy lands – the impression of a people united in its resolution to fight to the end. During the first eighteen months of the war, they could play to residual enthusiasm for the war, which was reflected in the broad appeal of these events across the social spectrum. As the burdens of war accumulated, the festivals became more focal in the mobilization of patriotism, and the techniques they employed became more refined. The events also became more parochial. They appealed increasingly to people who looked socially like the convenors, while the sentiments invoked in the rituals began to ring artificial. The interpretive claims of the patriots strained to accommodate a war that refused to end in its second year.

The campaigns of 1915

Erich von Falkenhayn had been War Minister at the outbreak of the war; and in the fall of 1914 he moved into Moltke's position as Chief of the General Staff, which had now taken on the title of Supreme Command of the Army (OHL). In his role as operational head of the Germany army, Falkenhayn oversaw the last desperate German efforts to turn the allied flank in Flanders. His nerves were stronger than his predecessor's; and he needed all of his composure to deal with the staggering dilemmas that now descended upon the German military leadership, as well as the rivalries that these dilemmas spawned.

Plate 2   Erich von Falkenhayn (reproduced courtesy of the Hulton
Getty Picture Collection Limited)

The failure of Schlieffen's grand design represented a strategic catas-trophe. German armies were already at war on two fronts. The coun-try's commitments to its allies among the Central Powers – primarily to Austria-Hungary, but also to Turkey – threatened fighting on several additional fronts in southern and eastern Europe, to say nothing of the small wars that the Entente powers were waging against German colonial holdings in Africa and the Pacific.[16] The combined military and economic resources now arrayed against Germany far exceeded anything the coun-try could hope to mobilize; and Germany's disadvantage promised only to grow with the continuation of the war. The question that haunted German strategic planning for the war's second year was accordingly no longer how to win a spectacular military victory, but rather how to bring the conflict to an acceptable end.

Falkenhayn embodied the predicament.[17] Late in 1914, he confessed his belief to the chancellor that Germany could not win the war militarily. This confession was based on a sober assessment of the new realities of industrial war. The conclusions that Falkenhayn drew from these military calculations, however, were tortuous and politically misconceived; and in the end, they offered no resolution to the strategic problem. "If we do not lose the war," he was heard to say at this juncture, "we will have won it."[18] Germany could not, he believed, win on both fronts. A military decision on the eastern front was in all events impossible, for he was convinced – with the experience of Napoleon as a guide – that the vast open spaces and resources of Russia made this land unconquerable. He reasoned accordingly that the western front represented the war's pivotal theater. Here Germany faced its most dangerous and determined foe, which he thought to be England. This conclusion, which reflected current popular passions as much as it did military calculation, then defined the priorities towards which Falkenhayn's decisions stumbled during the next year. To persuade England of German invincibility, he envisaged a massive German offensive in the west, coupled with submarine warfare against British commerce. The success of these ventures depended in turn, Falkenhayn thought, on a separate peace in the east. This goal he hoped to achieve by means of a diplomatic offensive in conjunction with a limited offensive on that front, which would inflict what might be called a

[16] Wolfgang Petter, "Der Kampf um die deutschen Kolonien," in Wolfgang Michalka (ed.), *Der Erste Weltkrieg: Wirkung, Wahrnehmung, Analyse* (Munich and Zurich, 1994), 392–411; William Roger Louis, *Great Britain and Germany's Lost Colonies, 1914–1919* (Oxford, 1967); Woodruff Smith, *The German Colonial Empire* (Chapel Hill, NC, 1978), 221–33; Charles Miller, *Battle for the Bundu: The First World War in East Africa* (New York, 1974).
[17] Holger Afflerbach, *Falkenhayn: Politisches Denken und Handeln im Kaiserreich* (Munich, 1994).
[18] *Ibid.*, 198.

"moderate defeat" on the Russian army. The German war effort in 1915 was to be apportioned accordingly. While German peace-feelers ventured quietly towards Russia, the German position in the west was to be built up as a basis for decisive offensive operations.

The thinking of Falkenhayn's rivals in the German military leadership was burdened with no such subtlety.[19] Paul von Hindenburg and Erich Ludendorff, the soldiers who had overseen the only German triumphs of 1914, envisaged a more brilliant scenario for 1915. They called for the military annihilation of Germany's weakest opponent, which they insisted was Russia. In their view, this goal required a massive maneuver of envelopment, which would penetrate deep into the rear of Russian positions in Poland, cut the Russian armies off from their bases, and destroy these forces. Then, with the eastern front secure, the full weight of the German forces could be thrown at the western powers, whose armies would await a fate similar to that of the Russians. In advocating a campaign that was framed in *Vernichtung* (annihilation by means of strategic envelopment), Hindenburg and Ludendorff could lay claim to Schlieffen's legacy, even if they adjusted his geographical priorities in line with their own experience in the eastern command.

The success of Hindenburg and Ludendorff as commanders of the eastern armies in 1914 lent enormous weight to their views, as it turned them into folk heroes. In the debates that took place at the end of the year over military priorities, these generals also had the support of Bethmann Hollweg, who, like Falkenhayn, hoped for a diplomatic settlement with Russia but who, like the eastern commanders, reasoned that a massive offensive in the east was the best way to achieve this end. But Falkenhayn also had allies. Alfred von Tirpitz and the naval command advocated commercial warfare against England. More significantly at this stage in the war, Falkenhayn enjoyed the support of the emperor and his entourage, who (with good reason) feared Hindenburg as a potential rival for popular loyalties. In this atmosphere, the debates over strategic priorities turned into intrigue before the issue could be resolved.

The decision in favor of the east was due to other circumstances. The war had not gone well for Germany's principal ally in 1914. In fact, the difficulties that plagued the military alliance of the Central Powers were already in evidence by the year's end.[20] The Austrians had not been privy

---

[19] Heinz Kraft, *Staatsräson und Kriegführung im kaiserlichen Deutschland 1914–1916: Der Gegensatz zwischen dem Generalstabschef von Falkenhayn und dem Oberbefehlshaber Ost im Rahmen des Bündniskrieges der Mittelmächte* (Göttingen, 1980).

[20] Gordon A. Craig, "The World War I Alliance of the Central Powers in Retrospect: The Military Cohesion of the Alliance," *Journal of Modern History* 37 (1965), 336–44; Gary W. Shanafelt, *The Secret Enemy: Austria–Hungary and the German Alliance, 1914–1918* (New York, 1985).

to the specifics of the Schlieffen Plan, nor were their operations in 1914 coordinated in any meaningful way with the Germans' designs. The performance of the Austrians in the initial campaigns of the war had done nothing to raise the regard in which the German military leaders held their ally. The defeat of Serbia obsessed the Austrian commander, Franz Conrad von Hötzendorff, to the point of clouding his judgment. In action against Serbian forces, however, Austrian armies had quickly stalled in the fall of 1914. More significantly, against the Russians in Galicia, a far more ominous opponent, the Austrians suffered major defeats and territorial losses, which included the great fortresses of Lemberg and Przemysl. The campaign on this eastern front also brought the decimation of the Austrian officer corps and revealed the extent of ethnic disaffection among the troops, particularly among the Czech contingents. Fears for the collapse of the Austrian army were not exaggerated; and they prompted the German command to send reinforcements to the south at the end of the year, as the operational subordination of the Austrians to the German command grew apace with their diplomatic dependence on their German ally. In the German leadership, however, anxiety over Austria's survival bred sympathy for the entreaties of the Austrian commander, who now pleaded that dramatic military success in the eastern theater would revitalize his army. This course of action promised finally to impress the governments of Italy and Rumania, which were both leaning towards intervention on the side of the Entente.

Falkenhayn thus agreed, albeit with skepticism and reluctance, to major offensive operations in the east. Four new reserve corps, which had been recruited in the fall of 1914, were committed to this theater, along with an additional corps from the western front and large stocks of artillery and machine guns. By early 1915, German forces in the east had grown to more than 600,000, which were now deployed in three armies. The offensive began in two sectors of the long eastern front (see map 5). Late in January, combined German and Austrian forces launched an attack to the south, into Galicia, which dislodged the Russians from the passes of the Carpathian mountains before it stalled. To the north, the Germans advanced some forty miles into Russian Poland from lines in East Prussia, before this attack stalled, too.

In the aftermath of this action, whose territorial gains hardly validated the enormous losses that the Austrians sustained to desertion and the winter, dissension returned to German headquarters. The issue now was the scope and goal of the next attack on the Russian positions. With the support of the Austrian commander, Ludendorff and Hindenburg argued in favor of a grand new Cannae, a massive flanking attack whose northern arm would sweep north and east of Kovno, deep into Poland.

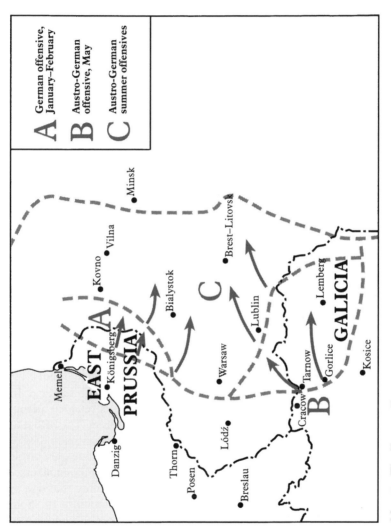

Map 5   The Eastern Front, 1915

A German offensive, January–February

B Austro-German offensive, May

C Austro-German summer offensives

In Falkenhayn's view, however, the demands that this plan made on Germany's limited military resources were as objectionable as was its likely impact on the Russians' interest in a negotiated peace. In hopes of forestalling the broader ambitions of his eastern command, Falkenhayn accordingly agreed to a more modest plan, a smaller-scale envelopment to follow an assault on Russian lines in western Galicia, in a sector marked by the towns of Tarnow and Gorlice.

The ensuing campaign yielded the most sensational German victories of the entire war. In one of the few frontal assaults to bear fruit in this war, a joint German–Austrian force broke through the Russian lines around Gorlice in May. Russian troops thereupon evacuated most of Galicia, when in July two German armies attacked in the north. The Russian retreat now became general; German troops occupied Warsaw in August, and by the end of September all of Poland, as well as Lithuania and Latvia, was in the hands of the Central Powers. It was a breathtaking spectacle. At a cost of more than 750,000 casualties, the Russian armies had fallen back up to 250 miles. The campaign gave the lie to the impression that the First World War lacked strategic mobility, but it also reflected the special circumstances that reigned in this theater. The thin Polish front extended some 600 miles over flat, sandy terrain; so it could not be defended with the sophisticated concentration that became the rule to the west. The most telling feature of the campaign was the vast technical superiority that the Germans enjoyed over the Russians. The Austro-German army that attacked around Gorlice in May was equipped with 1,272 pieces of light artillery and 334 heavy guns; the corresponding figures for the Russians who defended this sector were 675 and 4.[21] This advantage compensated for the numerical superiority of the Russian armies, which was, however, great enough to sustain even the staggering losses of 1915.

Ludendorff and Hindenburg were not the only ones who believed that the Germans could now, with sufficient support and strategic audacity, win the war in the east. Falkenhayn, however, disagreed. The difficulty, to which he was more alive than his eastern commanders, was that the Germans were also under enormous duress in the west. Here their armies enjoyed no such advantages as in the east, and the more equal balance of forces had already cast combat into the terrible immobility that was the hallmark of the western front. From the English Channel to the Swiss border, the front extended some 450 miles over rolling hills and forests. Much of the front was situated atop firm clay or chalk soil which accommodated deep, dense labyrinths of trenches. These were home to more than 8,000,000 soldiers on both sides, who were dedicated, trained, and

---

[21] Fritz Klein, *et al.*, *Deutschland im Ersten Weltkrieg* (3 vols., Berlin, 1968–69), vol. II, 76.

equipped to construct and man the most forbidding defense systems yet devised.

The unhappy role of demonstrating the formidability of these defenses fell in 1915 to the French and British armies (see map 6). The presence of German armies on Belgian and French soil dictated an offensive strategy to the western powers. The Germans launched but one major attack. This action, which took place in April in Flanders, was note-worthy for the Germans' introduction of poison gas on the western front, but its principal object was to screen the offensive then being launched on the eastern front against Gorlice. The French, by contrast, attacked German lines repeatedly in the Champagne district, while British and French forces did the same to the west, in the Artois region. Although these offensives reached several high points of intensity in the late winter, spring, and early fall, combat on the western front was already assuming its characteristic guise; and it was difficult to judge when one battle ended and another began. Extended artillery barrages on opposing trenches were the ritual prelude to what was called infantry attack, the headlong dash by masses of unprotected footsoldiers to their slaughter. The architecture of the trench systems proved resilient in the face of shelling, and its capstones, barbed wire and machine guns, consistently defied infantry assault. The mechanics of combat in this style condemned the attackers to casualties that were increasingly difficult to justify. Allied offensive operations near Arras in May and June 1915 opened with a storm of more than 2,000,000 shells on the German lines. The British and French attackers nonetheless suffered 132,000 casualties during their several weeks in front of the German trenches. That the German defenders lost 73,000 in this action disclosed the frightful toll taken by artillery, even when it failed to destroy entrenched defenses.[22] The German losses were also due to the reluctance of German commanders to abandon territory in tactical retreats to more secure defense lines.

For the Central Powers, 1915 was the best year of the war. Despite commitments to several fronts, the Germans had frustrated repeated allied offensives in the west. To the east, the Germans had achieved a spectacular strategic breakthrough in Poland and bolstered the armies of their Austrian ally. In the southeast, their Turkish allies had thwarted an allied effort to turn the strategic flank with an invasion of the Dardanelles peninsula. In the fall came more good news, when Bulgaria entered the war on the side of Central Powers. Bulgarian troops then joined Austrian and German forces in the final subjugation of Serbia at the end of the year – an operation that provided an overland link to Turkey, as well as

---

[22] *Ibid.*, 84.

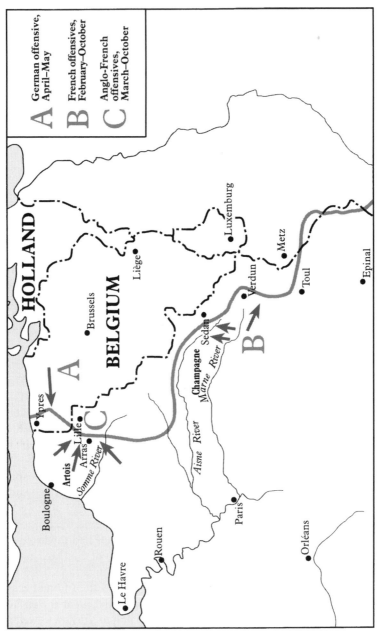

Map 6   The Western Front, 1915

A German offensive, April–May

B French offensives, February–October

C Anglo-French offensives, March–October

HOLLAND

BELGIUM

Brussels

Liège

Luxemburg

Metz

Verdun

Toul

Epinal

Sedan

Champagne

Marne River

Aisne River

Ypres

Lille

Arras

Artois

Somme River

Boulogne

Le Havre

Rouen

Paris

Orléans

to yet another theater of war far to the southeast, in Mesopotamia.[23] Here a German military mission attempted to foment rebellion against England and Russia, the imperial powers that dominated this part of the world.

If the developments of 1915 offered some immediate grounds for optimism in Germany, the long-term implications of the war's second year were less encouraging. The pattern of conflict in 1915 was the same as it had been in the previous year – triumph in the east, stalemate in the west, and no end to the war. The strains on German resources mounted as the conflict broadened. In May 1915, despite desperate German diplomatic attempts to forestall it, the Italians entered the war on the side of the Entente. A series of Italian offensives against Austrian positions in the Tyrol and along the Isonzo River demonstrated the particular formidability of defensive warfare in an Alpine setting. Despite their failure, the Italian attacks tied down sixteen Austrian and German divisions. At the end of the year, German troops were thus in action in the Tyrol, Serbia, Poland, Russia's Baltic provinces, Asia Minor, and Africa, as well as in Belgium and France.

Commitment to these many theaters was calculated to deplete German resources; and it defined the country's strategic dilemma throughout the rest of the war. The grand eastern offensive of 1915 halted in the exhaustion of German troops. The demands of the western front made it impossible for Falkenhayn to assign sufficient reinforcements to the eastern theater, even had he believed in the possibility of destroying the Russian army. However, the Russians' ability to bear enormous losses confirmed the German commander's belief that the key to winning the war did not lie on the eastern front. In 1916 he planned to prove his point in the west. Here, however, he faced a dilemma of a different kind, for the dynamics of battle frustrated the kind of offensive action that victory seemed to require. And by the beginning of 1916, many of Germany's leaders were questioning the wisdom of Falkenhayn's thinking, for political as well as military reasons.

Falkenhayn and Bethmann Hollweg

Soldiers commanded respect and power in Imperial Germany. The term "militarism" connotes this problem, which had a long history in

---

[23] Ulrich Trumpener, *Germany and the Ottoman Empire, 1914–1918* (Princeton, 1968); Frank G. Weber, *Eagles on the Crescent; Germany, Austria, and the Diplomacy of the Turkish Alliance, 1914–1918* (Ithaca, 1970).

Germany.[24] Conflicts between the military and civilian leadership had figured large in the wars of national unification in the middle of the nineteenth century, when the great Bismarck had fought for the principle of civilian supremacy in political councils. In the new German empire, which was the product of the soldiers' triumph, the military enjoyed immense prestige, and Bismarck's successors were less successful in resisting the claims of the military leadership to political influence. Schlieffen formulated his plan with no heed for its massive political consequences; and the most important German policy-maker during the ultimate stages of the July crisis in 1914 was arguably General von Moltke.

By virtue of his training and background, General von Falkenhayn also believed in the supremacy of the military, above all in time of war. He was a capable and ambitious soldier. His tolerance for ambiguity was unusually honed for a German officer, and it reflected his extended experience in foreign lands before he was named War Minister in 1913. In this role, he had nonetheless made no secret of his disdain for the views of his civilian colleagues in the ministry and the politicians in the Reichstag, whom he routinely antagonized with his arrogance. His manner also antagonized his military colleagues, however, so he had few friends anywhere when he took over Moltke's position in the fall of 1914. His decisions about the 1915 campaign earned him additional enemies. Given the political circumstances in Imperial Germany, the most important of these enemies were themselves soldiers.

Falkenhayn's immediate political antagonist was not a soldier but the chancellor.[25] The two leaders represented an interesting contrast. Bethmann Hollweg had advanced through the ranks of a classic bureaucratic career.[26] By temperament he was a ponderous, occasionally melancholy man, who found it easier to soften conflicting views through equivocation or compromise than to choose among them. In part for this reason, he conveyed different impressions to different people. Temperamental differences played a role in the growing conflict between him and Falkenhayn. The general was not prepared to suffer the interference of civilian politicians in strategic planning; and he withheld information from them.

---

[24] The classic studies of this problem are Gerhard Ritter, *Sword and Scepter: The Problem of Militarism in Germany* (3 vols., Coral Gables, FL, 1969–73) and Gordon A. Craig, *The Politics of the Prussian Army, 1640–1945* (Oxford, 1955).

[25] See, in addition to Afflerbach's biography of Falkenhayn, Karl-Heinz Janssen, *Der Kanzler und der General: Die Führungskrise um Bethmann Hollweg und Falkenhayn (1914–1916)* (Göttingen, 1967).

[26] Konrad H. Jarausch, *The Enigmatic Chancellor: Bethmann Hollweg and the Hubris of Imperial Germany* (New Haven and London, 1973); Günter Wollstein, *Theobald von Bethmann Hollweg: Letzter Erbe Bismarcks, Erstes Opfer der Dolchstosslegende* (Göttingen and Cologne, 1990).

The absence of any institutional forum to coordinate strategy and policy was consistent with German political traditions; but it exacerbated this problem. The chancellor in turn had doubts about Falkenhayn's competence to lead the German armies; and he questioned the general's strategic priorities. He also feared that Falkenhayn had designs on the chancellorship. By early 1915, he was scheming to have Falkenhayn replaced.

Bethmann's concerns reflected political difficulties that made Falkenhayn's strategic dilemmas look almost easy. Every phase of the war burdened the chancellor. The military conduct of the war had to concern him, as did the views (and moods) of the Kaiser, Germany's relations to other countries – whether allies or enemies – and the growing pressures on the homefront, which had by 1915 begun to find political expression. In the first instance, however, the chancellor had to preserve the domestic truce that was forged in the summer of 1914.

Despite the impressions of popular unity in the early days, the consensus in favor of the war was fragile from the start, vulnerable to pressures from both the left and right. The most sensitive problem was the Socialist labor movement.[27] The Socialist party's vote in favor of the war in August 1914 masked deep reservations among industrial workers, whose support was critical for the war effort. The Socialists were persuaded that Russian aggression against Germany had caused the war. To their supporters, leading Socialists argued that the defeat of this reactionary, autocratic power would lead to democratic reform of the constitution in Germany after the war. Socialists advocated a negotiated peace as soon as the war's basic defensive purpose was achieved. The continuation of the war into a second year made the tensions within this party increasingly difficult to contain; and in December 1914, Karl Liebknecht, the leader of its left wing, broke party discipline and voted in the Reichstag against authorizing further public loans to finance the war. As the advance of German armies deep into Belgium, France, and Poland made it harder to portray the war as a defensive struggle, the Socialists began to call for specific domestic reforms in order to reward the continued loyalty of workers to the war effort. One such reform was securing the legal validity of collective-bargaining agreements. Another was the democratization of the suffrage and the establishment of ministerial responsibility in parliaments in Prussia and the other German states.

To Bethmann Hollweg fell the task of convincing the Socialists of the German government's desire for a moderate peace, as well as its sympathy for some kind of domestic reform. However, the chancellor also had to

---

[27] Susanne Miller, *Burgfrieden und Klassenkampf: Die deutsche Sozialdemokratie im Ersten Weltkrieg* (Düsseldorf, 1974).

appease other groups. Right-wing forces insisted that a decisive victory, attended by appropriate territorial annexations, could alone justify the frightful sacrifices that Germans had already born in their own defense. In a series of memoranda, which arrived on the chancellor's desk in the first months of the war, the advocates of these war aims laid out a program of demands so ambitious that they anticipated, in notable respects, the German goals in the next European war. Buttressed by vast annexations in eastern and western Europe, Germany would, in all events, have emerged as the hegemonic power on the continent. Bethmann sympathized in private with the idea of large-scale annexations, but public statements to this effect were impossible.[28] Along with any prospect for a negotiated peace, they would destroy the tenuous domestic consensus as surely as would public commitment to democratic reforms at home.

Managing this dilemma required all the chancellor's arts of evasion, as he parried entreaties from proponents of the conflicting positions. Support for a moderate peace and constitutional reform was concentrated in the Reichstag – principally in the Socialist party, but also among the middle-class Progressives, and the left wing of the Catholic party, the Center. Bethmann Hollweg sought in vague terms to assure these political leaders of his support, for they could make life uncomfortable for him: these three parties potentially represented a majority coalition in the federal parliament. The periodic convening of the Reichstag to authorize additional war loans provided a public forum for criticizing official policy; and, as the costs of the war mounted, so did the criticism.

But the Reichstag was itself deeply divided. The Conservatives and National Liberals, the right-wing parties that represented in turn the landowning nobility and the upper bourgeoisie, called for a *Siegfrieden*, a victorious, uncompromising peace with lavish territorial rewards for the victor. Beyond the parliament, the advocates of this position were entrenched in the structures of power in Imperial Germany, so they enjoyed an influence altogether out of proportion to their numbers. They included the business leaders who controlled the country's economic mobilization. They dominated the public bureaucracies; and they were well organized in the patriotic societies. These nationalist organizations, which had called for an aggressive German foreign policy before the war, easily embraced a vast program of annexations as soon as the war broke out. Finally, advocates of annexations could be confident of the support of the military leadership, particularly in the eastern command. Most of

---

[28] One such memorandum, which advocated breathtaking annexations, originated in his own office. This document, the "September Memorandum," is the principal piece of evidence that Bethmann Hollweg planned the war to achieve German hegemony in Europe. See Fischer, *Germany's Aims in the First World War* (New York, 1967), 98–106.

Imperial Germany's prewar political and social elites thus congregated in this camp. They anticipated that military triumph would vindicate their own leadership of the country and hence forestall demands for domestic political and social reform.

Controversy thus quickly erupted over Germany's aims in the war. The early German advances suggested that the war was about more than national defense; they also raised specific political questions that were difficult to evade – such as the future of Belgium and Poland. Besieged in the first weeks of the war by a "flood of memoranda and petitions" with specific recommendations, Bethmann Hollweg moved to suppress the debate before it could jeopardize the domestic political truce.[29] He decreed a moratorium on all public discussion of war aims. The guidelines that he then laid down to the censors provided vaguely that Germany would emerge from the war secure against Russian despotism (a concession to the Socialists) and British plots to achieve world hegemony (a concession to the right).

Although several of the loudest and most aggressive nationalists were muzzled, enforcement of the moratorium was anything but balanced. Bethmann had no power over the Deputy Commanding Generals, who controlled the censorship in their districts and sympathized with the right-wing nationalists. Left-wing pamphlets and circulars were hence more vulnerable to confiscation than were those that circulated with extravagant demands for annexations. To the chancellor's consternation, the annexationists also enjoyed access to officials in the highest circles of government. The army's eastern command sympathized with their views and communicated its sympathies to the press. Early in 1915 the annexationists found another ally in Tirpitz, who was anxious to encourage popular support for an all-out submarine offensive against allied commerce, which could alone, he argued, break the strategic stalemate. The chancellor saw only the diplomatic perils of a military course that would antagonize the neutrals, above all the United States – as the furious outcry that followed the sinking of the *Lusitania* in May made clear. Not for the last time, he struggled to discourage the idea. To deprive Tirpitz of his popular forum, he persuaded the emperor to limit the admiral's autonomous powers of censorship over naval affairs. It was but a temporary success, and it earned the chancellor an important enemy in uniform.[30]

Falkenhayn remained another one. Tensions between him and Bethmann grew during the campaign of 1915, in part because of the general's

---

[29] Mommsen, *Bürgerstolz*, 574.
[30] Raffael Scheck, *Alfred von Tirpitz and German Right-Wing Politics, 1914–1930* (Atlantic Highlands, NJ, 1997).

support for Tirpitz's position. The chancellor also believed that the general's preoccupation with the western front was ill founded, that a decisive victory in the east was not only possible but the only realistic prelude to any kind of peace with the western powers. Bethmann Hollweg thus gravitated towards the camp of the so-called "easterners" and a dangerous alliance with the two heroes in uniform who held sway there. The alliance was consummated in 1916, and it had profound consequences for the remainder of the war.

3 The war grows total

Military historians have used the term "total war" to describe the dramatic growth in the scope and intensity of warfare during the last two centuries.[1] The term is geared to historical processes that, since the French Revolution, rendered wars larger, longer, and more costly. The growing difficulties of reaching a decision by arms and the expanding needs of modern armies placed growing demands on homefronts – to the point where, in the world wars of the twentieth century, civilians were scarcely less central than soldiers to the prosecution of war; and their pivotal roles in these wars made them just as vulnerable to systematic and calculated acts of enemy action, whether by means of commercial warfare or strategic bombardment from the air.

The First World War occupies a special place in this scheme. The term "total war" was the product of this great conflict. French leaders first used the term "*la guerre intégrale*" in 1917 to announce their government's intention to abandon all restraint in mobilizing French society for war. Their announcement signaled less a radical departure than the ruthless intensification of efforts that had begun in 1914 – in all of the belligerent lands. In all events, as a characterization of institutions and practices that marked the second half of this struggle, the term "total war" was no less valid for developments in Imperial Germany.

In this light, 1916 was a pivotal year. The land battles of 1916 were the most monstrous ever fought. New military leaders came to power in Germany, and they did aspire to achieve the total mobilization of society's resources and energies. The measures that they inaugurated to achieve this end brought the brutal reorganization of the economy for the purposes of making war. Then, at the close of the year, the German leadership decided upon a course of military action that expanded the scope of war to include all of the world's major powers.

---

[1] Roger Chickering, "Total War: Use and Abuse of a Concept," in Manfred Boemeke, *et al.* (eds.), *On the Road to Total War: The United States and Germany, 1871–1914* (New York, 1998) 15–28.

The land campaigns of 1916

The German victories in the east in 1915 failed to shake Falkenhayn's belief that the war could be won only in the west. The year's experiences on both the eastern and western fronts had confirmed his belief, however, that the war would not end in a great battle of annihilation. While he remained convinced that Britain represented the country's most implacable foe, he reasoned that endurance and attrition – or what the Germans called "*Ermattung*" – held the key and that the struggle would end only when the British leadership had concluded that the German army was invincible in the field.

These calculations lay at the basis of the German commander's plans for 1916. He was determined to undermine the British resolve with a two-pronged offensive. The one prong, which was aimed at the commercial underpinnings of the British war effort, was to launch unrestricted submarine warfare against all seaborne traffic with that island. He did not share the concerns of the civilian leadership that this course would bring the United States into the war, for he believed that the other prong of his strategy would by then have settled the whole issue. He planned a land attack in the west that would devastate Britain's weaker partner.

There was more than a little wishful thinking in Falkenhayn's calculations. His ideas about the effectiveness of submarine warfare were fanciful enough that the civilians were able, at this stage in the war at least, largely to parry them. His thinking about the land war carried more force, but it was only a little less fanciful. The campaigns of 1915 on both fronts had suggested that overwhelming superiority at the point of attack offered the only hope of success in offensive operations. Despite the massive industrial build-up at home and the broadening conscription of military manpower, the German army on the western front remained in significant respects weaker than its antagonists. The German military leadership raised an additional twenty-two divisions in 1915, but it purchased this result by reducing the number of regiments in each infantry division from four to three and the number of artillery pieces in each battery from six to four. At the end of the year, the Germans could deploy 2,350,000 men in the west, in 118 divisions; but these troops confronted 145 divisions, which comprised 3,470,000 enemy soldiers.

Falkenhayn was undeterred by these numbers. He had devised an offensive strategy that was appropriate, he believed, to a theater in which the defense was indomitable. The object was quickly to seize a point in the French line. This point was to be of such strategic or political significance that the French leadership would be compelled to recapture it – in circumstances that afforded all the advantages of the defense to the

Germans. The result, Falkenhayn reasoned, would be losses so hideous that the exhausted French would sue for peace, leaving the British isolated and in an untenable position.

By the force of this logic at least, Verdun was an ideal place to attack. It was one of a chain of fortresses that the French had built up in the late nineteenth century in order to deter another German invasion like the one of 1870. Because the original citadel was the handiwork of Vauban, Louis XIV's great military architect, the fortress had a patriotic aura that transcended its strategic significance. In early 1916, however, it appeared vulnerable. After the fall of Liège had thrown doubt on the invincibility of all such great fortresses, the French had stripped off most of Verdun's artillery for use in more active sectors of the front. Falkenhayn thus calculated that a swift strike would succeed here and that the public outcry in France would demand the recapture of the fortress. Despite the lessons of the allied failures in 1915, he planned to saturate the sector with an artillery bombardment so intense that, as he explained, "not even a mouse could survive."[2] Accordingly, German footsoldiers would have only to occupy the remains of the fortress. By February 1916, the Germans had thus assembled a force of 140,000 men and nearly 600 pieces of heavy artillery along an eight-mile sector opposite the fortress, which consisted of a system of forts on both sides of the Meuse Valley (see map 7). French forces in the sector numbered about half the German; and they had but 43 pieces of heavy artillery.

The battle began on 21 February with eight hours of German artillery fire.[3] German infantry thereupon advanced against light French resistance on the right bank of the river. Four days later, Fort Douaumont, the anchor of the entire system, fell to the Germans. If the first days of the battle vindicated the German hopes, the loss of Douaumont, which many observers had once thought to be the strongest fort in the world, prompted the French to react just as Falkenhayn had anticipated. The call went out for a vast French build-up in the Verdun sector. By the end of the month, large reinforcements had slowed the German advance; and by the end of the campaign, nine months later, two-thirds of the entire French army had seen action in this part of the front. Because they had not achieved their goals when the French defenses stiffened, the Germans, who now had to reinforce the sector massively themselves, found the dynamics of battle shifting to their great disadvantage, as they had to press the attack. As the German offensive broadened in the next weeks

[2] Quoted in Afflerbach, *Falkenhayn*, 361.
[3] Alistair Horne, *The Price of Glory: Verdun 1916* (New York, 1962).

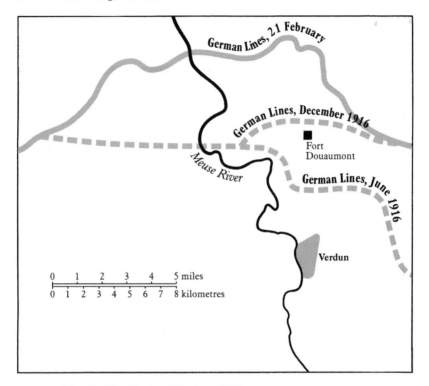

Map 7   The Battle of Verdun, 1916

onto both sides of the river, the battle became the quintessential battle of attrition, the western front in microcosm. The two sides exchanged roles repeatedly in the furious rituals of attack and counterattack. These purchased meters of empty land – sanitized in battle of every living thing – with millions of tons of material and tens of thousands of human lives. By early July, when the Germans achieved their furthest advance, each of the armies had expended about 250,000 casualties – the French a little more, the Germans a little less.

The crisis came in the early summer of 1916, when the Germans were reminded of their many strategic commitments elsewhere. On 4 June, to the desperate pleas of their French allies, the Russians launched their most successful operation of the war. The so-called Brusilov Offensive was directed against Austrian positions in the southern sector of the eastern front (see map 8). It resulted in dramatic gains along a 200-mile front, where the dispirited Austrian defenses collapsed. As Russian troops pushed 100 miles westward into Hungary, the Austrian army lost 350,000 soldiers, most of them to desertion. Falkenhayn responded to this

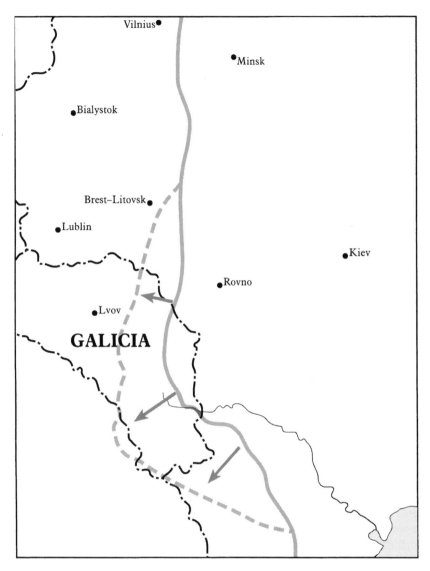

Map 8   The Brusilov Offensive, 1916

challenge as the French had hoped. As the Austrian command removed
troops from the Italian front, the Germans dispatched most of their strategic reserve, about 200,000 men, to salvage their beleaguered ally. Corruption, ill planning, and an absence of operational coordination among
the Russian armies then saved the Germans, whose strategic position

would have been desperate had a sustained Russian offensive followed against German positions to the north. Duress in the east nonetheless sapped the force of the German effort at Verdun.

So did events to the west of this fortress. The Anglo-French offensive at the Somme River stands out in the annals of this war. The nearly 60,000 British soldiers who fell before the German trenches on 1 July 1916, the first day of the infantry attack, were tribute to the most mindless defiance of the new realities of combat. By the end of the year, when the campaign limped to an end, the Allied casualties had grown to ten times this figure in the conquest of a patch of barren landscape. The British misadventures have overshadowed the dreadful costs that this action inflicted upon the Germans. The Battle of the Somme was the model contest of *matériel*, the *Materialschlacht*. It opened in a hail of 1,500,000 artillery shells, which fell around the clock on German positions for a full week. In enduring this and subsequent barrages, in defending their positions against repeated Allied infantry assaults, and in their own repeated counterattacks, the Germans themselves expended more than 150,000 artillery shells a day; and they lost close to 500,000 men.

Pressures from the Somme and the eastern front translated back to Verdun, where the German attack stalled in the summer of 1916. In October the French launched a carefully prepared counteroffensive, which retook what little remained of Fort Douaumont, before the German lines rallied in defense. When the campaign expired in general exhaustion at the end of the year, the German positions lay about three miles forward of where they had been in February. The cost of this exchange was about 750,000 casualties, almost half of them German. In all theaters, German casualties in 1916 totaled nearly 1,500,000 men.[4]

The German Supreme Command could take little comfort in the fact that these losses were less than those of their antagonists. The prodigious campaigns of the year not only demonstrated the bankruptcy of Falkenhayn's plans for a "small" western offensive; they also appeared to confirm the futility of all offensive operations in that theater, given existing technologies. The two sides seemed condemned to an extended ordeal of attrition – a prolonged, massive investment of men and *matériel* with negligible strategic returns. While this prognosis pleased the generals nowhere, it was particularly disquieting to the Germans, for it meant that they were eventually going to lose the war. The Germans faced a coalition that could, as the Battle of the Somme had already demonstrated, outproduce them in every area that was relevant to combat in this mode – whether munitions, machinery, food, or men.

[4] Reichsarchiv, *Der Weltkrieg 1914 bis 1918* (14 vols., Berlin, 1925–44), vol. XI, 41.

By the time the German leadership had digested these unhappy prospects, Falkenhayn was no longer in charge of the German armies. He had banked his fortunes on the success of his western campaign in 1916; and by the summer it was clear that his strategic conception had collapsed beyond hope. The final blow came in August 1916, in another development that the German commander had failed to foresee. The Rumanians entered the war on the side of the Entente, opening yet another front on which German troops were required. At the end of the month Falkenhayn fell from power. His mantle fell to the only generals who could boast a record of sustained success.

Hindenburg and Ludendorff

The fall of Falkenhayn marked epochal changes in the German prosecution of the war, as well as in the dynamics of German politics. Falkenhayn fell victim to machinations that had begun almost the moment he took over the Supreme Command from Moltke in the fall of 1914, but his departure signaled above all the alarm of the German leadership – the growing fear in Berlin that only a dramatic change of course could prevent the eventual defeat of the Central Powers. The campaigns of 1916 demonstrated that the scale of Germany's exertions was only going to grow. The plight of Austria-Hungary verged on desperation in the summer of 1916, after the Brusilov Offensive had eventuated in almost 1,000,000 losses to the army and stifled an Austrian offensive on the Italian front. In the aftermath of these ruinous operations, the German military leadership imposed a joint supreme command on their ally, while German units, along with staff and line officers, were distributed as bracing throughout the Austrian army. Rumors circulated nonetheless of Austria's imminent defection from the war.

Rumania was the last straw. The new setback deprived Falkenhayn of all his popular support. Most of the Reichstag demanded a change in the Supreme Command, as did the leadership of both the navy and the army. So did Bethmann Hollweg, who had reasons of his own. Falkenhayn's strategy, he believed, offered no prospect for military victory, while the unpopular general himself was an obstacle to a negotiated peace. Such a peace now beckoned to the chancellor as the most feasible way to end the war. Bethmann accordingly hoped to install popular leaders atop the army, in the calculation that they could make a negotiated settlement more palatable to the general public. He got his way with the new appointments, but he miscalculated fundamentally in the other respect, for the new Supreme Command was in no way interested in a negotiated settlement.

Plate 3   The Kaiser (centre) studying maps under the guidance of
Paul von Hindenburg (left) and Erich Ludendorff (right) (reproduced
with kind permission of the Trustees of the Imperial War Museum,
London)

The two soldiers who made up the so-called "third OHL" provided an
intriguing contrast. Paul von Hindenburg embodied the Prussian military
class.[5] He was born in 1847, the son of an army officer. His own military
experience began at the age of eleven, when he was sent to boarding
school as a cadet. He was then commissioned as a second lieutenant in
the Prussian army at the age of eighteen and spent the rest of his active
career in it. He fought with distinction in the war of 1870. He then made
his way up the ranks to a generalship and the command of an army
corps, until he retired in 1911 at the age of 64. His principal traits were
his stolidity, a limited intelligence, loyalty to his calling, and a lack of all
pretension. The outbreak of war in 1914 prompted his recall to service,
now at the head of German forces in the eastern theater. The leading role
in the ensuing campaigns, however, fell by calculation to his chief of staff
in that theater.

[5] John W. Wheeler-Bennett, *Hindenburg: The Wooden Titan* (London, 1967); Walter Görlitz,
Hindenburg: Ein Lebensbild (Bonn, 1953); Rudolf Olden, *Hindenburg: Oder der Geist der
preussischen Armee* (Hildesheim, 1982).

This was Erich Ludendorff.[6] In significant respects, this soldier represented the polar opposite of his nominal superior, as well as the symbol of a new dynamic in the German military profession. Ludendorff was not noble. Eighteen years younger than Hindenburg, he joined the army in 1882. His advancement through the ranks in the General Staff exposed him to the army's reigning social prejudices against middle-class officers. These prejudices he defied with his talent, as well as with the ferocious energy and willpower that made him a temperamental contrast to Hindenburg. He was also known for his broad knowledge of military engineering and technology – fields of technical learning which were disdained in the aristocratic ethos of the officer corps.

Under Moltke, Ludendorff became head of the operations section in the General Staff, and in this capacity he was the driving force behind the massive expansion of the German army in the years immediately prior to the war. This effort aroused the apprehensions of most of the army's leaders, who feared the dilution of the officer corps with non-aristocrats and the dilution of the troops with Socialists. Ludendorff, however, heeded only the technical imperatives of warfare; and he overpowered these objections, arguing that the Schlieffen Plan made no sense without a vast increase in force. His role in reducing the Liège fortresses in the opening days of the war then established his military reputation. He was immediately appointed chief of staff to Hindenburg in the eastern theater.

They made a good team from the start.[7] Ludendorff provided the impulse and operational imagination, but he would have been far less effective but for the stabilizing force of his senior colleague. Ludendorff also benefited from Hindenburg's immense popularity and the authority that it brought to the team in their dealings with military and civilian rivals. Ludendorff's rise was, in sum, inconceivable without Hindenburg.

After the Battle of Tannenberg, Hindenburg quickly became a semi-divine presence in Germany. He had the aura of a hero. He was a massive, grandfatherly figure – the symbol of determination and military success bathed in stern benevolence. The mobilization of morale in Germany was wedded to this figure, who became the focus of popular adulation. Parents named their children after him. By the end of 1914, a "Hindenburg cult" had taken root. Its rituals played out in town squares in Berlin and

---

[6] Wolfgang Venohr, *Ludendorff: Legende und Wirklichkeit* (Berlin, 1993); Roger Parkinson, *Tormented Warrior: Ludendorff and the Supreme Command* (New York, 1978); D. J. Goodspeed, *Ludendorff: Genius of World War I* (Boston, 1966).

[7] Robert B. Asprey, *The German High Command at War: Hindenburg and Ludendorff and the First World War* (New York, 1991); Trevor Dupuy, *The Military Lives of Hindenburg and Ludendorff of Imperial Germany* (New York, 1970).

elsewhere, where huge wooden statues of the commander were erected, then plated with metal nails purchased by townspeople with contributions to the Red Cross. "Our Hindenburg" was soon an omnipresent image, a symbol of charismatic authority, and a source of growing concern to the emperor and his entourage.

It was thus a measure of the distress in the German leadership that the emperor finally agreed in August 1916 to call Hindenburg and Ludendorff in from the east. To popular jubilation, which extended into the ranks of the Socialist party, Hindenburg became officially the head of the Supreme Command, while Ludendorff moved in as his chief of staff, although he took the title of first quartermaster. The dynamic of their relationship persisted. With the symbolic sanction of Hindenburg, Ludendorff became the dominant factor in the German military effort for the rest of the war; and Ludendorff's priorities became a compelling force in the evolution of politics and society on homefront.

These priorities deserve some comment. Ludendorff was a pure soldier. He regarded war as the foundation of human affairs. In an age of social Darwinism, he was by no means alone in this view, but he pursued its implications with a relentlessness that was unusual among German soldiers, most of whom were more bound by the conventions of their profession. In the twentieth century, Ludendorff believed, war had become an all-encompassing endeavor, and its claims on belligerent societies were absolute.[8] War demanded the ruthless mobilization of a nation's entire resources, for it knew no distinction between the home and fighting fronts: the civilian producers of weapons were no less essential to the war effort than were the soldiers who fired them. Ludendorff's convictions disdained the social traditions of German militarism, which had served the privileged exclusivity of an aristocratic military class as much as they did the prosecution of war. In Ludendorff's thinking, organization for war respected no social or political convention; the sole determinant of power and status was military proficiency. This proposition led finally to the conclusion that all politics was subordinate to military affairs, hence that government should be guided by soldiers, the experts in matters of war. The general's claims thus did not halt at the authority of the civilian chancellor – or the emperor. Military dictatorship was the political hallmark of the modern age.

---

[8] Hans Speier, "Ludendorff: The German Concept of Total War," in Edward Mead Earle (ed.), *Makers of Modern Strategy: Military Thought from Machiavelli to Hitler* (New York, 1966), 306–21; Michael Geyer, "German Strategy in the Age of Machine Warfare, 1914–1945," in Peter Paret (ed.), *Makers of Moden Strategy: From Machiavelli to the Nuclear Age* (Princeton, 1986), 537–54.

During his tenure in office, Ludendorff put many of these precepts into practice. The Supreme Command became the dominant force in German politics, and no civilian politician could effectively oppose its authority.[9] Beyond his claims to professional expertise and the support of the army, the principal source of Ludendorff's power was the charismatic authority in which he partook by virtue of his association with Hindenburg. His power thus had a plebiscitary component, and it remained unchallenged as long as he could sustain the popular belief that his armies were going to win the war.

Aspects of Ludendorff's rule anticipated the dictatorial system of government that the Nazis installed some years later. But the similarities ought not to be overdrawn. Even the term "military dictatorship" is deceptive, for Ludendorff confronted more poles of competing authority than Hitler had to suffer. The power of innumerable federal, state, and local bureaucratic offices confounded Ludendorff as much as it had his predecessors, although he soon introduced more effective control over the Deputy Commanding Generals. He could ignore the views of neither Hindenburg nor the emperor, who remained his superiors in the chain of command. Finally, the financial powers of the Reichstag made this institution more than an annoyance, and he could not disregard its sentiments. Thus the power equation remained complicated during the last two years of the war. Still, its dominant element was the Supreme Command; and Ludendorff was the most powerful man in Germany.

The new Supreme Command brought an immediate sense of renewed energy to the war effort. To deal with the strategic setback that had occasioned their coming to power, Hindenburg and Ludendorff organized a brilliant offensive in the southeast. German forces joined Bulgarian armies in the invasion of Rumania in the fall of 1916. The campaign resulted in the swift defeat of the Rumanian army and the occupation of Bucharest in December. The campaign also produced an irony. The leader of one of the German armies in the assault was Falkenhayn. His vindication came not only on the field of battle, for despite the continued success of German armies in the east, Hindenburg and Ludendorff quickly converted to their predecessor's views about Germany's strategic priorities. A trip to the west in September, as titanic battles raged on the Somme and at Verdun, persuaded the new military leadership of the centrality of this theater to the war's outcome.

The trip also sobered them about the possibility of another German offensive in the west. Their attentions turned as a consequence to the

[9] Martin Kitchen, *The Silent Dictatorship: The Politics of the German High Command under Hindenburg and Ludendorff, 1916–1918* (New York, 1976).

prospects of resuming unrestricted submarine warfare. The commanders also decided to reinforce German positions on the western front in anticipation of an extended period of reconsolidation and defensive warfare here, before a final grand offensive could be launched. After calling off German offensive action in the Verdun sector, they accordingly began to build up troop strength in the west. They called in forces from the east and called up older men from homefront garrisons. An order in November to lower the age of conscription to eighteen made clear both the determination of the new leadership and the severity of the Germans' plight, as it added 300,000 to the class of young men who were scheduled for induction in 1917.

The measures that were geared to the battlefield paled in comparison to preparations taking place elsewhere. The prerequisite for military victory was the mobilization of material resources to a degree hitherto unimaginable. The Supreme Command's plans thus prescribed a formidable agenda for the German homefront.

The Hindenburg Program

Immediately upon taking over the Supreme Command, Hindenburg and Ludendorff announced the total mobilization of the German economy for war. During the next three months, the generals oversaw negotiations in which the institutional framework emerged for an immense campaign of military production, which was christened the Hindenburg Program. In a series of letters to the chancellor, the War Minister, and other officials, the Supreme Command called for doubling the stores of munitions, tripling the supply of artillery and machine guns, and concentrating 3,000,000 additional workers in the arms sector. All this, they insisted, was to be accomplished by the spring of 1917.

This colossal productive effort implied the drastic reorganization of the German industrial plant, the concentration of every available resource in the manufacture of arms and munitions. All "non-essential" industries were to be shut down – a category that comprised firms that were not directly involved in war production, as well as many smaller firms that were. Capital investment, raw materials, and manpower were to be channeled into the firms that survived this ruthless purge. The direction of the effort was finally to be lodged in a centralized agency, directed by soldiers.

This program represented an attempt to realize Ludendorff's vision of war. The Germans' response to the campaigns of 1916 was to decree the total mobilization of resources, cost what it might. The campaign was conceived in images of national unity, the ultimate common exertion for the sake of victory. The realities of the situation were more complicated.

The Hindenburg Program rested ultimately on fantastic premises; and the bitter disputes that surrounded its execution laid bare the material disadvantages that Germany faced, as well as the social conflicts that the war had exacerbated.

The Hindenburg Program was designed to restructure industrial mobilization in the interests of greater efficiency. It was directed in the first instance, however, against the War Ministry, the agency that had coordinated industrial production during the first two years of the war. While the achievements of this agency had been considerable, several areas of friction consistently troubled relations between the planners and the industrialists who were charged with carrying out the plans. One area concerned the prices that the ministry was willing to pay for weapons and munitions, as employers made no secret of their displeasure over contracted price levels that they thought too low. Another area of friction was more complex and sensitive. It had to do with industrial manpower; and the goals of the Hindenburg Program made it acute.[10]

Labor was in theory but another factor of production, like investment capital, fertilizer, or magnesium, whose supply and allocation responded to market forces. The outbreak of war brought profound disruptions to the labor market, where the supply was finite and the manpower requirements of the armed forces gorged the demand. The problem became obvious the moment in 1914 when the advance of the German armies stalled at the Marne. Many of the men who marched in these armies had left peacetime employment in war-related industries. The munitions shortage in the fall of 1914 emphasized this dilemma, which was basic to industrial warfare, and hastened the return of many of these soldiers to the workplace. The War Ministry thereupon took charge of balancing the imperious, competing claims of generals and industrialists for manpower. It established guidelines for exempting and reclaiming manpower from the armed forces for service in war industries; these guidelines were then reflected in the contracts let though the Ministry's War Materials Section. The Ministry was not empowered to enforce its decisions, however, so the allocation of industrial labor became the regular object of negotiations between employers and local military authorities, who were responsible to the Deputy Commanding Generals.

The problem had an additional dimension. It was necessary not only to allocate labor for jobs essential to the war effort, but also to keep workers at these jobs, loyally laboring for war. Regulating and disciplining the workforce was an explosive issue, which had for decades violently unsettled industrial relations in Germany, from the Hamburg dockyards to the

[10] Gerald Feldman, *Army, Industry, and Labor in Germany 1914–1918* (Princeton, 1966); Robert B. Armeson, *Total Warfare and Compulsory Labor: A Study of the Military-Industrial Complex in Germany during the First World War* (The Hague, 1964).

coal mines of the Ruhr. The issue touched not only on workers' freedom of movement, but also their rights to representation, organization, and collective bargaining. To many employers, however, the war offered an alluring solution to the problem, the prospect of punishing recalcitrant workers with the trenches. Militarizing the industrial workforce, placing workers formally in the army's jurisdiction, would subject labor to military command, discipline – and (low) military wages.

This brutal device did not appeal to leaders in the War Ministry, who feared that it would exacerbate long-standing social tensions to the point of violence and undermine the war effort. They recognized the urgency of a loyal workforce, but they preferred gentler means of pacification. With uncommon foresight, and to the consternation of the industrial employers, they decided to enlist the trade unions as agents in the management of labor. The unions themselves had abetted this decision at the outbreak of the war, when, in the spirit of the *Burgfrieden*, they renounced strikes for the duration of the conflict. Union leaders thereupon became regular visitors to the War Ministry and other agencies of the government. Here officials enlisted their aid in determining guidelines for exemptions and reclamations of workers. These officials also encouraged the unions to organize in the war industries, even in the public-employment sectors, such as the railways, where unions had long been proscribed. The same officials promoted arbitration committees to resolve grievances between employers and employees; and they were often inclined to support workers' claims in wage disputes. The role of the unions, in turn, was to keep labor docile and to maintain industrial peace and the loyalty of the workforce.

The strategy appeared to succeed. The first two years of the war were remarkably free of industrial unrest. But the employers' frustrations with the War Ministry festered – over prices thought too low, manpower allotments thought too small, and official policies thought to coddle the labor movement. This last category of grievance was the most disquieting, for employers feared more than the impact of generous wages on their profit margins. In their view, the ministry's approach to workers smacked of dangerous social experimentation; it threatened to subvert the authority of employers in their own firms, to aggrandize organized labor, and to revolutionize industrial relations after the war. A factory owner could no more "permit his workers to make decisions about basic factory questions," complained one industrialist, than could "a colonel in the trenches permit negotiations with his troops."[11] This analogy was hardly fortuitous. In the army's leadership, the industrialists' hymns to authority,

---

[11] Quoted in Feldman, *Army, Industry and Labor*, 74–75.

hierarchy, and discipline had a natural resonance; and the employers found a sympathetic response to their complaints among some of the Deputy Commanding Generals even before Ludendorff and Hindenburg took power in 1916. Given the assurances of the leading industrialists that they needed only a proper "production policy," that they could, in agreeable circumstances, fulfill the vast targets set by the new mobilization program, the new Supreme Command was inclined to provide them not only with the price structures and manpower allotments they wanted, but also with the army's support in their dealings with labor.

A major institutional reshuffling in the fall of 1916 announced the new priorities. Hindenburg and Ludendorff first installed a new War Minister, Hermann von Stein, a soldier of whose loyalty they could be confident. Then they prevailed on the Kaiser to empower the War Minister at last to issue commands to the Deputy Commanding Generals in matters relating to economic mobilization. Finally, they created a new agency, the Supreme War Office (*Kriegsamt*) to oversee the entire undertaking. The head of this office was another capable and technically trained middle-class officer, Wilhelm Groener, who had with great skill overseen the railroad section of the General Staff.[12] Groener's new agency was located formally within the War Ministry, so he could himself claim delegated powers to command the Deputy Commanding Generals; but he was in practice the subordinate of the Supreme Command. With branches in each of the Military Districts, the new War Office was supposed to plan and control all facets of economic mobilization, including the reorganization of the economy foreseen in the Hindenburg Program. To this end, the office amalgamated most of the agencies of mobilization that had reported to the War Minister, including the War Materials Section and offices of military procurement, export, and labor exemptions.

Groener's office was also designed to administer the most controversial feature of the Hindenburg Program. The Supreme Command was determined to mobilize every able-bodied man in Germany for war-related service. The means was to be a civilian draft. The decision to ask the Reichstag to approve this dramatic measure was a sign not only of the importance that Ludendorff and Hindenburg attached to the step, but also of their desire to enact it amid a demonstration of popular unity and resolve. They soon had reason to regret their decision. The Reichstag had become home to every manner of discontent over the privations of war, from food shortages to censorship; and the labor movement had representatives not only in the SPD, but also in the Catholic and Progressive

---

[12] Dorothea Groener-Geyer, *General Groener, Soldat und Staatsmann* (Frankfurt am Main, 1954).

parties. The government nonetheless submitted the so-called Auxiliary Service Law to the Reichstag in November. The bill provided for the conscription of all men between the ages of 17 and 60 for war service, and it drastically restricted the freedom of workers to change jobs. Given prevailing thinking about gender roles in Germany, the absence of women from the bill's provisions proved less controversial than the question of how – and by whom – the civilian draft was to be administered. The bitter struggle that ensued revealed the growing recalcitrance of the parliament, which transformed the bill to the great benefit of organized labor. The Reichstag approved civilian conscription and the restriction of workers' mobility, but it accorded labor an essential role in the administration of its own fate. Representatives of labor sat in the committees that in each military district assigned workers to firms, determined exemptions, and arbitrated the claims of workers who sought to change jobs. In all firms with more than fifty workers, the law also established joint committees of labor and management, which were charged with settling disputes over wages and conditions of employment. Finally, the unions won the right to organize in war industries and, for the first time in German history, collective bargaining agreements were given the force of law.

Passage of the Auxiliary Service Law on these terms was a gesture to the burdens brought by the war to the homefront. The law had far-reaching implications for the position of both the Reichstag and organized labor in Germany. It marked a significant amplification of parliament's voice in the prosecution of the war; and it ensured the loyal support of the unions for the duration of the conflict.

The act was also the most important – and unintended – consequence of the Hindenburg Program, which otherwise disappointed the extravagant expectations of those who had conceived and promoted it. The addition of the Supreme War Office to the bureaucratic network of mobilization in many ways compounded the confusion.[13] Issues of responsibility continued to cloud relations between the Deputy Commanding Generals and the local branches of Groener's office. Questions of closing down "non-essential" industries resulted in an administrative nightmare, the mobilization of an army of advocates – from local chambers of commerce to members of the state and federal parliaments – who pressed the claims of imperiled firms at every level of bureaucracy. Finally, frictions plagued relations between Groener's office and the industrialists over questions of profits and the allocation and administration of manpower. Groener was critical of soaring industrial profits, and he revealed

---

[13] Hermann Schäfer, *Regionale Wirtschaftspolitik in der Kriegswirtschaft: Staat, Industrie und Verbände während des Ersten Weltkrieges in Baden* (Stuttgart, 1983).

progressive social views of his own in his dealings with labor. His attitudes were anathema to the employers and their allies, including his own military superiors. He was fired in August 1917.

By this time the failure of the Hindenburg Program was difficult to deny. Quotas were not met. Despite its lucrative inducements, German industry produced less steel in February 1917 than it had six months earlier, on the eve of Falkenhayn's dismissal. The reasons for the failure had to do with both the bureaucratic chaos and the simple limits of Germany's industrial resources. These limits drew the war's imperious appetites into the household and other private places. In the effort to mobilize materials for conversion to war use, pewter plates and cups yielded up their tin, lightning-rods and roofing their copper, bicycle tires their rubber; churches sacrificed their organ pipes for brass and their bells for bronze. The Auxiliary Service Law failed to mobilize much additional labor, for there was little additional (male) labor to mobilize – except from the army. In keeping with the dictates of the Hindenburg Program, thousands of soldiers thus returned from the front for service in industry. While their transfer home boosted industrial output, it emphasized the limits of Germany's resources, for it weakened the field strength of the army and further tied up the country's overtaxed railroads.

Other than manpower, the most difficult problem was coal, the principal source of industrial energy in this war. The coal supply had long been a source of anxiety, before shortages became critical during the hard winter of 1916–17, in part because the transfer of workers from the pits to the trenches had bred disrepair in the mines. The guidelines of the Hindenburg Program, which called for constructing new plants to produce arms and munitions, brought additional strains to the coal supply and the transportation network, whose locomotives themselves consumed this precious resource even as the trains distributed it. Coal was the lifeblood of the German war effort, and rationing it became the War Office's most effective means of shutting down non-essential industries.

The Hindenburg Program could be sustained only on the defiant neglect of basic economic realities. Even Ludendorff seems to have suspected as much in the spring of 1917, when he ordered the further consolidation of German defenses on the western front and a limited strategic withdrawal. Meanwhile, the German economy was thrown into ever greater dislocation in the desperate effort to produce more machines of war than resources would permit. By the end of the war, more than 90 percent of the German firms still in business were struggling to manufacture materials of war. "The new Supreme Command represented the triumph not of imagination, but of fantasy," writes Gerald Feldman. "In his pursuit of an ill-conceived total mobilization for the attainment of irrational goals, Ludendorff undermined the strength of the army, promoted economic instability, created administrative chaos, and set loose an orgy of interest politics."[14] Harsh words these: but they hardly exaggerate the toll taken by the militarization of the German economy. The toll was borne by other parts of Europe as well, which had fallen under German control and were now themselves geared to the fantasies of the Hindenburg Program.

Occupied Europe

German forces occupied extensive parts of western and eastern Europe for much of the war. Most of Belgium and northeastern France came under German control in the first weeks of the conflict, while the eastern offensives of 1915 brought Russian Poland and large segments of the Russian Baltic provinces into the German realm. The opportunities offered by these acquisitions were vast, as were the political dilemmas they raised – and the burdens they imposed on the native inhabitants of these territories.

It is difficult to remove this story from the shadow cast by German actions in occupied Europe during the Second World War. Aspects of German rule during the First World War did anticipate the Nazi "population policy" of the next war, the attempt to reengineer society in the occupied lands according to racial principles. During the Great War, however, this motif remained peripheral in the broader scheme of German policy, which was somewhat more circumspect and devoted, in the main, to principles other than race. The principal concern throughout was to harness the economic resources of occupied Europe to the German war effort, but the exploitation of these areas raised perplexing questions about means. Both within the German government and without, loud voices called for the annexation and pitiless exploitation of the occupied territories for the immediate purposes of war. Other leaders reasoned that German interests would be better served by more indirect, informal, and humane forms of rule and by policies that accommodated the interests of the indigenous peoples. In this respect, too, the coming of the third Supreme Command to power signaled a turn in the war.

In the occupied territories to the west, the opportunities for exploitation were lavish.[15] Rich reserves of industrial raw materials awaited the conquerors, as did a modern capital plant for extracting them – thanks

---

[14] Feldman, *Army, Industry, and Labor*, 150.
[15] Frank Wende, *Die belgische Frage in der deutschen Politik des Ersten Weltkrieges* (Hamburg, 1969); Ludwig von Köhler, *Die Staatsverwaltung der besetzten Gebiete: Belgien* (Stuttgart, Berlin, and Leipzig, 1927).

in part to large German investments in these areas before the war. The deposits of iron ore in the fields of Longwy-Briey, in French Lorraine, were thought to exceed all of the ore in Germany. The principal asset in Belgium was coal, although this land also contained large amounts of iron ore, as well as industrial chemicals. The pressures for putting these areas into the service of the German war effort were immediate; and they came from the German industrialists who had invested here before and now hoped to relieve the pressures on German producers.

The institutions of occupation looked much like the institutions of mobilization in Germany, and the explosion of competing jurisdictions fostered the same kind of confusion. Areas adjacent to the fighting front came under direct military control. To the rear was the realm of a governor-general, a soldier who was immediately responsible to the emperor. He ruled, like a super Deputy Commanding General, over a series of provincial governors, who were also soldiers. A parallel civilian administration, responsible to the Ministry of the Interior in Berlin, also arrived, as did representatives of the Raw Materials Section and the war corporations, which were responsible to the War Ministry. These arrangements provided ample room for the powerful German businessmen, such as Hugo Stinnes, who were its direct beneficiaries.[16] Industrial barons populated not only the war corporations, but also the committees that were set up to advise military and civilian officialdom throughout the occupied areas.

German policy was to operate as far as possible through indigenous agencies. In hopes of encouraging cooperation, the occupiers left local government in place while demanding contributions for the support of the occupying forces. The same principle suggested leaving businesses in local hands, while their operations were redeployed in the German war effort. In all events, appearances forbade outright German seizure of these firms, as did the prospect of reprisals against German assets held in enemy territories. French and Belgian firms thus remained the property of their owners, who were paid – at low, dictated prices – for what they were compelled by German managers to produce. The management of some 500 firms thus passed in practice into the hands of German businessmen, who contracted, much as they did in Germany, via the war corporations with the army's procurement agencies. Whatever the institutional formalities or initial hopes of cooperation, German exploitation resulted in the paralyzing dislocation of economic life in Belgium and northern France. The concentration of resources in the war industries

---

[16] Brigitte Hattke, *Hugo Stinnes und die drei deutsch-belgischen Gesellschaften von 1916* (Stuttgart, 1990).

came at the expense of "non-essential" sectors, notably agriculture and food-processing. Local industry suffered, too. The capital plant fell victim to disrepair, as growing quantities of raw materials – particularly coal – were sent directly to Germany for use.

The arrival of Ludendorff in power removed every appearance of moderation. The subjugation of economic life in the occupied areas now became ruthless in the service of policies fairly described as plunder. German businesses bought up Belgian utilities, port facilities, and industrial property on extortionate terms. Raw materials departed for Germany with no heed to the local consequences. Factories were worked to exhaustion, until they were dismantled and their metal skeletons transported to Germany for processing as scrap. Few businesses could survive these depredations. Of the 260,000 Belgian firms in operation on the eve of the war, 3,013 survived until the end. The collapse of employment attended this ordeal, as did the prospect of famine. The arrival of large-scale food relief from the United States helped avert the one catastrophe, while the Germans sought to capitalize on the other. During the first two years of the war, efforts to entice or prod Belgian workers to factories in Germany produced little success. Ludendorff, who was indifferent to appearances as well as international protest, moved in the fall of 1916 to a program of forced deportations. Before the war's end, more than 100,000 Belgians had in this way joined the cast of the Hindenburg Program in Germany.

The situation was marginally better in Poland, if only because this land was less developed economically.[17] The Germans and Austrians divided Russian Poland. In the German sector to the north, the army ruled directly, although a familiar roster of industrial committees oversaw the mobilization of the economy in the German interest. Poland offered fewer industrial riches than the western territories, although the large textile plants of Lodz and Warsaw fell under German management, as did electrical utilities and coal mines. The principal asset in Poland was agriculture, whose bounties Polish farmers were compelled to divert at low, administered prices to the service of the German food supply. Fodder crops, such as potatoes, clover, oats, and sugar beets, relieved critical shortages in Germany, as did Polish livestock, wood, cotton, wool, and flax. A resource that Poland shared with the occupied areas to the west was human. Ludendorff began to "recruit" Polish workers, too, in the fall of 1916. By the summer of 1917, some 600,000 had been enticed or forced westward, most of them to work on German farms.

---

[17] Werner Basler, *Deutsche Annexionspolitik in Polen und im Baltikum 1914–1918* (East Berlin, 1962); Martin Broszat, *Zweihundert Jahre deutsche Polenpolitik* (Munich, 1963); Werner Conze, *Polnische Nation und deutsche Politik im ersten Weltkrieg* (Graz and Cologne, 1958).

It is difficult to gauge the economic impact in Germany of resources from occupied Europe – a category that after 1916 included Rumania, with its rich wheat fields. That these resources helped alleviate shortages of crucial materials is beyond question, but so was the fact that depriving restive local populaces of these resources tied down large German occupation forces. So was the Germans' determination to retain some form of control over these areas after the war. This attitude was so pronounced in the discussions of war aims that one can almost speak of a consensus, at least to the right of the Social Democrats. The issue of Belgium revolved about the modes of domination – be it by annexation, as the nationalist right preferred, a customs union, or other indirect arrangements to guarantee the preponderance of Germans in the postwar Belgian economy. Hopes of winning indigenous sympathy for some such outcome persuaded the Germans to exploit long-standing tensions between the French-speaking majority in Belgium and the Flemish-speaking minority. Ethnic affinities between Flems and Germans provided the ideological pretext for this effort, which included patronage of several groups that favored Flemish independence or autonomy, supporting the use of the Flemish language in schools and local administration, and an attempt to establish a university with a Flemish faculty in the city of Ghent. While the policy prefigured the *völkisch* principles of the next war, it disappointed the expectations of its authors, for most Flemish-speakers so loathed the German occupiers that these blandishments provided no temptation to collaboration.

The political situation in Poland was much more complicated, for there were more interested parties to the debate. In 1914, the empires of Russia, Austria–Hungary, and Germany had all ruled over large Polish minorities for decades. The redefinition of Poland's status during the war thus carried far-reaching implications for Germany's relations not only with its enemy, but also with its principal ally. The military victories of 1915 brought all of Russian Poland under the control of Germany and Austria, making the Polish question central to their relations with one another, to say nothing of its bearing on a negotiated peace with Russia. While the German and Austrian armies occupied the land, opinions remained deeply divided in Berlin and Vienna over Poland's future. The most diplomatic option (and the most propitious for the alliance) seemed to be the so-called "Austro-Polish solution," which would cede sovereignty over Russian Poland to Austria in return for economic concessions to Germany.

The terms of diplomacy shifted, however, like much else, in the summer of 1916. Ludendorff, whom the first two years of the war had taught contempt for the Austrians, was interested only in the immediate military implications of the Polish question. He reasoned that concocting a sovereign Polish state out of the Russian sector would appeal to Polish nationalists and win large contingents of Polish soldiers to the side of the Central Powers. Accordingly, he dismissed both the protests of the Austrians and the objections of Bethmann Hollweg, who clung to the hope of a separate peace in the east. In November 1916 the Germans proclaimed the birth of a Polish kingdom, to be governed – with German assistance – by a parliament and an executive council of leading Polish politicians. The Germans' intentions were transparent, and, despite the announcement of plans to establish a Polish university in Warsaw, German domination proved little more palatable to Poles than to Belgians. Calls for Polish volunteers produced disappointing results. The Polish military contribution to the Central Powers never exceeded a few thousand men, who fought indifferently as a contingent alongside the Austrians; the great majority of Poles concluded that an Allied victory represented the best hope for genuine independence.

As if they recognized the obstacles to winning Polish collaboration, the Germans also laid the foundations for different, more ominous modes of rule in the east. With the support of leading civilian officials, including the chancellor, the army undertook plans to establish a long border strip in western Poland, which was to be purged of its native Polish – and Jewish – inhabitants and resettled with Germans.[18] The function of this so-called *Grenzstreifen* was to provide a sanitized ethnic barrier between Germany and the Slavic peoples to the east. The idea was no aberration in this war. Preparations for similar large-scale resettlement of ethnic populations accompanied the intensive economic exploitation of Courland and Livonia, two of the Baltic regions that the German army ruled directly, like a colony, after 1915.

Whatever the modalities of their long-term subjection, the occupied territories in the east and west were pivotal in German plans for postwar Europe. These plans were the object of debates that burst into the open in the fall of 1916, when, in hopes of encouraging morale with visions of triumph, Ludendorff removed the ban on public discussion of Germany's war aims. Although views differed on the specifics, a large segment of opinion embraced the vision of a postwar German *Mitteleuropa* – a colossal customs union, whose core was to be the empires of the Hohenzollerns and Habsburgs, and whose satellites were to span the continent, from Belgium to Turkey, and join in political or economic dependence on the core. The leading public advocate of this project was

---

[18] Imanuel Geiss, *Der polnische Grenzstreifen 1914–1918: Ein Beitrag zur deutschen Kriegszielpolitik im Ersten Weltkrieg* (Lübeck and Hamburg, 1960).

the head of the Progressive party, Friedrich Naumann, who was more eloquent and benign in his thinking than many of the others who joined him in a broad coalition, which reached from Ludendorff and the Pan-Germans into the ranks of the Social Democrats.[19] *Mitteleuropa* promised to eliminate, once and for all, the problem of German access to foreign markets and resources. The project seemed to offer the foundation on which Germany could compete for power on a worldwide scale not only with the empire of Great Britain, but also with the colossus on the other side of the Atlantic.

The fateful decisions undertaken by the German Supreme Command at the end of the year were thus less inconsistent with the premises of this grandiose project than with its timing. In all events, the strategic logic of a war against Great Britain propelled Germany early in 1917 into war with the United States of America.

The war at sea

Naval operations in the First World War resembled the face of battle on land, insofar as they, too, took planners everywhere by surprise and failed to produce a decisive engagement.[20] Navies had figured centrally in the deterioration of diplomatic relations between Germany and Great Britain before 1914, when competition to build battle fleets reflected a widely held belief that in any future war, vital issues of national power and security were to be settled at sea. The reigning philosopher of naval power in both countries was an American, Alfred Thayer Mahan, who foretold a cataclysmic battle between surface fleets dominated by huge battleships and battle-cruisers. To the victor in this great clash would go command of the sea, the coveted prize that would guarantee eventual triumph in the broader war. The Anglo-German naval race began in 1897, when the Germans concluded that they might one day prevail in such a battle. The relentless growth of the German battle fleet predictably fed the enlargement of the Royal Navy. The centerpiece of the British effort was the introduction in 1906 of ultra-modern, fast and heavily armed battleships called *Dreadnoughts*. These presented a technological challenge that the Germans, in turn, could not resist. But the escalation of naval force altered only the dimensions, not the basic concept of the

[19] Henry Cord Meyer, *Mitteleuropa in German Thought and Action, 1815–1945* (The Hague, 1955).
[20] Paul G. Halpern, *A Naval History of World War I* (Annapolis, 1994); Holger H. Herwig, *"Luxury" Fleet: The Imperial German Navy, 1888–1918* (London and Atlantic Highlands, NJ, 1987), 143–257.

titanic sea battle, which loomed, as if in a maritime Schlieffen Plan, as the decisive moment in a future war.

From the perspective of the German naval leadership, the war broke out too soon. In 1914 the core of the German High Seas Fleet consisted of sixteen state-of-the-art battleships. The British had twenty-five of them. Given this ratio of force, the British appeared to enjoy a prohibitive advantage in any concentrated showdown in the North Sea. The British, however, were also reluctant to risk a confrontation, despite these odds. Instead, they conceded much of the North Sea to the Germans, as they removed their fleet to the north, to Scapa Flow, and blockaded the German coast with ships and mines from the safe distances of Scotland and the English Channel. These moves made a major engagement unlikely, for the German fleet was hesitant to venture far from the sanctuary of its own shores. The first months of the war accordingly brought several skirmishes between elements of the two fleets but no strategic decision, except to prolong the confinement of the German fleet to its ports.

Stalemate thus quickly descended at sea as well as on land. To Admiral von Tirpitz and other leaders of the German navy, this situation was a source of particular frustration, for it emphasized their own marginality in the great exertions that were taking shape on land. The German navy played no role in the Schlieffen Plan, for there had been no interservice planning whatsoever. After the failure of this initial offensive, the direction of the German war effort remained in the hands of the generals, who were convinced that the decision-at-arms would come on land and were largely indifferent to the navy's concerns. Virtually from the beginning of the conflict, the navy's leaders were therefore compelled to search for a new role.

Discussions of this issue were bitter throughout the war, for the naval leadership was united more in restless exasperation than in a strategic concept to vent it. While one faction clung to the hope of a great surface battle, for which their traditions and training had prepared them, another group concluded that Germany was now involved in a different kind of war, in which naval action had become subsidiary to commercial warfare – that the principal targets of German naval operations would not be enemy warships but the merchant vessels that maintained enemy armies in the field. Commercial warfare had traditionally been the business of smaller warships; and German cruisers and other surface raiders scored some notable successes against British shipping in the first months of the war. These successes drew attention to an arm of the German fleet that had not figured much in prewar plans. Submarines had proved effective in early action against both merchant shipping and older British warships.

They could be built quickly – some classes in a matter of months – and far more cheaply than surface warships. The submarine thus promised relief for at least one of the navy's frustrations, for it seemed to offer an effective means to retaliate against the British blockade.

These prospects were decisive to admirals who were eager for action of any kind. In February 1915 they were rewarded when the German government proclaimed the waters surrounding the British isles to be a war zone, in which German submarines were empowered to attack without warning every merchant vessel they encountered, whether these ships flew the flags of enemies or neutrals. Announcement of this bold step was rewarded with jubilation on the German right, where frustrations were also rife. But the new strategy raised more problems than it resolved. At the moment of the proclamation, the German navy counted only thirty-seven submarines of all descriptions. Given the fact that an average of six of them were daily at sea during the spring of 1915, the initial results of their campaign were impressive. In March, April, and May they sank 115 ships with more than 250,000 tons, losing but five of their own. These figures lent urgency to building more of them as rapidly as manpower shortages in the German shipyards would allow.

A more serious problem was diplomatic; and it inhered in the very features that made the submarine such a formidable weapon. War at sea was governed in 1914 by an elaborate body of maritime law, which had taken shape in an era when submarines prowled only the minds of visionaries. This law, to which the Germans were party, prescribed that only specific categories of goods were subject to interdiction, that ships were not to be sunk without warning, and that the safety of the crews of the unfortunate vessels was to be assured. In 1914, submarine warfare quickly made mockery of the law. During the early months of the conflict, German commanders learned that warning merchant vessels and inspecting cargoes sacrificed the stealth that was the submarine's principal advantage, while it put their own ships at dire risk. Escorting captured crews to port in submarines was simply ludicrous. Well could the Germans argue that the British were also defying maritime law in enforcing their blockade. The Germans failed to appreciate, however, that inflated definitions of contraband goods and the many other forms of chicanery with which the British sought to throttle the German economy were directed against property, while the German response also took lives. "Germany's malpractices on the high seas," as Professor Chambers put it, "were more criminal and spectacular than England's."[21]

---

[21] Frank P. Chambers, *The War Behind the War: A History of the Political and Civilian Fronts* (New York, 1939), 199.

The German declaration of submarine warfare laid bare all these problems. A series of incidents in the spring of 1915 drew howls of protest from neutral countries whose shipping and nationals were falling victim to the German submarine offensive, which was in fact calculated to sow terror in these quarters. The loudest protests came from the neutral country that mattered the most, to the British and Germans alike. When in May 1915 a German submarine sunk the British passenger liner *Lusitania* with over 100 Americans on board, Germany and the United States reached the point of a diplomatic rupture. At this stage of the conflict, a break with the United States seemed like too high a price to pay; and the German government relented with measures first to limit the submarine blockade around the British isles and then, in September, for most intents and purposes to call it off.

These decisions were not easily reached. Submarine warfare had become another element in the struggles that raged in the German capital over strategic and political priorities. The suspension of the blockade represented a temporary victory for Bethmann Hollweg and the diplomats in the Foreign Office, who feared drawing both Holland and the United States into the war on the allied side. While the decision provoked bitter opposition from Tirpitz and the rest of the navy's leadership, it also lent new life to the idea of a naval Armageddon with the British surface fleet.

The debate over these questions continued for more than a year. The decision to renew the submarine blockade in the spring of 1916 represented a facet of Falkenhayn's grand strategic concept for that year, but it was so freighted with compromise that it provoked the general's disgust and Tirpitz's resignation. Despite procedures that were carefully defined to avoid attacks without warning on passenger ships and other unarmed vessels, the submarine offensive nonetheless brought another crisis in relations with the United States the moment several American passengers died on a torpedoed French steamer in the English Channel. When the chancellor thereupon concluded that the diplomatic risks were still too grave, the government again lifted the submarine blockade, tipping the balance in the German naval leadership to those who longed for the great surface battle.

They got their way. At the end of May 1916, the main elements of the German and British surface fleets, some 250 warships on both sides, met in the North Sea for the only time in the war in the so-called Battle of Jutland, the largest direct clash among surface vessels in modern history.[22] Few sea battles have been the subject of as much controversy

22 V. E. Tarrant, *Jutland: The German Perspective: A New View of the Great Battle, 31 May 1916* (London, 1995).

or retrospective analysis, for the stakes were as enormous as the opportunities that were squandered in miscommunication on both sides. The "Trafalgar of the First World War" it was not. After several hours of brawling, the two fleets disengaged intact. Judged on the numbers alone, the results of the encounter registered a victory for the German High Seas Fleet, whose ships and gunners consistently outperformed their counterparts in the larger British Grand Fleet. The British lost six capital ships to the Germans' two, and they sustained more than twice the Germans' casualties. Announcement of these statistics unleashed popular celebrations throughout Germany, but the numbers were irrelevant to the battle's strategic outcome. In this respect, the Germans suffered an unambiguous defeat, for the strategic balance in the North Sea, which had kept the German navy paralyzed, remained unaltered. The German navy returned to port, while the British returned to the business of the blockade. The prisoners had attacked their jailer, noted a journalist on the morrow of the battle, but in the end they were safely back in jail.[23]

So the balance tipped again in the summer of 1916 back to the advocates of unrestricted submarine warfare.[24] This time, however, the change accompanied a dramatic shift in the political climate in Berlin. It was no surprise that Hindenburg and Ludendorff favored resuming the blockade of the British isles, nor that they were willing to risk war with the United States, for they were convinced that without American supplies the British could not long continue to fight. Nor was it surprising that the industrial leaders and their nationalist allies favored the same course. More surprising was the broad resonance that resumption of the submarine offensive found among the other parties, including factions of the Social Democrats. Amid the same frustrations and illusions that gave birth to the Hindenburg Program in the fall of 1916, the submarine underwent a metamorphosis in the popular imagination. It became a panacea, the wonder weapon whose all-out employment promised to resolve the war and bring the British to their knees.

The chancellor remained more skeptical, but he was under mounting pressure to bow to popular sentiment. The showdown came at the end of the year, once the end of the Rumanian campaign freed the Supreme Command to address the larger picture. A memorandum from Henning von Holtzendorff, the Naval Chief of Staff, brought enticing prospects to Hindenburg's attention in December. Admiral von Holtzendorff reasoned that submarine warfare could, if ruthlessly directed against commerce with Great Britain in the English Channel and the North Atlantic,

---

[23] Halpern, *A Naval History of World War I*, 328.
[24] Bernd Stegemann, *Die deutsche Marinepolitik 1916–1918* (Berlin, 1970).

sink 600,000 tons of shipping per month and frighten off most of the remaining neutral traffic. Five months of this punishment would, he predicted, reduce total tonnage to Britain by 39 percent and force the starved enemy from the war. He dismissed as irrelevant the objection that this strategy would draw the United States into the war against Germany. The submarine, he explained, would block the transport of American soldiers to Europe; and by the time they did arrive in Europe in significant numbers, the war would in all events be over. The memorandum revealed that Hindenburg and Ludendorff were not alone in the land of fantasy, for Holtzendorff proposed to accomplish this breathtaking feat with about 100 submarines, of which only forty could be put to sea at a given time. Hindenburg and Ludendorff nonetheless embraced the admiral's calculations during their bitter assault on Bethmann Hollweg's opposition, which they concluded in victory in early January 1917. The emperor endorsed the position of the generals; and on 1 February 1917 the Germans officially resumed unrestricted submarine warfare.

Popular celebration at the announcement of the renewed offensive could not long hide the folly of the whole idea. Not only did submarine warfare bring war with the United States within two months, but the assumptions on which it was predicated were preposterous. While destroyed tonnage corresponded to German projections in the spring months, the figures plummeted once the British navy, whose own traditions had resisted the new realities of commercial warfare, organized merchant traffic into convoys, which were escorted in increasing numbers by ships of the American navy. German submarines sank only two-thirds of their monthly quota for the rest of the year, whereupon allied shipping, which now included the American merchant fleet (and some fifty German ships that had been interned in the US), grew significantly. By 1918, British and American shipyards were producing twice the tonnage that the Germans were sinking. The situation in Great Britain had been briefly scary in the middle of 1917; but the British food supply was never in jeopardy. The British proved no less agile than the Germans in adjusting to shortages. Nor was a single American troop transport sunk. The German submarine offensive was a failure.

Not for the first time in this war had the German leadership taken a leap in the dark. This one ensured the country's eventual defeat, for it invited the world's leading industrial power, whose productive capacities the German leaders gravely misjudged, into the ranks of the Germany's enemies, which now numbered most of the rest of the world. The indices that mattered had less to do with the numbers of American troops who arrived fresh for combat on the western front in 1918 than with the industrial bases of combat.

Table 2 *Raw-material production in 1918*

	Production in 1918 (millions of tons)		
	Coal	Iron	Steel
Great Britain	231	9	10
France	26	1	2
USA	615	40	45
Allied total	872	50	57
German total	161	12	12

Source: Fritz Klein, *et al.*, *Deutschland im Ersten Weltkrieg* (3 vols., Berlin, 1968–69), vol. III, 313

The German figures were themselves impressive, but they paled in the context of the Supreme Command's great gamble in 1917, which defied the dimensions and degree of their enemies' industrial superiority. The German figures reflected in all events an extraordinary campaign to exploit limited economic resources, a collective exertion that brought comprehensive disruption and took a frightful toll on the lives of practically every German who endured it.

4 The war embraces all

In October 1914 a story circulated in the German press about Peter Edlbauer, a seventy-six-year-old man who lived alone with his fifty-year-old
daughter deep in the woods of southeastern Germany. He received neither mail nor newspapers, so he remained oblivious of the war for two
months, until a passing tourist broke the news to him. Incredulous, he
went to town to inquire at the local garrison, where he learned of German
successes on several fronts. "Things will be all right," the old gentleman
remarked, then returned to his retreat.[1] The press did not report about
his subsequent fate, but even a hermit could hardly have long remained
impervious to this war's impact. The dispatch of millions of young men
to the fighting fronts, the wrenching reorganization of the economy
for military production, and mounting deprivations and shortages of
every description touched everyone in Germany in the most profound
ways.

The fact that no one was exempt from these exertions and disruptions poses formidable challenges to the social history of the war. The
adversities were comprehensive, but no two Germans endured them in
the same way. Edlbauer's detachment represented an extreme. It was
far less typical than the devastation visited on the historian Georg von
Below in Freiburg, whose family suffered through the deaths of two sons
in combat. The hermit represented an extreme case in another respect.
The vast majority of Germans lived through the war not in isolation but
as members of social groups, whether these were marked out by class,
confession, gender, generation, or geography. This proposition applies
to *Kriegsalltag*, to the banal routines of life in wartime, as well as to the
war's dramatic moments.[2] It applies especially to the war's many burdens,
for social groups were vulnerable to different degrees and in different
ways.

---

[1] "Einer, der vom Krieg nichts weiss," *Volkswacht* (Freiburg im Breisgau), 14 October 1914.
[2] Peter Knoch (ed.), *Kriegsalltag: Die Rekonstruktion des Kriegsalltags als Aufgabe der historischen Forschung und der Friedenserziehung* (Stuttgart, 1989).

Warriors

The war opened amid the promise that social divisions would dissolve into a transcendent national community. The most conspicuous embodiment of this community was the soldiery, the 13,123,011 Germans who served in the army between 1914 and 1918. This group, whose badge of membership was the military uniform, was defined by gender and age, for most of the men who served were between the ages of twenty and forty. The great majority of them – over 80 percent – were linked above all, however, in the common experience of combat on one or more of the several European fronts. They were pioneers in the new forms of warfare; most of them endured first-hand the paralysis imposed on mass armies by the lethal new machines of destruction. In this role, however, they were paradoxically members of a broader, international community, which the English writer Vera Brittain characterized as a "tragic profound freemasonry of those who accepted death together" on both sides of the front.[3]

Like the British and French troops who faced them, German soldiers watched helplessly as the new modes of fighting made mockery of the visions of adventure that had underwritten initial enthusiasm for the war. Strategic immobility rendered the war instead a continuous siege, which offered the proximity of boredom and death – the monotonous tyranny of daily routine alongside the prospect of its sudden, horrible termination. Images of individual heroism survived only in the sky, in the figures of aviators like Willi Boelcke and Manfred von Richthofen, whose celebrity was the issue of a wedding between modern aerial technology and medieval modes of combat, which themselves soon receded into the anonymity of squadron tactics. Heroic images had no relevance, however, for the masses of the footsoldiers, who were more aptly portrayed as the proletarians of industrial war, or as animals that burrowed into muddy labyrinths for shelter until they emerged – in what were called offensives – to offer pale challenge to the modern machines that ruled the battlefield and blocked access to enemy trenches.

This numbing, frightful experience put enormous strains on the power of conventional ideas and language. In this respect, too, in trying to find a "symbolic key" to make sense of the slaughter, German soldiers confronted the same problems that plagued their enemies.[4] During the first

---

[3] Cited in Susan Kingsley Kent, "Love and Death: War and Gender in Britain, 1914–1918," in Frans Coetzee and Marilyn Shevin Coetzee (eds.), *Authority, Identity and the Social History of the Great War* (Providence and Oxford, 1995), 165.

[4] Robert Weldon Whalen, *Bitter Wounds: German Victims of the Great War, 1914–1939* (Ithaca and London, 1984), 45. The German experience of combat awaits an analysis comparable to Paul Fussell's study of the British case: *The Great War and Modern Memory*

two years of the war, while it was still possible to hope that the next great battle might be the last, the theme of heroic sacrifice survived as a guide for Germans under fire on the ground. The theme found its most poignant and resonant symbol in the "Battle of Langemarck."[5] This label attached to a series of German infantry attacks on French and British positions near the Belgian town of Ypres in the fall of 1914. The action was of no particular strategic significance, and the wholesale carnage inflicted on the attackers, many of whom were ill-trained reservists, was already a standard feature of this war. The official German report from the front combed out these aspects of the action; it told instead of youthful volunteers who successfully rushed enemy positions singing "*Deutschland, Deutschland über alles.*" Whether or not it had any basis in fact, this representation of the action exerted enormous popular appeal, for it transformed defeat into moral victory, highlighting the enthusiasm and sacrifice of young warriors who had carried the "spirit of 1914" onto the battlefield.

Metaphors of heroism and sacrifice depended on a belief in transcendent moral purposes, which gave meaning to death on the battlefield as the vehicle of collective redemption and renewal. The demise of this belief during the monster battles of 1916 summoned up new motifs that were stripped of idealism. To judge from the newspapers that circulated in the trenches, the prevalent imagery now emphasized the soldier's stoic endurance of adversity in hopes of an early peace.[6] The roots of an altogether different set of images could also be found in the trenches during the later phases of the war. This imagery later took on chilling energy in the writings of Ernst Jünger, a veteran who aestheticized industrial warfare into an apocalyptic experience, a "storm of steel," the quest for self-transcendence by a new breed of warriors, who were bereft of moral sentiment and honed to the violent rituals of death.[7]

Because all these images homogenized the *Fronterlebnis*, the "front experience," in an effort to lend it meaning, they tended to misrepresent

(London, 1975). But see Eric Leed, *No Man's Land: Combat and Identity in World War I* (Cambridge and New York, 1979); Klaus Vondung (ed.), *Kriegserlebnis: Der Erste Weltkrieg in der literarischen Gestaltung und symbolischen Deutung der Nationen* (Göttingen, 1980).

[5] Karl Unruh, *Langemarck: Legende und Wirklichkeit* (Koblenz, 1986); Bernd Hüppauf, "Langemarck, Verdun and the Myth of a New Man in Germany after the First World War," *War and Society* 6 (1988), 70–103.

[6] Anne Lipp, "Friedenssehnsucht und Durchhaltebereitschaft: Wahrnehmungen und Erfahrungen deutscher Soldaten im Ersten Weltkrieg," *Archiv für Sozialgeschichte* 36 (1996), 279–92. See also the testimony in Bernd Ulrich and Benjamin Ziemann (eds.), *Frontalltag im Ersten Weltkrieg: Wahn und Wirklichkeit* (Frankfurt am Main, 1994).

[7] Ernst Jünger, *In Stahlgewittern: Aus dem Tagebuch eines Stosstruppführers* (Leipzig, 1920); translated into English as *The Storm of Steel: From the Diary of a German Storm-Troop Officer on the Western Front* (London, 1929).

the diversity of military experience in this war. The most indelible images originated on the western front, where the world's most modern armies clashed in circumstances that brought strategic stalemate to its senseless fulfillment. Other conditions governed combat on the eastern front. Here great disparities of military power among the contending forces bred a much more mobile war, which appeared to develop with more strategic purpose and less unremitting direct engagement. Many of the soldiers who saw action in this theater helped as well to rule the strange, vast territories that fell under German occupation.[8] Some 75,000 Germans who served in the navy experienced the war on still different terms. Because the surface fleet was confined to its ports on the North and Baltic Seas for most of the contest, the men who populated these warships endured the tedium of war without the intermittent excitement. When the marginality of the surface fleet translated into reduced rations for the sailors, frustrations below deck began to fester towards turmoil.

In the official imagery, service in the armed forces united Germans of all stations in defense of the fatherland. The reality of the situation was different. The common experience of military life failed to suspend divisions and tensions that had unsettled German society before the war. Suspicion, ill will, and mutual incomprehension were common in the relations among units that displayed the linguistic peculiarities or confessional preferences of the different regions from which they were recruited. Ethnic friction was particularly sensitive. Regiments recruited in Alsace-Lorraine or Prussian Poland were deployed as far from home as possible, for fear of their desertion to units of co-nationals in the French or Russian armies. The most widespread tensions, however, were social. The German army faithfully replicated the basic class distinctions of peacetime society. Most of the officers in the army (and navy) came from families of property, education, or high birth; most of the non-commissioned officers and common soldiers or sailors did not. The privileged university students who enlisted during the first weeks of the war transgressed this principle, but the brutality and chicanery that they experienced at the hands of their sergeants and fellow recruits betrayed class resentments that were as a rule directed by common soldiers at commissioned officers.[9] The arrogance and arbitrary exercise of authority by officers headed a long list of grievances, which included the preferential treatment that officers routinely enjoyed in matters of quarters, food and supplies,

[8] Vejas Liulevicius, *War Land on the Eastern Front. Culture, National Identity and German Occupation in World War I* (Cambridge, 2000).
[9] Bernd Ulrich, "Die Desillusionierung der Kriegsfreiwilligen von 1914," in Wolfram Wette (ed.), *Der Krieg des kleinen Mannes: Eine Militärgeschichte von unten* (Munich and Zurich, 1992), 110–26.

battlefield decorations, and access to bordellos behind the lines. The perception that corruption and "connections" worked to the special advantage of these officers compounded the resentments, which were directed in all events with special intensity towards officers in staff or administrative positions who evaded combat.

The persistence of regional, confessional, and class tensions fed the misery of life at the front. The mounting adversities did not, however, produce any organized collapse of discipline in the German army like the mutinies that terrified the French high command in 1917. But more subtle forms of resistance did suggest the growing difficulty of setting intellectual bearings for the front experience. The fraternization of German soldiers with their enemies in no-man's land on Christmas day in 1914 represented the spontaneous suspension of military discipline; and alarmed German officers took pains to prevent its recurrence, for it seemed to repudiate the war's very premise. The practice then modulated into informal agreements across the trenches, which kept large sectors of the front quiet, except for ritual exchanges of fire undertaken in order to appease the officers. Self-mutilation offered an escape to the common soldier that was difficult to brand as indiscipline, however suspicious the circumstances. It was much less common than the several varieties of emotional disorder, the so-called "war neuroses," which baffled military doctors and outraged officers. The number of these cases – over 600,000 of them were reported – pointed less, however, towards calculated acts of resistance than to intellectual disorientation of massive and clinical proportions. The signs of indiscipline, disorder, and resistance all increased significantly during the second half of the war, as the burdens of combat accumulated amid the decimation of military units and the mounting shortages of basic supplies, particularly food and clothing. These material deficiencies testified to another grave problem, for most of the supplies came from home, where the war was also taking a terrible toll.

Homefront and battlefront

The homefront and the fighting front were inextricably married.[10] The performance of the German armies in the field defined the central mandate of civilian efforts, and it affected the material circumstances of civilian life. The impact of war on the homefront was less immediate than on the front lines, simply because of the distances that separated civilians from the fighting; but the experience of war at home was no less massive

---

[10] Benjamin Ziemann, *Front und Heimat: Ländliche Kriegserfahrungen im südlichen Bayern 1914–1923* (Essen, 1997).

or comprehensive. The homefront and the fighting front were also linked in constant communication. The attempt of the censors to police this link met with only mixed success, for numerous channels of communication kept civilians and soldiers abreast of one another's fortunes.

The direct experience of war on the German homefront did not match the terrors of the next European conflict, although there were several exceptions to the rule. Germans in the southeastern parts of East Prussia endured several hard months of Russian occupation in the fall of 1914. Apart from small areas in Alsace, the west remained unoccupied until war's end; but the western front ran close enough to the border in several places that German civilians experienced the sights and sounds of combat. Residents of towns and villages in the upper Rhine region, in Baden, could hear and see artillery exchanges along the Alsatian sector of the front, which ran along the crest of the Vosges mountains. Residents in a number of west German cities, such as Düsseldorf, Cologne, Mainz, Strassburg, Mannheim, and Karlsruhe, received a foretaste of the next war in a series of bombing raids by French and British airplanes, which operated out of eastern France. The material damage inflicted by these small aircraft was no more significant than the harm brought by German aircraft to civilian targets in France and England. Allied bombers visited the university town of Freiburg twenty-five times and killed thirty-one people.[11] In all, 768 Germans perished in enemy raids throughout the war. Still, these episodes provided an ominous introduction to the ordeal of strategic bombing. Most of them took place randomly at night, so families were evacuated from sleep into cellars or makeshift shelters in public buildings. Anti-aircraft fire was primitive, as much a danger to civilians nearby as to enemy airplanes.

Occupation and strategic bombing were the most immediate channels through which the war came home, but they represented exceptional experiences, which were confined to regions of the country near the frontier. Other forms of communication brought the war more commonly to the homefront.

The war was about dying. The censors could suppress the aggregate statistics, but the death of an individual soldier could not be concealed from those at home who were directly affected – a category that comprised the families of about 2,000,000 men. During the first stage of the war, news of death and injury arrived publicly. Lists of casualties were posted in public places, such as police stations and newspaper offices, before the growing length of these documents invited discouraging public

---

[11] Heiko Haumann and Hans Schadek (eds.), *Geschichte der Stadt Freiburg im Breisgau* (3 vols., Stuttgart, 1992–96), vol. III, 263.

speculation about the war's course. So the communication of tragedy was banished to the more private channels provided by the postal service, where it remained, unless families chose to publish notices of their bereavement in the newspapers. As in other armies, the painful duty of communicating the news of death at the front fell to junior officers, who resorted to a set of sterile formulas to describe deaths that were proud, heroic, and quick. The language of these letters validated the official reading of the war, but the ritual quickly lost its power to disguise the grisly circumstances in which soldiers were dying at the front. Uncertainty often compounded the family ordeal. The heavy weapons that shaped the face of battle in this war were not "clean." About half of the soldiers who died in combat were destroyed beyond identification. In these cases, the dreaded letter home brought news only of a loved one "missing in action," if it arrived at all.

The war was also about injury. Some 4,000,000 German men were wounded in various degrees of severity, and evidence of their misfortune was far too abundant to conceal. The most serious cases were transported back to Germany to makeshift hospitals, which the army or the Red Cross set up in schools, auditoriums, theaters, or other large buildings. Trains and horse-drawn carts filled with wounded soldiers thus became common sights in localities near the eastern and western borders of Germany, which initially played host to most of the casualties. Convalescing soldiers were also a common sight here. Many of them survived thanks to advances in antisepsis and other medical arts that matured in this war; and many of these survivors were frightfully disfigured, protected only by the shields that a new, thriving prosthetics industry had devised for them.[12] The sights and sounds of men in uniform were constant reminders of combat in far-away places, as more enthusiastic or anxious young men on their way to war mixed with these forlorn ambassadors from the front.

The predominant mode of communication in this war remained the written word. Beyond carrying news of death or injury, letters constituted the great bulk of the traffic to and from the battlefront, the principal medium in which the experience of war was given expression in both arenas. A staggering amount of mail traveled in both directions. Including the so-called *Liebesgaben*, or "care-packages" of food, liquor, clothing, tobacco, and other essentials for the soldiers from home, the deliveries in both directions numbered close to 30 billion during the war. Close to 7,000,000 of them went homeward every day.[13] The volume

[12] Wolfgang U. Eckart and Christoph Gradmann (eds.), *Die Medizin und der Erste Weltkrieg* (Pfaffenweiler, 1996).

[13] Bernd Ulrich, "Feldpostbriefe im Ersten Weltkrieg – Bedeutung und Zensur," in Knoch, *Kriegsalltag*, 43.

of packages, letters, and cards complicated the efforts of frontline officers and censors at home to prevent the exchange of military secrets or
negative feelings about the war. The mails could only be screened selec-
tively, so they offered a more authentic view of the war than did censored
newspapers, which also went to the front to tell of life at home.

Like the newspapers, the *Feldpostbriefe*, the letters from the front,
announced the elation of the early months. Even as they spoke of the
hardship and brutality of combat, they embraced the official language to
represent the war in terms of the bravery, heroism, sacrifice, and the common exertions it evoked. "There can be nothing more beautiful for me,"
read a typical outpouring from a young officer, soon to be killed, "than to
sacrifice my earthly happiness on the altar of the Fatherland."[14] Early letters like this one were welcome to censors and newspaper editors alike as
instruments of homefront propaganda. Many of these documents found
their way into the press or the dozens of anthologies that appeared in the
first two years of the war. Collected letters of university students, Saxons,
Socialists, or assorted other groups of soldiers admonished resolve on the
homefront and underscored the unity that was supposed to reign among
all sectors of German society.

This genre did not survive the campaigns of 1916, nor did the sentiments that had inspired it. The letters home were no longer published,
for their disillusionment and cynicism conveyed a much drearier picture
of war. The subversive potential of these letters was of great concern to
the censors, who were already occupied with another dimension of the
same problem, the so-called *Jammerbrief*, the letter of complaint in the
other direction, which detailed the growing hardships of life on the homefront. The censors feared the impact of these letters on frontline morale,
for the welfare of the homefront represented not only the premise of a
defensive war, but – probably in the eyes of most soldiers – also the only
compelling grounds for holding out. The situation bred its ironies. During their offensives of early 1918, German soldiers raided allied supply
depots and dispatched much of the bounty eastward, as *Liebesgaben* for
the beleaguered homefront.

Despite their complex dependencies, experiences on the homefront
and fighting front were geared to different phases of the war. The
gulf between the two worlds bred resentments, which fed through the
Jammerbrief and another channel of communication homeward, the fur-
lough. Soldiers ordinarily received two weeks' leave at home after a year of

---

[14] Quoted in Reinhard Rürup, "Der 'Geist von 1914' in Deutschland: Kriegsbegeis-
terung und Ideologisierung des Krieges im Ersten Weltkrieg," in Bernd Hüppauf (ed.),
Ansichten vom Krieg: Vergleichende Studien zum Ersten Weltkrieg in Literatur und Gesellschaft
(Königstein im Taunus, 1984), 4.

frontline service. These visits often became occasions of more discomfort than solace, and they left soldiers yearning to return to the front. Furloughs brought direct contact with the privations faced by loved ones on the homefront, as well as the grumbling and apparent ingratitude of civilians, who had little comprehension of life at the front. Two figures, who symbolized the problem, became the focus of the soldiers' resentments of the homefront. The first was the profiteer, the greedy businessman with the war contracts, to whom the war had brought riches amid the general misfortune. The other figure was the blustering home-front patriot, like the headmaster in Remarque's *All Quiet on the Western Front*, who had not himself served in the army and whose understanding of the war had, as a consequence, frozen in the summer of 1914. Soldiers found this loud, arrogant patriotism repugnant, for it no longer provided an adequate interpretive framework for the experience of the front. Nor, for that matter, did it make much sense of the crippling costs that the war was extracting from nearly everyone at home.

Paying for war

The costs of the war were incalculable – less because of their magnitude, however difficult this aspect was for Germans to comprehend, than because of their variety and long-lingering consequences. They included direct demographic costs, which registered as several ugly indentations in the twentieth century's population curve, depreciation costs to plants and equipment, and the less tangible emotional costs of deprivation in its various forms. One category of costs did have to be counted, however; and accounting for these expenses had far-reaching social consequences.

Every gun, shell, sandbag, cartridge box, horseshoe, belt buckle, and boot nail carried a price tag. The government, in the guise of the War Ministry, paid out these costs in the form of war contracts. The immediate consequence was an astronomical increase in the outlays of the German federal government. By 1918, direct war-related expenses stood at more than ten times the total federal budget on the eve of the war (see figure 1).

These direct outlays totaled nearly 150 billion marks over the course of the war. They represented but the beginning. The federal government was by no means the only public agency that paid out the price of war. State and local governments took on the immense ancillary costs. Cities and communes supported the families of soldiers in the field, and they shared with the federal government the costs of pensions to the families of those who were killed or incapacitated in action, as well as caring for the wounded. Local governments provided subsidies in cash or rations to the poor, a category that by war's end comprised about half the population.

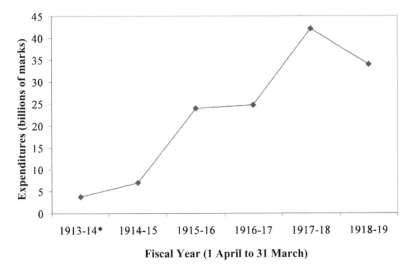

* Total expenditures

Figure 1   War-related expenditures of the German government (*source*: Gustav Stolper, *The German Economy: 1870 to the Present* [New York, 1967], 57)

These agencies also paid the full salaries of public officials who were serving in the military, as well as partial wages to other classes of public workers who were in the field. In the absence of these employees, however, the responsibilities of local governments increased. From the pool of those who were not at the front – a group made up largely of women – public offices expanded their staffs to coordinate the rationing of food and other essential goods, as well as to replace departed workers whose services were indispensable. The women who donned uniforms to collect fares on the tramways in Karlsruhe, Munich, and other cities symbolized both the social and financial implications of this situation. State governments provided some subsidies, while the federal government agreed to indemnify both state and local governments after the war for the expenses that they had accumulated; but as long as the war continued, these agencies needed enormous revenues of their own in order to finance their daily operations.

Public agencies from the top down thus faced an urgent problem: how to raise the money to cover these staggering costs. Collections and donations, like the purchase of the nails to emboss Hindenburg's wooden statue, served important symbolic functions but raised negligible revenues. Two options remained: to tax or to borrow. Taxation was unpopular. Persuasive voices in the German government, foremost among them Karl Helfferich, the federal Minister of Finance, argued that Germans were already under such duress from the war that increasing the burden of taxation would threaten morale. They also feared that a debate over new federal taxes would raise intractable issues of social equity, which were best avoided in the interests of national unity. Proponents of increased federal taxes encountered an additional, constitutional obstacle, for the federal government had historically levied only indirect taxes, such as excises and tariffs, so no apparatus was in place to administer direct federal taxes. States and communes, which were under no such limitation, did increase the levels of taxes that they levied on property and income, although the communes nonetheless found themselves some 2 billion marks in debt by the fall of 1917.[15] In all events, the actions of these bodies further discouraged the idea of direct federal taxation. Only in 1916 was a major federal tax introduced to help finance the war. It too was indirect, a value-added tax; and it was levied against a vulnerable target, the war profiteers, who were taxed at a sliding rate on their "excess profits." War contractors soon found ways, however, to pass these additional costs on in their negotiations with procurement agencies. Because of the government's reluctance to tax or to deal ruthlessly with the businessmen who supplied essential materials, taxation covered only about 15 percent of the direct outlays for the war.

That left borrowing. The German government faced obstacles here as well. Unlike the British and French, the Germans found themselves practically excluded from foreign financial markets, after an attempt to float a major loan on Wall Street failed in 1914. The only alternative was domestic borrowing; and it became far and away the major vehicle for raising revenue during the war. It took place in several forms. The most publicized was the *Kriegsanleihe*, the selling of war bonds. Nine times during the war, once every six months, the Reichstag authorized additional war credits, which were then issued in the form of public bonds. Most of these sold at a rate of 5 percent and were redeemable over ten years in semi-annual payments. These bond issues were accompanied by extravagant displays of patriotism, which were calculated to increase subscriptions. The bonds sold at banks, credit institutions, and post offices. Children were released from school to canvass door-to-door for individual subscribers. Banks invested in them; so did parishes and voluntary associations. Businesses and public offices purchased quantities of them, which they then encouraged their employees to buy with advanced wages.

---

[15] Otto Ziebill, *Geschichte des Deutschen Städtetages: Fünfzig Jahre deutsche Kommunalpolitik* (Stuttgart, 1956), 225.

In part because of the tremendous public pressure, in part too because of popular commitment to the war, the bond issues raised enormous amounts of money. Over the course of the war, the federal government generated in this fashion close to 100 billion marks.

The difficulty was that this money was directed only at federal expenditures; and it covered only about two-thirds of these, while the interest on the bonds themselves represented another, accumulating expense which claimed further resources. The German government planned to present the defeated enemy with the entire bill at the conclusion of the war; but until then, it discovered no alternative to funding its mounting deficits by manufacturing its own money. The process required only that the *Reichsbank*, the German national bank, discount short-term treasury bills with bank notes to the government's credit. While this practice addressed the immediate requirements of the federal government for credit, the national bank refused to accord the same service to state and local governments, whose need for credit to meet their own current expenses also burgeoned. With this problem in mind, the Federal Council passed a law in the first days of the war that established a network of loan bureaus (*Darlehenskassen*) in localities throughout the land. These institutions were empowered to lend money to states and local government agencies, as well as to private borrowers, on more liberal terms – with less collateral but higher rates of interest – than the national bank provided. To this end, the loan bureaus were allowed to issue their own notes. These had the same legal status as the notes of the national bank and hence circulated in increasing numbers as paper money, once gold coins were called in (to provide coverage for national bank notes) and silver coins disappeared to hoarding (see figure 2).

These policies conjured paper money out of nowhere. It became common practice to use war bonds at the loan bureaus as collateral for loans whose sole purpose was the purchase of additional war bonds. The national bank in turn used notes of the loan bureaus to cover additional issues of its own notes. These rituals provided thin cover for the government's resort to the printing presses to fund the war. The consequences were direct and obvious. The growth of the money supply meant that more money pursued fewer goods. Hence the government's monetary policies fueled strong pressures already being exerted by shortages of basic goods, like food. Prices rose (see figure 3).

Inflation thus became an unremitting, omnipresent fact of life on the German homefront.[16] Despite administrative attempts to soften

---

[16] Gerald D. Feldman, *The Great Disorder: Politics, Economics, and Society in the German Inflation, 1914–1924* (New York and Oxford, 1993).

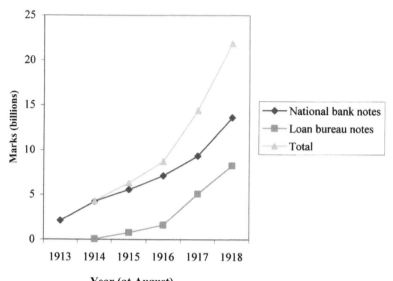

Figure 2   Bank notes in circulation (*source*: Ruth Andexel, *Imperialismus, Staatsfinanzen, Rüstung, Krieg: Probleme der Rüstungsfinanzierung des deutschen Imperialismus* [Berlin, 1968], 50–51)

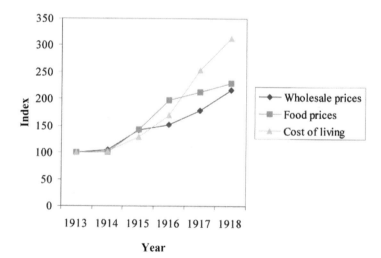

Figure 3   The rise of prices and the cost of living (*source*: Jürgen Kocka, *Klassengesellschaft im Krieg: Deutsche Sozialgeschichte 1914–1918* [Göttingen, 1973], 17)

its impact with price ceilings, it affected everyone. It also delivered the bill for the war to the German people, for it confiscated their wealth as surely as taxation did. It did so, however, more deceptively and without the benefits of taxation, which in theory reduced the money supply and so discouraged inflationary monetary pressures. Every German whose wages, salary, rents, or investment earnings fell behind the rate of inflation paid the price for the war in the form of reduced real income and capital wealth. In this light, the sale of war bonds was especially pernicious, for it encouraged far more sacrifice than patriotic subscribers suspected. A war bond with a face value of 1,000 marks when purchased in the summer of 1914 still carried a face value of 1,000 marks in the summer of 1918, when its value, adjusted to current prices, stood close to 300 marks.

As it jeopardized standards of living and eroded wealth, inflation bred a pervasive sense of social anxiety on the German homefront. Its impact was socially divisive as well. Its root causes were remote and difficult to understand, so inflation invited suspicions towards more tangible objects of frustration, like the farmers and merchants who charged the ever higher prices. Finally, inflation also became a motor of social change, for some groups of Germans were more vulnerable to its effects than others.

War and social class

The war affected every German who endured it, but its impact was by no means uniform. The experience of war varied among the basic groups of which German society was composed. These groups displayed various characteristics in common, which bred shared experiences, a sense of shared identity, and common perceptions of the war's meaning. The most basic of these groups were social classes, which were founded on the common circumstances in which people labored in order to support themselves and their families. Class relations rested on material differences of income, property, and other wealth, as well as on the status and the access to education, privilege, and power that material advantages conferred. Along this axis of social relations, the war occasioned fundamental shifts as it distributed its hardships.[17]

The war mobilized vast resources for purposes of destruction. It commanded, in other words, the destruction of vast amounts of wealth. Four years of this enterprise resulted in general social immiseration. The vast majority of Germans had less real wealth at the end of the war than they

[17] Jürgen Kocka, *Klassengesellschaft im Krieg: Deutsche Sozialgeschichte 1914–1918* (Göttingen, 1973).

had at the beginning. A rise in the cost-of-living index of 200 percent between 1914 and 1918 meant that anyone whose income failed to keep pace suffered a net material loss during the war. Nearly everyone did. The costs, however, were not equally shared. Some groups lost significantly more than others, and social relationships became unsettled.

The war generated a massive shift of material resources towards the sectors of the economy that produced the tools of destruction. The social "winners" were to be found here. The war provided good business for the firms that were directly engaged in producing arms and munitions, the great industrial plants that dominated the war corporations and fed on the generous terms of war contracts (and on the indifferent efforts of the government to regulate the attendant profits). By 1917, the net profits of the Krupp steel works had increased two and a half times over the prewar average. Profits were up a comparable amount in the Cologne Gunpowder Factory and ten times over prewar levels in the mammoth Rhine Metal Works in Düsseldorf. Adjusting for inflation, dividends were up an average of 175 percent among companies that processed iron on a large scale and almost 200 percent in the chemical industry. These figures documented an obvious social truth: certain branches of German industry did very well during the war, as did their owners, stock-holders, managers, and other leading employees. Germans who were in the economic orbit of the large companies that dominated mining and metal processing, chemicals, and electrical equipment were thus in the best position to withstand the social ravages of the war.

The further an enterprise was removed from this orbit, the more perilous became the condition of those who were associated with it. While the war encouraged the concentration of industrial power in huge concerns that were directly involved in the production of weapons and munitions, firms that were devoted to less essential manufactures tended to be smaller. These firms faced myriad problems. While the value of their capital plants provided some protection against inflation, a distorted market made survival difficult amid rationed supplies and controlled prices, reduced sales and profits, and the departure of workers and owners to the army or other, more essential and better-paying industries. The plight of these firms registered in the fluctuation of their workforce. While the number of workers rose 44 percent in war industries between 1913 and 1918, it fell 21 percent over the same period in "intermediate" firms, which produced for both civilian and military purposes; and it declined 40 percent in firms that produced only for civilian purposes.[18] In Barmen, the number of workers in the textile plants declined 60 percent during

[18] *Ibid.*, 13.

Table 3 *Industrial wage indices (male workers), 1914–1918*

Male workers in:	Wage index, 1914	Wage index, 1918	Cost of living index, 1918
War industry: metals, machinery, chemicals, electrical	100	252	313
Intermediate: stone, wood, leather, paper	100	209	313
Civilian: food, textiles, clothing, printing	100	181	313

Source: Jürgen Kocka, *Klassengesellschaft im Krieg: Deutsche Sozialgeschichte 1914–1918* (Göttingen, 1973), 14

the war, while it rose over 50 percent in the metalworking factories.[19] These figures reflected the collapse of countless small businesses, whose owners or workers were drafted into the army or whose supplies of coal and other essential materials dwindled. Particularly after the Hindenburg Program intensified the purge of non-military production, closure was a common fate among small firms (and many larger ones) that had produced or processed food, textiles, reading materials, and buildings. In Wesel, a fortress town of about 20,000, some 300 artisans and other small businessmen were inducted; and by the winter of 1916–17, about half of them had been compelled to shut down their operations.[20] At the same time, however, many small businesses did persevere as contractors or subcontractors in the many niches of the war economy. Saddlers, locksmiths, watchmakers, box-makers, and other craftsmen learned that the price of survival was the quick adjustment of their shops and output to the tastes of the military procurement offices.

Proximity to war production not only governed the material fortunes of owners, managers, and stockholders of industrial firms; it affected workers as well. Here the statistics told an unambiguous story (see table 3). Although their wages failed to keep pace with the rise in the cost of living, male workers who were employed in war production fared significantly better than others, particularly when their labor was skilled, as it was in many phases of metal-processing and electrical work. Because their labor was essential to the war effort, most of the workers employed in these critical plants were well treated by employers and government officials.

[19] Jürgen Reulecke, *Die wirtschaftliche Entwicklung der Stadt Barmen von 1910 bis 1925* (Neustadt an der Aisch, 1973), 69.
[20] Bernhard Sicken, "Die Festungs- und Garnisonsstadt Wesel im Ersten Weltkrieg: Kriegsauswirkungen und Versorgungsprobleme," in Bernhard Kirchgässner and Günter Scholz (eds.), *Stadt und Krieg* (Sigmaringen, 1989), 207.

Table 4 *White-collar wage indices, 1914–1918*

	Pay index, 1914	Pay index, 1917 (1918)	Cost of living index, 1917 (1918)
Shop clerks	100	118*	285*
High-level public officials	100	147	313
Mid-level public officials	100	172	313
Low-level public officials	100	218	313

* 1917

Source: Jürgen Kocka, *Klassengesellschaft im Krieg: Deutsche Sozialgeschichte 1914–1918* (Göttingen, 1973), 72–4

These workers were encouraged to organize and, in part because of the protection that unionization brought them, they were relatively well paid – often in food and other material provisions, as well as wages. The median wages for skilled metalworkers in Düsseldorf nearly trebled during the war. The higher wages reflected as well, however, the long hours that prevailed in the armament factories, like the Düsseldorf Pipes and Iron Rolling Works, where twelve-hour shifts were not unusual.[21]

Workers who were employed in firms less immediately involved in war production faced greater jeopardy from the erosion of their livelihoods. The most vulnerable category of employee comprised so-called white-collar or clerical workers, who typically worked for salaries or commissions in non-manual occupations. Their vulnerability was due to central characteristics of their social existence in war: they tended to lack capital assets and the protection of collective bargaining. Some statistics suggested the dimensions of the problem (see table 4).

All categories of these white-collar employees lost real wealth to inflation – even those who were employed by Siemens, the giant electrical firm that played host to innumerable military contracts. Moreover, excepting only the lower-level public officials, all clerical and public employees found their incomes more severely eroded in the rising cost of living than did industrial workers as a group.

The war brought material hardship to nearly everyone. Even workers in the war industries had to contend with increasing shortages of the most basic commodities; and no one's wages kept pace with inflation on the black market. Still, no one starved. Other kinds of social problems, which were psychological as well as material, were more subtle

---

[21] Elizabeth H. Tobin, "War and the Working Class: The Case of Düsseldorf 1914–1918," *Central European History* 17 (1985), 269, 276.

and durable. These had to do with collective identities or self-perceptions among social groups. The war drew attention to the broad gulf that separated the rich from the poor – the Germans with wealth and property from those without. In 1916, this second group received official bureaucratic designation as "*minderbemittelt*" – people of "lesser means," who earned less than a subsistence income and were accordingly entitled to public subsidies. This group, which comprised a significant majority of the men, women, and children in virtually every German city, endured the worst failures and humiliations of the rations system, for they lacked the resources to circumvent it. As the war continued, these experiences nourished resentment among this official lower class against the privileges of wealth, which were emphasized daily by the absence of the rich – those Germans for whom "price plays no role" – among those who queued up for rations.

A second critical focus of tension lay along the divide that marked off Germans "of lesser means." The war threatened to close the social fissure that had separated salaried from non-salaried employees, white-collar from blue-collar workers – or, in the terms in which these distinctions were conventionally defined, the lower tiers of the middle class from the industrial working class. The claims of salaried employees to higher social status had traditionally rested on the purported respectability and independence of their work and lifestyle. White-collar workers did not work with their hands, nor for hourly wages. They did not bargain collectively in unions; they had generally earned more than manual workers, and some at least had modest savings. The war eroded the material foundations of these self-perceptions and status claims. Many white-collar workers fell during the war into the category "of lesser means." Inflation hit them as a group harder than it did industrial workers. Major sectors of the proletariat emerged from the war earning more money than salaried employees, who not only tended to disdain unionization but had also invested their savings in war bonds.

Among these salaried public employees, the higher officials – from judges to university professors – represented a special case. Their claims to social distinction were based on their academic credentials – the fact that they had studied at a university. They, however, faced the greatest relative erosion of their material circumstances; not only did their salaries stagnate and their savings dwindle, but they also could not qualify for the public subsidies that helped support their lower-ranking colleagues. They shared this fate with many highly educated professionals, such as lawyers and journalists. The consequence was to breed special insecurity among this articulate group, which comprised much of the country's cultural and political leadership. Although it did not reach catastrophic proportions until the hyperinflation of the postwar era wrought the financial ruin of much of Germany's middle class, the seeds of social crisis were planted during the war. One clear sign of trouble was the growing frequency with which public officials and other groups of salaried employees began to organize – and even to strike – towards the end of the war, for this step represented a fundamental departure from behavior prescribed in the social image of these people.

The war thus promoted important shifts of social power in Germany even as it emphasized class divides. In the reorganization of the economy, social survival seemed to require strategic location, size, and organization. The benefits of this principle accrued to selected sectors of the industrial bourgeoisie and the blue-collar workforce, which could exploit their central positions in the war economy at least to temper their immiseration. Large segments of the German lower middle class, both small businesspeople and salaried employees, were not so fortunate. Not only did they bear the brunt of the inflation, but the war also challenged their sense of respectability and social distinction. Images of smallness, duress, and helplessness – of a petite bourgeoisie squeezed between big capital and big labor – circulated now with special power in these sectors of society. Images like these provided at least a sense of bearings for the vulnerable, as the war assaulted long-standing relationships among social groups that had been defined by differences of material circumstance. But class represented only one category of relations that the war challenged.

Gender

Like class, gender was a basic condition of social experience during the war. It was geared to a different, physiological order of circumstances. The relationship between class and gender was nonetheless a cultural phenomenon, and it was inextricably reciprocal. Patterns of gender relations were governing characteristics of class, just as social factors conditioned the experience – and even the definition – of gender. The classic instance of this truth was the doctrine of "separate spheres." In segregating the private from the public realm, and in defining "proper" women as inhabitants of the home, this doctrine sanctioned gender roles that were more prevalent – and possible – among middle-class families in Germany (and elsewhere) than among working-class households, which depended to greater degrees on the gainful employment of women.

It contradicts none of these principles to observe that German women experienced the war in fundamentally different terms than men did.

Women did not face death in combat. The proposition that they were by nature weak, gentle, nurturing creatures was far too culturally entrenched to permit even the thought of conscripting German women into the armed forces. In fact, the same proposition was an effective block to the systematic mobilization of women into the industrial workforce; and it accounted for the exclusion of women from the civilian draft that the Auxiliary Service Law sought to impose in late 1916. The precept that women were care-givers, whose proper sphere was the home, proved extraordinarily resilient in Germany, even amid material circumstances that had made mockery of it long before the war. Paradoxically, the war encouraged this thinking. While the men departed for combat, the women remained behind – on the "home" front. The role of women was perforce supportive. They not only cared for families in the absence of husbands, brothers, and fathers, but – as the war dragged on – they also provided essential material succor for the warriors at the fighting front. The feminization of the homefront thus inhered in the war's gendered oppositions, but it was also a social fact: the homefront was largely a female phenomenon. Women bore the principal brunt of its privations, and – despite the ideological obstacles to the process – they became an indispensable force in the war economy.

Generalizations about women in the war are nonetheless risky. Class distinctions bore on women's experiences of the conflict no less than they did on men's. While women of all social stations contended with the absence of male heads-of-household and other loved ones, working-class women faced harsher circumstances as a rule than did women of the higher classes. They were usually poor to begin with, so the departure of a principal provider for the front meant immediate hardship, as these women abruptly found themselves at the head of households. Although they were criticized in some quarters as an invitation to squander money, public subsidies to the wives of soldiers provided a measure of compensation, as did public aid to the families of the poor; but inflation and growing shortages of most basic items made support of a household by a lone working-class woman an increasingly desperate concern.

Although patriotic appeals and other moral enticements contributed to it, the growing prominence of women in the workforce was thus driven in the end, as it had been before the war, by material hardship. By the end of the conflict, over one-third of the industrial workforce was female, and well over 2,000,000 women were employed in factories with more than ten workers. The market, not the state, drove this trend, whose most remarkable feature was the dramatic increase of women in the high-paying war industries, like the metal-processing plants of the Rhineland and Westphalia, where the number of women in the workforce grew from

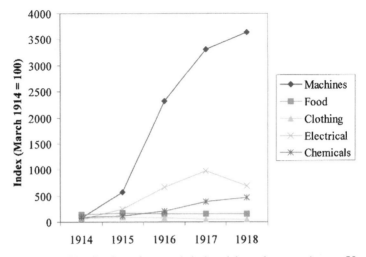

Figure 4   Distribution of women's industrial employment (*source*: Ute Daniel, *Arbeiterfrauen in der Kriegsgesellschaft: Beruf, Familie und Politik im Ersten Weltkrieg* [Göttingen, 1989], 47)

19,000 in 1914 to 106,000 at the war's end.[22] In the Krupp works, women made up nearly 40 percent of the workforce.[23] The aggregate statistics confirmed the pattern (see figure 4).

These figures long buttressed the argument that the First World War brought the real beginnings of women's emancipation to Germany, that it provided millions of women with an essential, rewarding role in the war effort, as well as an opportunity to acquire a sense of occupational identity.[24] The argument comported well with the coming of women's suffrage to Germany in 1919, but it has not withstood recent scrutiny.[25] The female industrial workforce grew 17 percent during the war, but prewar trends suggested that it would have grown almost as much had there been no war. The statistics indicate that the war instead occasioned a significant movement among women who were already in the workforce,

---

[22] Jürgen Reulecke, "Wirtschaft und Bevölkerung ausgewählter Städte im Ersten Weltkrieg," in Reulecke (ed.), *Die deutsche Stadt im Industriezeitalter: Beiträge zur modernen deutschen Stadtgeschichte* (Wuppertal, 1978), 123.

[23] Ludwig Preller, *Sozialpolitik in der Weimarer Republik* (Kronberg and Düsseldorf, 1978), 8.

[24] Ursula von Gersdorff, *Frauen im Kriegsdienst 1914–1945* (Stuttgart, 1969); Stefan Bajohr, *Die Hälfte der Fabrik: Geschichte der Frauenarbeit in Deutschland 1914–1945* (Marburg, 1979).

[25] Ute Daniel, *Arbeiterfrauen in der Kriegsgesellschaft: Beruf, Familie und Politik im Ersten Weltkrieg* (Göttingen, 1989).

that women deserted jobs in domestic service or in industries such as textiles and food-processing, where they had long constituted a major portion of the workforce, for places on assembly lines that fashioned fuses, shells, and grenades. Labor here was both strenuous and dangerous. An explosion in a munitions factory in Fürth claimed the lives of forty women workers in the spring of 1917; thirty perished in similar fashion shortly thereafter in Cologne. That labor in these circumstances afforded women much sense of occupational identity or fulfillment is dubious. Owing to the mechanization of weapons production, the employment that they found here often required little training, skill, or responsibility; and they were paid on average about half the wages of their male peers. Many of these women found adjustment difficult to the regimentation of labor in the war industries, where they could expect to work fifty-five hours a week. The army established child-care facilities for them in more than 800 of the larger armament factories, but the support that these facilities provided was scarcely adequate; the 700,000 women workers in these factories shared the services of 630 nurses.[26] Finally, virtually all the women in the war industries understood well that their employment would terminate the moment the men returned from the front.

Still, women in the war industries enjoyed the highest wage rates among all women workers, and their lot improved in the later stages of the war, as they joined trade unions in increasing numbers – to the point that they constituted one-quarter of the Socialist unions' membership in 1918. As a rule, women who worked in other sectors, like male workers in these sectors, earned significantly less. Women in textiles earned on average only about two-thirds the wages of women in metal-processing. Most vulnerable were the women who populated the domestic industries that took on new life in the war economy. These women, many of whom were wives of soldiers, did piecework as subcontractors to the army, producing baskets, belts, and other items for military use. In Constance, to cite one example, 2,000 of them produced sandbags and canvas strips as subcontractors to a local textile firm.[27] Despite its low pay, many working-class women preferred this mode of employment, for it kept them close to home, where the ordeal of feeding, clothing, and otherwise supporting their households consumed much of their time.

[26] Rolf Landwehr, "Funktionswandel der Fürsorge vom Ersten Weltkrieg bis zum Ende der Weimarer Republik," in Rolf Landwehr and Rüdiger Baron (eds.), *Geschichte der Sozialarbeit: Hauptlinien ihrer Entwicklung im 19. und 20. Jahrhundert* (Weinheim and Basel, 1983), 87.

[27] Lothar Burchardt, "Konstanz im Ersten Weltkrieg," in Burchardt, *et al.*, *Konstanz im 20. Jahrhundert: Die Jahre 1914 bis 1945* (Constance, 1990), 20.

It is more difficult to generalize about middle-class women during the war, for their work experiences were more diverse and less publicly supervised (hence less accessible to statistical review). Many of these women were compelled to join the workforce, too, although not as a rule in factories. Clerical positions in sales or secretarial work continued, as they had before the war, to offer more suitable employment opportunities for middle-class women, who had now also to fend financially with inflation and the departure of male providers. The war itself created additional opportunities for them, above all in nursing, both at home and near the front; but many found a demand for their clerical skills in the local public bureaucracies that oversaw rationing systems and other social services.

The war also offered opportunities to women who did not need to supplement their household incomes. Wealth softened the anxieties of these women about feeding and clothing their families, for it bought easier access to scarce goods. Their servants stood in line for purchases that were legal, and the black market was available for purchases that were not. Women of the upper-middle classes had long been anchors in Germany's many charitable associations, whose local networks comprised women's clubs of assorted confessional and political colorations. These groups had traditionally provided care for unwed mothers, orphans, alcoholics, and other categories of unfortunate people. The war opened vast new challenges to women's charitable organizations, whether Catholic, Jewish, feminist, or nationalist; and it transformed their status. Often in conjunction with the Red Cross, they came together in towns and cities to offer their help to beleaguered local officials, who were grateful to accept. Christened the "National Women's Service," alliances of women's organizations thereupon began to oversee all manner of services, including hospitals, soup kitchens, child-care centers, classes in running a frugal household, and agencies for collecting old clothing and shoes. In Mannheim, the alliance comprised seventy-two different women's organizations, which oversaw, among other things, 600 children of working women in twelve child-care centers.[28] In Berlin, the participating organizations in the National Women's Service provided the city government with 1,400 volunteers.[29] These activities turned private associations in these cities and elsewhere into semi-public corporations. Their members received at most nominal pay for their work, but they now participated in public authority and administered public money. Their public contribution was essential, and it raised problems. The spectacle of women in

---

[28] Friedrich Walter, *Schicksal einer deutschen Stadt: Geschichte Mannheims 1907–45* (2 vols., Frankfurt am Main, 1949–50), vol. I, 212, 241.
[29] Landwehr, "Funktionswandel," 81–82.

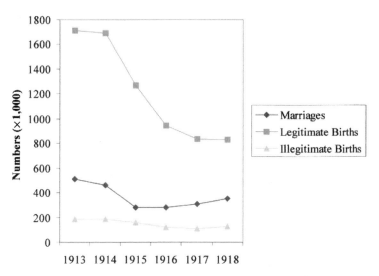

Figure 5   Marriages and births (*source*: Ute Daniel, *Arbeiterfrauen in der Kriegsgesellschaft: Beruf, Familie und Politik im Ersten Weltkrieg* [Göttingen, 1989], 129, 135)

prominent public roles was as novel to these women as it was to the men who formally supervised them, so the energy and enthusiasm with which women performed these roles became a frequent source of exasperation and jurisdictional friction. Nonetheless, terms like "emancipation" and "fulfillment" were not entirely incongruous to the wartime experience of women who, like Johanna Bungert, one of Meta Scheele's fictional "Women at War," lent their services in such capacities to the national effort.[30]

The war affected the relations between women and men in other, more basic ways. It resulted in the long-term, if not permanent, separation of millions of men and women who had been in sexual relationships, or would have entered them. The impact registered in the statistics (see figure 5). A flurry of quick marriages accompanied the beginning of the war, some of them products of impulse, others calculated to qualify a new bride for public subsidies. The rates of marriage and births thereupon dropped precipitously for the duration of the war. Conjugal intimacies were confined to letters, where they were exposed to the censors' gaze, or to furloughs home.

The war did not, however, suspend sexual relations, either at the front or at home. It encouraged instead its own regimes, which challenged the

[30] Meta Scheele, *Frauen im Krieg* (Gotha, 1930).

polarities that had traditionally ordered gender roles. That the fighting front, the realm of male aggressiveness, required an institutionalized outlet for male sexual drives seemed self-evident. The presence of millions of German soldiers thus turned prostitution into a massive industry near the front in Belgium, France, and Poland. Brussels, Lille, Antwerp, and other cities were home to hundreds of public bordellos, as well as to countless "free" prostitutes, who were easy to find in the notorious "*estaminets*" or coffee houses of the region. The military authorities made no effort to discourage prostitution, for they themselves subscribed to conventional stereotypes and believed in its benefits for the morale of the soldiers under their command. They were alarmed only by the venereal disease which the institution made rampant.[31] Fearing the degeneration of the army's fighting strength, they attempted to regulate the producers. They shut down the more informal avenues of prostitution and tried to confine it to the public houses, which were supervised medically. Their efforts to regulate the consumers of prostitution were more controversial. They ordered the medical inspection and supervision of soldiers who visited the bordellos, as well as a campaign to educate soldiers in safe practices, including the use of contraceptive devices. These efforts quickly drew protests from home, however, from women who pointed out that the army was promoting infidelity among married soldiers.

Male infidelity at the fighting front threatened conventional thinking about sexuality a great deal less than did female infidelity on the homefront. The dimensions of this problem were impossible to determine statistically, but images of the faithless *Kriegerfrau*, the soldier's adulterous wife, were ubiquitous – the subjects of jokes and cartoons, as well as serious commentary. These images were too widespread to lack foundation. They spoke in all events to major anxieties, which had to do with the dichotomies that underpinned several orders of relationships. The motif of betrayal challenged the supportive bond that ordered relations between home and the battlefront. The images spoke in addition to visions of sexual disorder, the reign of aggressive sexuality among German women. Visions of social disorder were at play, too, for promiscuity, prostitution, and the public display of sexuality were conventionally associated with women of the working class. While these visions fed on homefront prostitution, which flourished in places, like Düsseldorf, where soldiers were barracked or paused in transit, the most disquieting image was accordingly the adulterous *Kriegerfrau* from the middle class, whose passive

---

[31] Lutz Sauerteig, "Militär, Medizin und Moral: Sexualität im Ersten Weltkrieg," in Eckart and Gradmann, *Die Medizin*, 197–226. See also Magnus Hirschfeld, *et al.*, *The Sexual History of the World War* (New York, 1934).

sexual purity was supposed to be the mark of her social station.[32] The circumstances of war encouraged these anxieties, which commonly focused on women's invasion of the workplace, the presence of French and Russian prisoners of war among the women who worked German farms, and that perennial dark figure, the *Schlafgänger*, the male lodger who provided a welcome supplement to the household income but then joined the family in other ways. He represented, however, but one of the many ways the war impinged on family life.

Generations young and old

The term "generation" refers to social groups that were not, like class or gender, marked out by social space, but instead by social time. Members of generational groups had the timing of their births in common, hence they shared experiences of events at comparable stages in their natural lives. Like class and gender, however, generations were constructed culturally. Not only the attributes of generational categories like "youth" and "old age," but their very definitions were dependent on the same cultural codes that governed – and wed them with – understandings of class and gender.

The First World War was a defining generational moment. Age conditioned the experience of war in many ways. It forged a "front generation" out of millions of German males who were born during the last quarter of the nineteenth century.[33] Age also impinged centrally, if less dramatically, on the experience of Germans who were younger and older than those whose age qualified them for the journey to the front.

Close to 10,000,000 Germans were born between 1902 and 1918. This group of young people was significantly smaller than projected, for the war shrank the population of the very young. The precipitous fall in the birth rate during the war was the principal cause of this demographic event, but manifold privations also encouraged the deaths of infants who did find their way into that troubled world. The statistics on infant mortality reflected the hazards of malnourishment and exposure that awaited them (see figure 6). The sharp rise in the curves at the end of the war registered the impact of an influenza epidemic, which added to the ordeal of Germans, adults as well as children, in the summer and fall of 1918.

For German children who survived the risks of infancy, the salient experience of war was neglect. The war did not so much foster child

---

[32] See Peter Hüttenberger, "Die Industrie- und Verwaltungsstadt (20. Jahrhundert)," in Hugo Weidenhaupt (ed.), *Düsseldorf: Geschichte von den Anfängen bis ins 20. Jahrhundert* (3 vols., Düsseldorf, 1989), vol. III, 245.

[33] See Robert Wohl, *The Generation of 1914* (Cambridge, 1979).

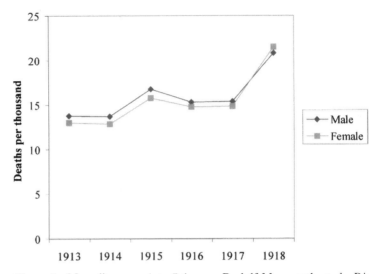

Figure 6   Mortality, ages 1 to 5 (*source*: Rudolf Meerwarth *et al.*, *Die Einwirkung des Krieges auf Bevölkerungsbewegung, Einkommen und Lebenshaltung in Deutschland* [Stuttgart, Berlin, and Leipzig 1932], 58–59)

abuse as it diminished the attentions and resources of adults who would in normal circumstances have provided nurture and supervision to children. Children were the principal victims of the food shortages, for their bodies most wanted the vitamins and proteins supplied in foods, like milk and fruits, that were in critical scarcity. The war deprived most families of an adult male, so children grew up in the company of females, who in 1915 made up 58 percent of all German households. In working-class families, adult females were frequently occupied outside the household as well, so the responsibilities of child-care fell to older siblings or cooperative day-care centers.

The experience of neglect extended well beyond the household. The war had a devastating impact on the public institution that normally supervised German children from the ages of six to fourteen. Schools yielded to more urgent demands. School buildings were transformed into hospitals, their former occupants banished into whatever quarters they could find. In the small city of Speyer on the Rhine River, for instance, every schoolhouse hosted the army's wards in the fall of 1914.[34] School teachers, too, heeded the call to the colors. In the town of Schwäbisch Hall in Württemberg, twenty of the school district's sixty-six teachers

[34] Hans Fenske, "Speyer im 19 Jahrhundert (1814 bis 1918)," in Wolfgang Eger (ed.), *Geschichte der Stadt Speyer* (2 vols., Stuttgart, 1983), vol. II, 263.

were called up.[35] By the end of 1915 one out of every four elementary school teachers in Germany was in the army; and the shortage of teachers became more paralyzing as the pressures of mobilization increased, despite efforts to recruit retired teachers back into the classroom. The shortage of teachers combined with shortages of space to make classes larger and instruction truncated. The dearth of farm labor recommended long vacations for school children in the summer and early fall, while coal shortages mandated long breaks from unheated schoolrooms in the winter. By the end of the war, children in many parts of the country were in school only a few hours a week.

The effect of some forms of neglect was palpable. The war made German children smaller physically. After the war, studies revealed that school children were on average several centimeters shorter and several kilograms lighter than prewar norms for their age groups.[36] Children also suffered disproportionately from diseases bred by malnutrition, inadequate shelter, and poor hygiene. Shortages of animal fats put soap in short supply; as a result, clothes, underclothes, and linens (to say nothing of bodies, young and old) remained dirty. Intestinal disorders, chronic anemia, and tuberculosis were rampant, as was rickets, which, by one estimate, afflicted nearly 40 percent of Germany's children. The fact that doctors observed great increases in nervousness and bed-wetting among children suggested that material deprivation exacted a psychological price as well, although it must remain a matter of speculation whether, as one historian has argued, the absence of millions of fathers left unresolved oedipal tensions in a "youth cohort," which was later drawn, as a consequence, to Hitler.[37]

Nonetheless, like the youths of Ernst Glaeser's fictional "Class of 1902," children and youths were left to undergo formative experiences of life and love in a world largely unsupervised by adults.[38] Military and civilian authorities soon grew alarmed at some of the consequences. To combat what they called the "moral dissolution" (*Verwahrlosung*) of Germany's youth, they enlisted young people into all manner of war-related activities, in hopes of providing constructive occupation for them and elevating morale on the homefront generally. Placing children in the fields at harvest time fell into this category, as did door-to-door canvassing

[35] Armin Müller, "Schwäbisch Hall 1914–1918: Eine Oberamtsstadt im Spiegel des I. Weltkrieges," *Württembergisch Franken* 76 (1992), 277.

[36] F. Bumm, *Deutschlands Gesundheitsverhältnisse unter dem Einfluss des Weltkrieges* (2 vols., Stuttgart, Berlin and Leipzig, 1928), vol. I, 121–3.

[37] Peter Loewenberg, "The Psychohistorical Origins of the Nazi Youth Cohort," *American Historical Review* 76 (1971), 1,457–502.

[38] Ernst Glaeser, *Jahrgang 1902* (Potsdam, 1929).

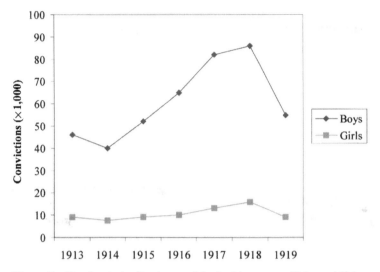

Figure 7   Youth criminality (*source*: Moritz Liepmann, *Krieg und Krim-inalität in Deutschland* [Stuttgart, Berlin, and Leipzig 1930], 98)

to promote war bonds or to collect donations of money, household objects made of metal, and old clothes for the poor. A network of paramilitary organizations occupied hundreds of thousands of older boys with pre-military training – and real weapons – under the supervision of reserve officers. Nonetheless, a dramatic increase in criminality among young Germans, particularly among German boys, nurtured the worst fears. Cutting school was the most common offense, and it reached epidemic proportions. In the city of Cologne the rate of unexcused absences among school boys rose from 15 percent to 48 percent during the first three years of the war. The court records documented comparable increases in more serious crimes during the war (see figure 7).

That neglect played a major role in driving these figures was hard to dispute. A survey of young criminals in Berlin revealed that in nine out of ten cases, the mother was employed outside the home, incapacitated, or otherwise absent. Young people thus sought the support of one another, and much of their criminal activity became organized. Many of the infor-mal youth clubs that took shape in German cities during the war became difficult to distinguish from gangs.

The war also provided its characteristic endings to the German rites of youth. Children of all social classes found that portents of wartime adulthood awaited them after the age of fourteen. For boys, the prospect of armed service loomed within three or four years. Boys in secondary schools prepared for this passage in regular military training, which became part of their curriculum. The relaxation of child-labor laws meant that many boys and girls of the working class experienced full-time employment in their early teens. By 1917 over 300,000 young people between the ages of fourteen and sixteen were at work in factories. Although many of them filled unskilled, low-paying positions, their wages represented an essential part of the family's budget. The spectacle of young workers with money in their pockets nonetheless conjured up additional anxieties about the breakdown of order. Particularly disquieting was the specter of the young male worker, "in his silk waistcoat picking up prostitutes," for his consumption challenged the social order, his promiscuity mocked the gendered order, and his impertinence was an affront to the authority of his parents.[39] These anxieties prompted the military authorities to address the temptations of youthful dissolution in a number of decrees, which imposed early curfews, barred young people from movie theaters, and forbade them to smoke in public. Lower-class youths were the targets of most of the prohibitions. The same young people were also the objects of the most mean-spirited of these measures, which operated in military districts that housed major industrial centers (including Berlin). It prescribed compulsory savings accounts, into which young workers were required to deposit the major portion of their wages. This arrangement mollified the social prejudices that had inspired it, but it provided only a gratuitous indignity and material hardship to the working-class families that depended on the wages that it blocked.

The war also weighed heavily on the elderly. Some 2,500,000 Germans who greeted the war in 1914 had been born before 1855. For them the ensuing experience was marked by many of the same hazards that afflicted the very young. They, too, were particularly vulnerable to malnutrition and exposure. Like children, they paid disproportionate costs for the decline in health care that accompanied the call-up of physicians for military duty. The mortality of the elderly would have been high in any circumstances because of their advanced age, but the war accelerated it, as the statistics showed (see figure 8). Elderly German women displayed consistently higher mortality rates than their counterparts on the British isles, who were spared the shortages of food and fuel in the degree that Germans endured. As these shortages accumulated in Germany, they

---

[39] Eve Rosenhaft, "Restoring Moral Order on the Home Front: Compulsory Savings Plans for Young Workers in Germany, 1916–1919," in Coetzee and Coetzee, *Authority*, 81–109.

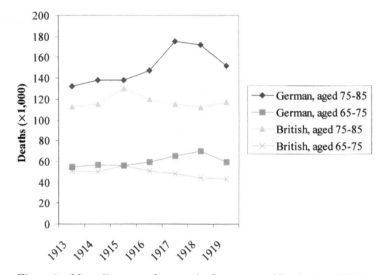

Figure 8   Mortality rates of women in Germany and England and Wales (*source*: F. Bumm *et al.*, *Deutschlands Gesundheitsverhältnisse unter dem Einfluss des Weltkrieges* [2 vols., Stuttgart, Berlin, and Leipzig 1928], vol. I, 53)

hastened the deaths of the elderly to respiratory diseases like tuberculosis and pneumonia, which thrived in the conditions of war, as well as to the influenza that visited Germany in 1918.

The war imposed other, less tangible cruelties on the elderly. Old age brought little joy even in peacetime. Imperial Germany had the most progressive system of pension benefits in the world, but payments were not available to all retired workers, nor were they remotely adequate to sustain a modest household, especially given the ravages of inflation. For Germans who were poor, old age usually meant long-term reliance on family and friends in any circumstances. The war increased the material and psychological burdens of this condition on everyone involved, particularly on the elderly themselves, for as their young relatives were being destroyed, their own labors were of little use even in the national emergency. Many of them found solace in church.

Confession

Social groups defined by generation, gender, and class transected still another category of social division in Germany. This one was based on confession – the social allegiances and practices that grew out of religious beliefs. Imperial Germany's confessional divisions were pervasive and deep-seated. They remained central to civic life in Germany, and they figured prominently in the experience of war. The civic truce that was proclaimed to patriotic jubilation at the war's beginning was supposed to suspend, if not to dissolve, confessional conflict in the great national community then taking shape. This dimension of the *Burgfrieden* was critical to the success of the war effort, for both Protestant and Catholic churches were central agents of moral mobilization. In the first stages of the war, hopes for confessional cooperation appeared to be vindicated. The German Catholic church proved almost as convinced in its support of the war as did the Protestant churches.

This was a considerable feat, for no sector of the population was more ardent a supporter of the war than the German Protestant churches.[40] The close tie between *Thron und Altar* molded the political loyalties of the clergy, as well as their thinking about war. Many pastors found a compelling theological justification for war in the doctrine of the "two kingdoms," which portrayed warfare as an inescapable feature of an earthly realm of sin and depravity. But the Protestant approach to war in 1914 was hardly fatalistic; it betrayed the ease with which Protestant theology had long lent its sanction to the aggressive designs of German nationalism. The fact that the coalition arrayed against Germany included Catholic France and Orthodox Russia supported the belief that the country was fighting in the name of the true – Protestant – Christianity and that the triumph of German imperial ambitions corresponded to the designs of God.

The outbreak of the war thus brought the amplification of themes that were already well defined in Protestant thinking, which now became known generally as *Kriegstheologie*, or "war theology."[41] Its tenets and tenor were well captured in the German curse hurled at the apostate Protestant power: "May God punish England!" War theology resounded throughout German Protestantism, from top church officials and theology professors to parish priests, for it provided a powerful representation of the war, which it framed in the light of divine will and German destiny. Apart from the blood-curdling sermons, many of which were published in order to quicken public morale, Protestant services were difficult to

---

[40] Karl Hammer, "Der deutsche Protestantismus und der Erste Weltkrieg," *Francia* 2 (1974), 398–414; Kurt Meier, "Evangelische Kirche und Erster Weltkrieg," in Wolfgang Michalka (ed.), *Der Erste Weltkrieg: Wirkung, Wahrnehmung, Analyse* (Munich and Zurich, 1994), 691–724.

[41] Günter Brakelmann, *Protestantische Kriegstheologie im Ersten Weltkrieg: Reinhold Seeberg als Theologe des deutschen Imperialismus* (Bielefeld, 1974); Wilhelm Pressel, *Die Kriegspredigt 1914–1918 in der evangelischen Kirche Deutschlands* (Göttingen, 1967).

distinguish from the patriotic rallies that secular authorities organized. Secular patriotic themes intruded into the liturgy, and patriotic songs were sung in lieu of hymns. These rituals continued throughout the war. They culminated in 1917, in an orgy of Protestant self-congratulation in connection with the *Lutherfeier*, the 400th anniversary of Luther's posting of the Ninety-Five Theses. There were only a few voices of doubt, caution, or moderation. The most important of these were associated with the journal, *Die Christliche Welt*, and its editor, Martin Rade, who taught theology at the university in Marburg.[42] But even when they were not censored, these voices were drowned out in a loud Protestant chorus that sang of annexations and a victorious peace until the bitter end.

The marriage of nationalism and Protestant theology accompanied the rejuvenation of parish life in Protestant communities after decades of growing secularization and religious indifference. Attendance increased at church services and other activities. Protestant churches became bulwarks of the war effort at home. Beyond stoking public morale, they provided private solace and spiritual support at a time when these services were in heavy demand. Parishes were centers of sociability for young and old. Protestant churches and their auxiliaries, particularly their women's organizations, had long been prominent in local charities; and the war brought the expansion of these efforts. Finally, the contribution of the Protestant clergy extended to the fighting front. Close to 1,000 Protestant clergymen served as chaplains to the army and navy, many of them frustrated that they could not, by law, themselves bear arms in combat.

Most of the generalizations that described the experience of the Protestant churches in wartime applied as well to German Catholicism.[43] The clerical hierarchy rallied to the war effort. Catholic parish life took on renewed vigor, as priests and lay organizations became props of both spiritual life and civic charity in a time of great duress. In Catholic parishes, too, as one clergyman noted, one heard "sermons that could have been given almost as easily in a patriotic assembly or a class in civic loyalty."[44] At the front, Catholic chaplains ministered to Catholic regiments. The vigor of Catholic support for the war betrayed a determination to show that their national loyalties were no less genuine than

---

[42] Johannes Rathje, *Die Welt des freien Protestantismus: Ein Beitrag zur deutsch-evangelischen Geistesgeschichte. Dargestellt an Leben und Werk von Martin Rade* (Stuttgart, 1952).

[43] Heinz Hürten, "Die katholische Kirche im Ersten Weltkrieg," in Michalka, *Weltkrieg*, 725–35; Heinrich Lutz, *Demokratie im Zwielicht: Der Weg der deutschen Katholiken aus dem Kaiserreich in die Republik 1914–1925* (Munich, 1963); Richard van Dülmen, "Der deutsche Katholizismus und der Erste Weltkrieg," *Francia* 2 (1974), 347–76.

[44] Hürten, "Die katholische Kirche," 730. See Heinrich Missalla, *"Gott mit uns": Die deutsche katholische Kriegspredigt 1914–1918* (Munich, 1968).

Protestants'. Catholic thinking on the subject of war was governed in principle by the doctrine of the "just war," the legitimacy of which was never
in question. In practice, this principle admitted of such flexible interpretation that German and French Catholics could alike appeal to it. The
German Catholic representation of the conflict resembled the Protestant
vision in remarkable respects. Catholics, too, insisted that the German
armies represented a special vehicle of God's will, which ordained, among
other things, the punishment of French Catholics, who had fallen from
the true faith into secularism, rationalism, and modernism. In the eyes of
some Catholics, the war offered the hope of healing the great schism in
German Christianity and the reconstruction of a single church on
German soil. This hope was baseless, but the readmission of the Jesuits
to Germany in 1917 kept alive the Catholic hope for some form of confessional reconciliation.[45]

Despite these wartime affinities with the Protestants, Catholic support
for the war proved less unequivocal. As the war dragged on, evidence of
fatigue surfaced at the grass-roots in sectors of German Catholicism that
bore the heaviest privations, particularly in its working-class wing, whose
political leaders began in 1916 to speak out in favor of a compromise
peace. In 1917, the position of German Catholics became more problematic. In August, Pope Benedict XV, who had assiduously guarded his neutrality in a conflict that had enveloped two-thirds of his entire flock, called
publicly for a negotiated end to the slaughter. This development, which
seemed to sanction Catholic opposition to the war with the church's highest authority, drove tensions into the open that had been building not only
within Catholicism but between Germany's leading confessional groups.
The Papal peace note encouraged left-wing Catholics who were advocating a negotiated peace, but they encountered little sympathy among
the Catholic aristocracy or upper bourgeoisie, nor among the high clergy.
The German Catholic leadership attempted to quiet the opposition, not-
ing that the Pope had spoken out not as the spiritual leader of Catholicism,
but as the secular ruler of the Vatican state. The specter of discord among
German Catholics over continuation of the war also revived other confessional tensions. Prominent Protestants, who had protested against the
return of the Jesuits to Germany, began publicly once again to question
the patriotism of German Catholics.

Whether or not Germany's 500,000 Jewish citizens constituted a confession was a principal object of debate during the war.[46] Prejudices
against Jews had been widespread in Germany on the eve of the war.

---

[45] See Róisín Healy, *The Jesuit Specter in Imperial Germany* (Boston and Leiden, 2003).
[46] Ulrich Sieg, *Jüdische Intellektuelle in Ersten Weltkrieg: Kriegserfahrungen, weltanschauliche
    Debatten und kulturelle Neuentwürfe* (Berlin, 2001); Christard Hoffmann, "Between

They took many forms, including systematic exclusion from public service; but only the radical nationalists were prepared to call for stripping German Jews of their civic rights, on the grounds that Jews belonged to a foreign ethnic or racial group. The vast majority of German Jews themselves argued that they were distinguished from other Germans by confessional differences alone, that Judaism represented a set of religious beliefs, like Protestantism or Catholicism. The war appeared at first to ratify this view. In the spirit of the *Burgfrieden*, German Jews, like German Catholics, demonstrated the authenticity of their patriotism. More than 10,000 volunteered for service in the first weeks of the war. As young Jewish men marched willingly to their deaths at the front, Jewish organizations of all descriptions joined in the mobilization of material and morale on the homefront. In the same spirit, the army's leadership removed a major barrier to Jewish civic equality when it agreed to commission Jewish officers, while the Deputy Commanding Generals suppressed the writings of prominent anti-Semites.

The spirit of accommodation soon dissipated amid the growing frustrations of war. Incidents of anti-Semitism multiplied in the army, and the restraints on anti-Semitic propaganda slackened at home, as old stereotypes adjusted quickly to new conditions. The stalemate, food shortages, and bureaucratic chaos begged explanation, which the figure of the Jew now offered as the symbol of profiteering, slacking, and defeatism. In 1916 the military authorities connived in this symbolism when they undertook a census of Jews in the army. Reports of the census became public; the results did not. The army thus lent credibility to the accusation that Jews were evading military service. The statistics, had they been released, would have showed this charge to be as baseless as the proposition that Jews stood out among the war's profiteers – an idea that rested largely on the fact, which was indisputable, that Walther Rathenau, who had organized the mobilization of raw materials, was a Jew.

The army's action brought a dreadful affront to Germany's Jews, some 12,000 of whom gave their lives during the war. Along with the rejuvenation of anti-Semitic stereotypes, the census provoked a renewal of a debate, among Jews and non-Jews alike, over the nature of "Jewishness." While racist themes surfaced with growing frequency in the anti-Semitic literature, German Jews themselves had increasing grounds to ponder the issue. The army's conquests in eastern Europe brought a large majority of Europe's Jews under German rule. The status of these Jewish communities, particularly the issue of whether Polish Jews constituted a discrete

Integration and Rejection: The Jewish Community in Germany, 1914–1918," in John Horne (ed.), *State, Society and Mobilization in Europe during the First World War* (Cambridge, 1997), 89–104.

national group, had important implications for occupation policy; it also bore immediately on the self-definition of Jews in Germany.[47] While most German Jews continued to insist on defining themselves and other Jews as a confessional community, both the encounter with east European Jews and the spread of anti-Semitism at home lent life to several German Zionist groups, which accepted the premise of the anti-Semites that Jews were fundamentally different from Germans.

Despite its auspicious beginnings, the war did not resolve tensions that had long reigned in confessional relations in Germany – and in other areas of German life. The *Burgfrieden* did not endure. The pressures of war exacerbated divisions not only among confessional groups, but also among generations, social classes, men and women, and soldiers and civilians. In these circumstances, the consensus in favor of the war was itself in jeopardy. During the last two years of the conflict, it collapsed.

---

[47] Egmont Zechlin, *Die deutsche Politik und die Juden im Ersten Weltkrieg* (Göttingen, 1969), 101–284.

5   The war breeds discord

The social burdens of war resulted in broadening discontent. In some sectors of German society discontent translated into organized protest and resistance to the war's continuation. Understanding the dynamics and patterns of this process begins best with a number of general observations about the organization and mobilization of sentiment to political ends.

Class, gender, generation, and confession all combined to structure basic communities of experience in wartime Germany. These communities provided frames of collective identity, as well as several different cultural vocabularies for making sense of the war. The common experience of combat defined one such community at the front, while the homefront played host to several others. These were nurtured in routine encounters among people who faced common problems, shared common lifestyles, lived in the same neighborhoods, and knew one another personally.

The most durable communities of experience on the homefront were those that were best organized; and these were defined historically by class and confession. They reflected the basic cleavages in German society and their institutionalization in rich networks of clubs and other kinds of voluntary associations, which the Germans called *Vereine*. Organizations of many descriptions had sprouted during the decades before the war, in order to serve a bewildering variety of purposes. They included chambers of commerce and local political organizations, trade unions and professional associations, women's groups, church auxiliaries, bicycle clubs, sharp-shooting societies, and groups devoted to the collecting of stamps, butterflies, or carrier pigeons. They tended, however, to replicate and reinforce the broader division of German society – in the first instance along lines of confession and class. The *Kulturkampf* drove the mobilization of German Catholics into their own organizations, which served the practical defense of Catholics' interests, as well as their spiritual needs and sociability. Then, in the 1890s, the spread of the German Socialist movement brought the further segregation of these organizations, now by class. Networks of working-class *Vereine* took shape in parallel with middle-class organizations, both Protestant and Catholic, in which many workers had not felt welcome. Localities throughout the land henceforth hosted multiple gymnastics clubs, women's auxiliaries, youth groups, and choral societies.

The war profoundly affected associational life in Germany. Many organizations collapsed or withered with the departure of dues-paying members to the front. Groups such as gymnastic societies and bicycle clubs, which appealed to able-bodied young men, were particularly vulnerable, as were trade unions in non-essential sectors of the economy. So were groups that had both male and female members – like choral societies, which found survival difficult without bass and tenor voices in their ranks. It was a fitting symbol of the problem that club trophies were then sacrificed to war production for their metal. In these arduous circumstances, German organizational life came into flux. Ties of confession and class survived as primary bonds, but the experience of war encouraged new solidarities and patterns of organization, of which military units were merely the most obvious.

Structuring and restructuring these communities of experience was a cultural process. It rested on shared meanings, which were constructed, represented, and communicated during the war in a rich variety of symbols and social rituals – the holy sacraments no less than the figures of Luther, Marx, and Hindenburg, the banner of the workers' glee club "Friendship" no less than the black-red-and-white of the Imperial German flag, and the singing of "The International" no less than the wearing of military uniforms. All these symbols and rituals conveyed representations of the war. They were vehicles in which Germans of all stations confronted the war's meaning and sought to locate their own experience within some broader interpretive framework, such as the nation's history and destiny, class conflict, or the promise of divine redemption.

Defining these communities of experience was finally also a political process. The war raised deep issues of social equity and the distribution of power, which could not long be hidden in the rhetoric of patriotic unity. Patriotism spoke to the most comprehensive of these communities – the one that united Germans as Germans. The language of patriotism represented the war as a supreme moment of crisis, challenge, and opportunity for every German. Patriotism provided the official interpretation of the conflict. The scenes of celebration early in the war suggested its power to accommodate diverse aspirations and to define the meaning of the war for groups of people who otherwise disagreed with one another about fundamental questions, such as those that related to class and confession. As the war dragged on, however, the power and credibility of this language diminished – in some communities more than others. Consensus thus eroded in misery, as the meaning of the war became itself the object of a bitter contest. Opposition grew.

The war and "culture"

The broad understanding of culture employed here, which stresses the symbolic construction and representation of shared meanings, is more familiar to anthropologists and cultural historians today than it was to Germans who endured the war.[1] To them the term "*Kultur*" referred instead to a phenomenon that was symbolized in the figures of Goethe, Kant, and Beethoven. German culture meant in the first instance "high culture."[2] It comprised the country's distinctive achievements in art, music, literature, and scholarship, as well as a set of collective virtues – like diligence, order, and discipline – that were thought to be characteristically German. This culture tended to find expression in the creative media and the scholarly treatise. It denoted a specific kind of cultural undertaking in the broader sense of the term. Its practitioners, too, sought to represent meanings; they did so, however, in specialized forms and languages of expression, like painting, poetry, or music, which normally required technical training.

To those who were most immediately associated with it, *Kultur* defined the central issue of the war. The great majority of Germany's leading writers, artists, composers, and academic scholars were passionately engaged in support of the war effort, which they portrayed as the defense of German culture. They affixed their signatures to manifestos that invoked German cultural superiority in order to justify the country's cause and claims, including the pursuit of expansive war aims.[3] One such document, which defiantly dismissed accusations of German barbarism in occupied Belgium, was addressed early in the war "To the Cultured World" and was decorated with the names of close to 100 of the country's leading intellectuals and artists, among them the writer Gerhart Hauptmann, the painter Max Liebermann, the biologist Ernst Haeckel, the theologian Adolf von Harnack, the economist Gustav Schmoller, the philosopher Wilhelm Windelband, the historian Friedrich Meinecke, and the composer Engelbert Humperdinck.[4] These and other figures were likewise

[1] See Lynn Hunt (ed.), *The New Cultural History* (Berkeley and Los Angeles, 1989).
[2] Georg Bollenbeck, *Bildung und Kultur: Glanz und Elend eines deutschen Deutungsmusters* (Frankfurt am Main and Leipzig, 1994).
[3] Klaus Schwabe, *Wissenschaft und Kriegsmoral: Die deutschen Hochschullehrer und die politischen Grundfragen des Ersten Weltkrieges* (Göttingen, 1969).
[4] Jürgen Ungern-Sternberg von Pürkel and Wolfgang von Ungern-Sternberg, *Der Aufruf an die Kulturwelt: Das Manifest der 93 und die Anfänge der Kriegspropaganda im Ersten*

prominent fixtures in the campaign to mobilize morale on the home-front. As the war stripped German universities of students and younger faculty, older scholars turned their efforts towards more popular forums; they offered their learned opinions in the press, contributed brochures for mass circulation, and spoke to large, appreciative audiences at patriotic rallies.

For these "culture carriers" (*Kulturträger*), the war offered an occasion for extended public meditation on the distinctive nature of German culture and their own social identity.[5] From the start, they cast the struggle between Germany and the western democracies in a set of dichotomies, which pivoted – to the great disadvantage of the latter term – on a polar opposition between "*Kultur*" and "*Zivilisation*." In this reading, "culture" represented the civic virtues that had found collective expression in the "ideas of 1914" at the outbreak of the war. Atop the list of these virtues were German creative idealism, heroism, self-sacrifice, and the willing subordination of the individual to a national community that bound its members by organic ties. "Civilization," by contrast, connoted the cause for which Britain and France had gone to war. It was linked to the ideals of the French Revolution, to the "ideas of 1789"; and these, in the German reading, implied superficiality, materialism, the pursuit of selfish interest, and political systems that gave primacy to the individual over the community. The dichotomy between "community" and "society," *Gemein-schaft* and *Gesellschaft*, which had figured centrally in the "ideas of 1914," modulated in this way into the basic motif of the wartime discourse on culture.

The German rhapsody to *Kultur* took many variations, as famous scholars elaborated on the contrast in idioms specific to their fields. According to the economist Werner Sombart, the contest pitted *Helden* against *Händler*. The Germans, he explained, were a nation of heroes, committed to the great deed, animated by Faustian drives; the English, by contrast, were a nation of traders, whose collective inclinations were practical, hedonistic, calculating, and base. The historian Karl Lamprecht portrayed the war as a conflict between a vibrant young German culture,

Weltkrieg (Stuttgart, 1996); Bernhard vom Brocke, " 'Wissenschaft and Militarismus': Der Aufruf der 93 'An die Kulturwelt!' und der Zusammenbruch der internationalen Gelehrtenrepublik im Ersten Weltkrieg," in W. M. Calder, III, *et al.* (eds.), *Wilamowitz nach 50 Jahren* (Darmstadt, 1985), 649–719.

5 Eckart Koester, *Literatur und Weltkriegsideologie: Positionen und Begründungszusammen-hänge des publizistischen Engagements deutscher Schriftsteller im Ersten Weltkrieg* (Kron-berg, 1977); Helmut Fries, "Deutsche Schriftsteller im Ersten Weltkrieg," in Wolfgang Michalka (ed.), *Der Erste Weltkrieg: Wirkung, Wahrnehmung, Analyse* (Munich and Zurich, 1994), 825–48; Wolfgang Mommsen, *Bürgerstolz und Weltmachtstreben: Deutschland unter Wilhelm II. 1890 bis 1918* (Berlin, 1995), 828–92; Kurt Flasch, *Die geistige Mobilmachung: Die deutschen Intellektuellen und der Erste Weltkrieg* (Berlin, 2000).

whose historical moment had arrived, and the tired, decadent values embodied in Anglo-French civilization. The richest and most perverse exploration of this theme came from the pen of Germany's greatest novelist, Thomas Mann, whose *Reflections of an Unpolitical Man* dwelt on the ethical, political, and aesthetic preferences (like a predisposition for musical creativity) that putatively distinguished German culture from the civilization of the west. In all its erudition, Mann's treatise reformulated the popular stereotypes of this war. Even its title was perverse, for in nearly all its forms, the dichotomy between culture and civilization was supremely political, a thin veil in defense of Germany's semi-authoritarian constitution against the claims of all democrats, whether abroad or at home.

These arguments appealed above all to the Protestant educated upper-middle class, the so-called *Bildungsbürgertum*, whose relationship to German *Kultur* was thought to be special. The distinguishing mark of this group was the experience of university education, which counted as the badge of being "cultured" (*gebildet*). Because academic credentials were also required for prestigious careers in the professions, education, and the upper public service, the *Bildungsbürgertum* supplied most of the country's elites. The group comprised the Protestant clergy and teachers in the humanistic secondary schools (*Gymnasien*), who numbered among the most ferocious patriots in Germany. Portraying the conflict in the language and media of *Kultur* resonated with particular force in these cultured circles, in which patriotism included patronizing local theaters and concert halls, where the dramas of Schiller and Hebbel testified, like the music of Mozart, Beethoven, and Wagner, to the righteousness of the German cause.

The forms of high culture percolated as well into the more popular media. The initial celebration of the war found expression in an explosion of poetry. During the first six months, several million war poems appeared in newspapers or popular anthologies. Most of the authors were amateurs, who lacked both talent and training, so their feat was remarkable principally for its enthusiasm and abundance. Although he was a poet of some distinction, Richard Dehmel fed this flood of patriotic verse which carried German soldiers (Dehmel among them) into battle. The wooden opening lines of his poem, "*Der Feldsoldat*" ("The Frontline Soldier"), typified the genre:

> Da alles ruht in Gottes Hand;
> wir bluten gern fürs Vaterland
>
> As all is safely in God's hand;
> we're glad to bleed for the Fatherland

The war invaded music halls, popular novels, and the fictional offerings in the *feuilletons*. The cinema, which had already become the most frequented medium of popular culture in Germany, also accommodated the war. A spate of propaganda films bestrewed the first year of the war – to quote Siegfried Kracauer – with "rubbish filled to the brim with war brides, waving flags, officers, privates, elevated sentiments and barracks humor."[6] As this genre waned along with the initial enthusiasm for war, feature films reverted to providing popular entertainment with titles like "Detective Joe Deebs," "The Dowry Hunter," and "Nanunta, the Rose of the Wild West." However, newsreels from the frontlines were ritual preludes to these diversions from the pressures of wartime. Film figured centrally in the propaganda of this war, although the Germans were slower than their enemies to realize the power of the new medium. Only in 1917, after Ludendorff had provided the stimulus, did the government impose central controls on the distribution and production of moving pictures. The most significant result of this official interest in the cinematic representation of the war was the founding, under the army's auspices, of the Universal Film Company (UFA), a private company that henceforth produced feature films, as well as newsreels, for consumption in Germany and abroad.[7]

The regimentation of the cinema late in the war brought a culmination to the campaign to control cultural expression. The principal powers of censorship in cultural affairs resided throughout the war in the hands of the Deputy Commanding Generals; and these powers encompassed not only movie houses, but other theaters, concert and music halls, libraries, bookstores, and art galleries. Although a succession of central offices attempted to impose uniform guidelines, different standards prevailed in the military districts, so some diversity of artistic expression survived. Films made outside Germany after the outbreak of the war were everywhere banned (a boon for the German film industry). Works by "enemy" authors met the same fate in most parts of Germany, unless the author in question had, like Shakespeare or Tolstoy, died before 1914 and securely entered the pantheon of high culture. Even works by German authors that were set in England or France were vulnerable.[8] Traditionalists used the opportunity to step up an attack, which had begun before the war,

---

[6] Siegfried Kracauer, *From Caligari to Hitler: A Psychological History of the German Film* (Princeton, 1947), 23.

[7] Klaus Kreimeier, *The Ufa Story: A History of Germany's Greatest Film Company, 1918–1945* (New York, 1996).

[8] Gary Stark, "All Quiet on the Home Front: Popular Entertainments, Censorship and Civilian Morale in Germany, 1914–1918," in Coetzee and Coetzee, *Authority*, 74.

against the art of French impressionists and post-impressionists that hung in German museums.

The censors, however, were as a rule less concerned about "elevated" works of art, which the educated classes tended to patronize, than they were about what the masses consumed. The fact that adventure on the battlefield (and above the battlefield) became a staple feature of pulp fiction and the movies offered the authorities an opportunity to renew an assault on what they had long called "smut" (*Schundliteratur* or *Schundfilm*). As it had before the war, the campaign reflected powerful social anxieties. It was calculated to prevent the cultural subversion of Germany's youth – in the first instance working-class youth. The military censors thus imposed stringent controls on the sale of cheap, sensationalist literature, much of which was easily available through colportage; movies – and the posters that advertised them – were objects of a similar battery of regulations.

Because culture, both high and low, was so allied to the mobilization of morale during the war, its political implications were transparent. Perhaps for this reason, the creative output of Germany's established cultural leaders was meager. Max Liebermann's most productive period lay behind him. The great dramatic and literary representations of the war (including Thomas Mann's *Magic Mountain*) awaited the aftermath of the conflict.[9] German composers produced few remarkable pieces, with the exception perhaps of the "Variations for Orchestra" by Max Reger (who died in 1916), Richard Strauss' *Frau ohne Schatten*, and Heinz Pfitzner's opera, *Palestrina*, which appealed in the Wagnerian tradition to nationalist sentiment.

Another, more fundamental difficulty was that the upheaval of war seemed to defy representation in the artistic idioms that these established figures had mastered. The *avant garde* was not handicapped in this way. Several years before the war, the movement known loosely as German expressionism had gathered young writers and artists in feverish revolt against prevailing styles, conventions, and modes of artistic expression. From centers in Berlin, Munich, Dresden, Leipzig, Cologne, and Hanover, they hurled challenges in verse and oil at established institutions. Whether they were poets, like August Stramm and Gottfried Benn, or painters, like Franz Marc and Max Beckmann, their works exuded a fascination with the primitive, violent, emotional, and irrational, which they portrayed in tension-filled language, drastic metaphors, jarring colors, and abstract imagery. This was the language of apocalypse

---

[9] See Scott D. Denham, *Visions of War: Ideologies and Images of War in German Literature before and after the Great War* (Berne, 1992); Martin Patrick Anthony Travers, *German Novels on the First World War and the Ideological Implications, 1918–1933* (Stuttgart, 1982).

and regeneration. In fact, a number of expressionist works, such as Georg Heym's chilling poem "War" (1911) or Ludwig Meidner's canvas "Burning City" (1913) prefigured the First World War better than did the Schlieffen Plan.

The outbreak of war in 1914 boded fulfillment.[10] Apocalyptic expectations adapted easily to the patriotic exhilaration of the first hours. Many of these artists and writers joined the colors – among them Stramm, Benn, Beckmann, Meidner, Otto Dix, Georg Trakl, August Macke, and Erich Heckel. The militant accents in their work soon modulated in the terrible tedium of war, but the creative language of expressionism proved well matched to the disorientation and periodic tumult of the frontline experience. Stramm set the horror and excitement of combat effectively to verse. The paintings of Beckmann and Dix, which were devoted to the same theme, are among the most enduring cultural documents of the war. "Almost breathtaking," writes Wolfgang Mommsen of "the intensity with which [these painters] attempted to represent the extraordinary, the unimaginable artistically."[11]

The war nonetheless confounded their expectations. Macke was killed at the Marne, Marc at Verdun. Others, like Georg Grosz, found the ordeal of the front insufferable and broke down emotionally. At home, disillusionment over the dreary stalemate began by 1916 to register in the German *avant garde*. Given the censor's vigilance, open opposition was difficult, but veiled criticism of the war surfaced in the pages of several cultural journals, of which Paul Cassirer's *Bildermann* was the most important. Anti-war readings, poetry, songs, and drama also found a forum in private homes and cabarets, which remained beyond the reach of the censor. This private milieu then provided the network through which more radical opposition spread into Germany during the last two years of the conflict. Born in Zurich, the Mecca of European resistance to the war, Dada, whose very name celebrated nonsense, embodied revolt without the claims of regeneration. Dadaist art was dedicated instead to portraying the utter absurdity of the war, as well as the senselessness of all the institutions and beliefs that had made the conflict possible. Dada's exuberant nihilism struck root in the German cabaret scene, particularly in Cologne and Berlin. But the censor kept German Dadism behind the doors of places like the "Club Dada" in Berlin, until it exploded at the war's end in the satirical savagery of Grosz and John Heartfield.

---

[10] Hermann Korte, *Der Krieg in der Lyrik des Expressionismus: Studien zur Evolution eines literarischen Themas* (Bonn, 1981); René Eichenlaub, "L'expressionisme allemand et la première guerre mondiale: À propos de l'attitude de quelques-uns de ses représentants," *Revue d'histoire moderne et contemporaine* 30 (1983), 298–321.

[11] Mommsen, *Bürgerstolz*, 862.

Resistance to the war among these German writers, artists, and intellectuals was an elite phenomenon from the first. The *avant garde* milieu never comprised more than a few hundred figures, and even they were by no means united in opposition to the war. Other sectors of the cultural elite, including most of the university professors, supported the German war effort to the end. Those cultural leaders who opposed the war did so on their own terms, which were largely unintelligible to the great majority of Germans. These painters and poets were thus but barometers of growing disaffection. The development of this disaffection into a significant political force in Germany was more commonly couched in the less abstract language of the street. Here it registered above all the deterioration of material conditions.

Cold and hungry

The omens in 1916 were not good. The great battles of the year redefined the scale and cost of combat. The reorganization of the German homefront turned merciless. Then outside factors intervened to compound the misery. The heavy rains came to central Europe in the late summer. They persisted until the early onset of frost in the fall. The ensuing winter was the coldest in memory, and the weather remained unseasonably cold until May 1917. Given existing shortages, the wet and cold joined forces at the worst time imaginable; and the attendant problems invaded the remotest corners of life in Germany.

One problem was to stay warm. Home heating, like industrial production, was dependent on coal, for most Germans heated their homes with coal-burning stoves. Even accounting for shipments from Belgium, coal production in Germany was 10 percent less in 1917 than it had been before the war. The figures reflected major shortages, which began to plague industrial production even as the Hindenburg Program reorganized it. In early 1917, as ice on the Rhine and other rivers complicated further the problem of distribution, the shortages of coal spread to the kitchen and living room, where claims to adequate rations were less compelling than in the war-related factories. The difficulties extended, however, well beyond the inconvenience of wearing gloves, overcoats, or blankets indoors. Another problem was to find warm clothing. Owing to the blockade, the demands of the army, and the mounting exhaustion of German agriculture, supplies of cotton, wool, and the other raw materials of textiles also dwindled. "Stretching" natural fabrics with substitutes, like paper, provided but limited relief (and, when the fabric was wet, more literal relevance to the word "stretch"). Meanwhile, the shortage of leather reduced many of the urban poor to wearing shoes with wooden soles, whose clapping on sidewalks became a common sound of war.

Still another problem was to stay clean. Because animal fats were also in short supply, so was soap. So was hot water for bathing, because it, too, was normally heated with coal. The public baths, the principal bathing sites for the poor, were among the first casualties to the mounting coal shortages. They shared this distinction with several other public services, like schools. Excepting only the few areas in Germany (such as the upper Rhine region) that were served by hydroelectric power, most municipalities acquired electricity from steam-powered turbines, which also required coal. The shortages compelled municipal governments to cut back or eliminate tram service, as well as to dim or turn off electric lighting in the streets. Beyond its immediate impact on military production, the coal shortage thus struck at features of daily life that had been taken for granted in a modern society, as it conditioned the physical experience of war on the homefront. The effects of the war could now be seen, felt, heard, and smelled.

They could also be tasted. The dearest casualty of the weather in 1916 was a prop of the German food supply. The potato was a wonderful, serviceable vegetable. It was cheap, easy to grow, flexible, and an efficient carrier of caloric energy. The war only emphasized its importance as a food crop. The potato occupied a central place in the kitchen – particularly in the lower-class kitchen – as a ready, palatable substitute for a growing variety of foodstuffs in short supply. A survey in 1915 found that municipal workers in Berlin and their families were consuming well over a pound of potatoes a head per day.[12] Ground into flour, the potato was also a vital supplement to cereal grains in the making of *K-Brot*, the critical component of the German diet that was variously known as "war bread" ("*Kriegsbrot*") or "potato bread" ("*Kartoffelbrot*"). But the potato was also a temperamental vegetable. It insisted on moderate climactic conditions, was easily bruised and difficult to store in bad weather. It reacted to the damp and cold autumn in 1916 succumbing to phytophtora, a fungus, which destroyed almost half of the German winter potato crop by the end of the year.

The impact of this blight was calamitous. The average per capita consumption of potatoes plummeted in 1917 by more than one-third from its level the previous year.[13] Particularly in the first half of 1917, before the harvesting of a new summer crop, the potato's absence brought a

---

[12] *Volkswacht* (Freiburg im Breisgau), 9 August 1915.
[13] Rudolf Meerwarth, *et al.*, *Die Einwirkung des Krieges auf Bevölkerungsbewegung, Einkommen und Lebenshaltung in Deutschland* (Stuttgart, Leipzig, Berlin, 1932), 448–49.

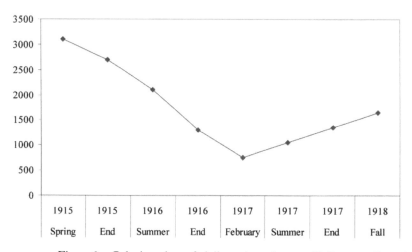

Figure 9   Caloric value of daily rations (*source:* F. Bumm, *Deutschlands Gesundheitsverhältnisse unter dem Einfluss des Weltkrieges* (2 vols., Stuttgart, Berlin, and Leipzig, 1928), 72)

food crisis in dimensions unknown in Germany for almost a century. The potato was not only basic to the human diet, it was also a central element in the ecology of German agriculture. It was a staple fodder crop, so farm animals suffered in the crisis, too. Their afflictions translated into the fertilizer supply, thence into diminished crop yields and shortages of essential foodstuffs like milk, eggs, fats, and sugar. Although harvests improved in 1917 and 1918, insufficient supplies in nearly all categories of food tormented the last two years of the war. Individual cows produced on average one-third less milk and fat in 1917 than they had the year before the war (when there were three times as many of them). Harvests of all grains in 1917 were down 30 percent from prewar levels.[14] Undernourishment reached alarming proportions, particularly in urban areas, among those who could neither produce food for themselves nor afford access to the black market. Rationing helped prevent the worst, but its fluctuations registered the problem (see figure 9). While they revealed that rations quickly fell below 2,800 calories a day – the amount thought to be sufficient for an adult – these figures understated the problem. The ration merely prescribed maximum quantities that could be purchased; it guaranteed the availability of nothing. For long periods, especially during the bleak winter months of 1916–17, difficulties of supply and transport kept available foodstuffs well below even their rationed levels.

[14] Friedrich Aereboe, *Der Einfluss des Krieges auf die landwirtschaftliche Produktion in Deutschland* (Stuttgart, Berlin, and Leipzig, 1927), 86–91.

Hunger became the overwhelming fact of life on the homefront, and it retained this status despite a number of attempts to temper it. Attention turned initially to another root vegetable, which rivaled the potato in versatility and nutritiousness but was more resistant to the weather. For humans and animals alike, this ersatz potato was the turnip. It was baked, fried, boiled, and put into soups. It was dried and ground into flour for use in war bread. It was used to make coffee, marmalade, a variety of other pastes, and in countless other capacities. An exhibition in the town hall in Charlottenburg featured recipes to disguise it in ninety different ways. So omnipresent was the vegetable in the German kitchen that the term "turnip winter" was sufficient to evoke the misery of early 1917: most Germans found the taste of this hardy warrior to be execrable.

The long, hard winter of 1917 lent new urgency to several institutions that municipal authorities had established, with the assistance of private charitable organizations, in order to relieve the hunger and hardship of the poor. Neighborhood centers made used clothing, blankets, and shoes (whether wooden or leather) available at reduced prices. The public soup kitchens, which drew on communal stocks of foodstuffs, were the most important of these institutions. Some 3,000 of them were in operation by the end of the war. Soup kitchens supplied 216,000 midday meals in Breslau in January 1917; in Hamburg they provided over 6,000,000 in April of the same year.[15] The activity of these agencies testified to the failure of the rationing system to provide equitable access to scarce food supplies. In the desperate circumstances of the turnip winter, however, considerations of equity yielded to more basic principles. Simply preserving the physical stamina of the workforce was more essential to the war effort, so rations were henceforth scaled in favor of those who performed heavy labor. Despite these measures, the physical condition of the men and women who produced the weapons of war remained a grave concern. "One has only to look closely at the workers," wrote one informed observer late in 1917, "to see that they are suffering to a great degree from undernourishment and that despite their purportedly high wages, misery stares from their eyes."[16]

The food scarcity weighed as well on the relationship between urban and rural Germany. The shortages seemed, on the one hand, to erase the practical distinction between country and town – between areas in which agriculture was the principal occupation and those areas where it was

[15] Skalweit, *Die deutsche Kriegsernährungswirtschaft* (Stuttgart, Berlin, and Leipzig, 1927), 43, 49.
[16] Cited in Lothar Burchardt, "Die Auswirkungen der Kriegswirtschaft auf die Zivilbevölkerung im Ersten und im Zweiten Weltkrieg," *Militärgeschichtliche Mitteilungen*, No. 1 (1974), 69.

not. This basic division of labor, which had marked the urbanization of Germany in the nineteenth century, retreated into the wholesale embrace of small-scale agriculture in cities and towns throughout the country. Backyards, municipal parks, and land on the outskirts of town reverted to the farming of fruits and vegetables, as well as the raising of small animals – goats, rabbits, chickens, even pigs – for meat and dairy products. Paradoxically, however, the war also broadened the gulf between town and country. This small-scale agriculture could never provide more than a supplement; and urban consumers remained profoundly dependent on rural producers for their food supplies. The shortages and the inflation of food prices, however, fueled antagonisms between town and country, as did the perception, which was almost universal among city-dwellers, that farmers were not only eating well, but were also exploiting urban misery to their own profit.

This perception was not entirely accurate. Farmers did have more secure access to food, but they faced a multitude of their own problems. The war drained farms of manpower and horses, leaving the arduous business of farming in the hands of women, children, and older men, as well as prisoners of war, close to 1,000,000 of whom were working German fields in 1918.[17] The bureaucratic controls that descended on the food supply affected farmers massively. By the middle of the war, regulations had reached into every phase of agricultural production; they dictated the supply and price of fertilizer and seed, the mix of food and fodder crops to be grown, the varieties and quantities of food crops and livestock to be raised and delivered, and the prices at which these commodities were to be sold. The farmers' loudest complaint, particularly after 1915, was that the controlled prices did not cover production costs; and it was too common to have lacked a basis in fact. Farmers were also notoriously well practiced in evading controls, but in the wake of the food crisis in 1917 they faced more ruthless compulsion in the form of confiscations of their crops and livestock. Smaller farmers in the south and west were particularly vulnerable to all these constraints, for their profit margins were smaller, their crop options fewer, their political influence less, and their access to prisoners of war for use as farm labor more restricted. These disadvantages reflected fundamental, long-standing social inequalities in the German countryside; and they had a regional accent, which surfaced in complaints about "the Junkers," who were said to "have government and power in their hands."[18] These tensions paled, however, in a community

[17] Fritz Klein, et al., Deutschland im Ersten Weltkrieg (3 vols., Berlin, 1968–69), vol. III, 303.
[18] Martin Schumacher, Land und Politik: Eine Untersuchung über politische Parteien und agrarische Interessen 1914–1923 (Düsseldorf, 1978), 70.

of rural experience, which was animated in the furious resentments that all farmers harbored not only against urban consumers and their importunate complaints, but – above all – against the state that had imposed a suffocating system of controls.[19]

A wartime community of rural interests could appeal to a long and powerful tradition in German public life. Its urban counterpart was also powerful, but it was rooted less in ideological tradition than in common experiences of wartime scarcity.[20] The resentments of urban consumers were directed in the first instance against farmers and "middlemen," the wholesalers and merchants whose intervention saddled the prices that consumers paid to producers. The establishment of a nationwide network of local consumer associations provided an organizational forum that bridged several constituencies, as it brought together Protestants and Catholics, working-class organizations, and women's groups of several descriptions. The forging of a common sense of consumer identity took place less, however, within this formal framework than it did – literally – in the streets, in the long lines that formed in front of shops and market booths that sold food and other precious supplies. The remarkable feature of this ritual, which was known everywhere in Germany as the "*Polonaise*," was the prominence of women in it. The image of the German consumer was female; and it inspired respect and fear among public officials.[21] In the community of experience that it symbolized, women were united across confessional and social divisions, at least to the extent that those who "danced the *Polonaise*" were not exclusively from the working class.

Even as the food shortages set urban consumers against rural producers, they resulted in a final paradox. They bred another, broader community of experience, which united both town and country in opposition to the state. This community corroded like no other the patriotic symbolism on which the German war effort was based. The war turned private concerns about food and diet into public problems. By the end of 1916, when the potato entered the list of rationed commodities, the free market for foodstuffs was long gone (at least in its legal form); in its place stood sprawling public bureaucracies. While farmers contended with requirements imposed by state officials, urban dwellers were dependent upon public agencies for virtually everything they consumed. Posted in public, in newspapers, or on kiosks, official bulletins announced in

---

[19] Robert G. Moeller, "Dimensions of Social Conflict in the Great War: The View from the German Countryside," *Central European History* 14 (1981), 142–68.

[20] See Christoph Nonn, *Verbraucherprotest and Parteisystem im wilhelminischen Deutschland* (Düsseldorf, 1996), 318–38.

[21] Belinda Davis, *Home Fires Burning: Food, Politics, and Everyday Life in World War I Berlin* (Chapel Hill, NC, 2000).

the morning what would (or might) appear on the kitchen table in the evening. Whether in the guise of the farm inspector, the policeman in the market square, or the petty official in the rations office, the state intruded into the daily life of every German, where its presence turned food shortages into a political matter.

The state was the public arbiter of hunger. It was also the symbol of the problem. "The population has lost all confidence in promises from the authorities," moaned the Deputy Commanding General in Nuremberg in September 1917, "particularly in view of earlier experiences with promises made in the administration of food."[22] Although much of the criticism of public officialdom was unfair, bureaucratic imperiousness and incompetence were convenient, omnipresent targets of popular frustration and anger. The situation was fraught with tension, for the public administration of hunger also forced unhappy people to congregate in circumstances calculated to make them more unhappy. The "*Polonaise*" was a dangerous phenomenon – the reason why public officials feared women consumers, who chafed increasingly in their role as objects of bureaucratic regimentation. During the last two years of the war, as the size and availability of rations became explosive issues, crowds of frustrated consumers in Nuremberg and elsewhere became the focus of spontaneous incidents of petty violence, some of which grew into food riots. These episodes spoke to deep problems.

Criminality and war

Protest sits awkwardly alongside criminality. The lines that separate criminal behavior from calculated political resistance are blurred, particularly in unstable times like wars. Studies of revolution have nonetheless identified criminality as an index by which the instability of a regime – its vulnerability to revolutionary assault – might be gauged. Criminality represents, in this reasoning, a refusal to abide by prevailing legal norms, hence an implicit statement of political opposition.

Exploring this proposition in wartime Germany encounters several difficulties. The most immediate is to determine the extent of criminality. Every society lives with a discrepancy between crimes committed and crimes prosecuted to conviction; but the statistics of criminality rely on the second category. This discrepancy yawned in the wholesale intrusion of the war into the German criminal-justice system – a network of institutions that radiated out from state capitals to encompass police,

---

[22] Cited in Klaus-Dieter Schwarz, *Weltkrieg und Revolution in Nürnberg: Ein Beitrag zur Geschichte der deutschen Arbeiterbewegung* (Stuttgart, 1971), 153.

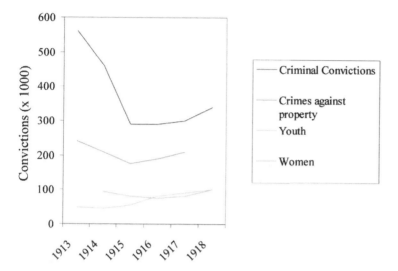

Figure 10   Wartime criminality (*source:* Moritz Liepmann, *Krieg und Kriminalität in Deutschland* [Stuttgart, Berlin, and Leipzig, 1928], 15, 56, 98, 134)

prosecutors' offices, courts, and prisons. In most places, police forces comprised young men in their twenties and thirties, many of whom were still in the military reserves. They were called up immediately, to join younger prosecutors and judges, as well as private attorneys and law students, who had volunteered or held reserve commissions. As a consequence, countless – and uncountable – crimes, which in ordinary circumstances would have been tried, remained unpunished, unprosecuted, or undetected. A second difficulty has to do with the nature of the "criminal class" in Germany. Prewar statistics from Germany (and other countries) made clear that most crimes were committed by young adult males, who also belonged to the group most likely to be removed into the armed services, where criminal behavior, if it occurred, became the concern of the military authorities. The logical consequences of this situation were two. It resulted in a decline in the number of crimes committed, as well as in the number prosecuted; and it altered the profile of the criminals. A much greater proportion of crimes was committed by "newcomers," those who stayed at home and had no prior convictions.

The statistics confirmed these generalizations (see figure 10). The number of crimes prosecuted fell significantly during the war. The precipitous decline at the onset reflected the atmosphere of popular elation, in which many minor infractions went unprosecuted. The rise in several categories of crime after 1915, however, suggested a correlation between criminality and protest, insofar as many of the criminal acts could be traced to the privations of the war.

The rise of criminality among male youths, whom the war had deprived of parental supervision, was one case in point. Another was the growth after 1916 of the crime rate among women. Women made up a much larger portion of those convicted than they had before the war. Most of their convictions fell into a single category of dereliction, crimes against property. This category in fact comprised about three-quarters of all convictions during the last years of the war. War drove women and men (and young people) to steal; and they stole the things they needed to survive, like food, clothing, shoes, and wood.

Was this sort of criminality political? Did it represent protest against the war or opposition to the "war-making" system? These questions beg a circumspect answer. The war led to a revolution in both the German economy and legal system, insofar as the market mechanism retreated before a command economy – a system of rations, production quotas, and price controls whose ultimate sanction was the law. Economic decisions – how much to produce or sell, and at what price – were determined in the first instance by regulations framed in administrative agencies and enforced by the police and courts. There were many, many new laws to break. Producers and merchants faced legal action for violating price ceilings, withholding goods from the controlled market, and participating in the black market. Punishments ranged from jail to fines or temporary suspensions of commercial licenses. Most of these cases, however, were handled in administrative action rather than the courts (unless they were appealed); so they did not register in the criminal statistics. They burgeoned nonetheless, for they were basic features of a new economic regime in which the public realm expanded, in the form of legal restraint and compulsion, into manifold phases of private life. The system itself nurtured criminality, if only because so many new laws invited violation.

And violated they were, ritually. "Everything is being stolen nowadays – literally everything," came the lament from a South German editor early in 1918. "Nothing – absolutely nothing – is secure. The 'big-fish' defraud the state of hundreds of thousands . . . the littler thieves naturally have to make do with less."[23] The rations system seemed almost calculated to breed a culture of crime. Its failure to provide for basic wants posed not only a temptation, but also an injunction to acquire goods illegally, whether by stealing, fraud, or otherwise circumventing the myriad of laws

---

[23] *Volkswacht* (Freiburg im Breisgau), 1 March 1918.

on which the controls rested. Farmers were merely the most practiced in evasion, but they were in good company. Merchants slipped extra supplies to their families, friends, and long-standing customers. Restaurateurs did the same. Consumers hoarded to the extent they could. The black market rivaled the ration system as a source of food and other scarce goods. Officials had little choice but to connive in the workings of this illegal system, without which scarcities would have been even more debilitating. In northern Bavaria and elsewhere, extra trains were scheduled to accommodate the (illegal) *Hamsterfahrt*. Officials in Munich estimated in March 1916 that the evening train from Dachau arrived every day laden with 20,000 illegal eggs.[24] During the last years of the war many major war contractors, like the Rhine Metal Works in Düsseldorf, trafficked routinely in the black market to supplement the rations of their workers. In Düsseldorf and elsewhere, as one official conceded of this practice, "the authorities closed their eyes to it."[25] That one broke the law was a fact of life. To this extent, criminality enjoyed a cultural sanction. And its ramifications were political. Criminal behavior eroded the authority of the state, which embodied laws that were so commonly defied.

Another category of criminal behavior also had political implications. "Crimes against public order" comprised various collective breaches of the public peace and defiance of the police, from unruliness to riots and acts of revolution. These cases were much less numerous than other types of crime, but their pattern was familiar (see figure 11). Before the war, this category had featured violent incidents that accompanied strikes and other forms of labor protest. During the war, it covered several additional kinds of behavior. In 1917, nearly half of the convictions pertained to acts of vandalism by youth gangs. Most of the rest, however, reflected the growing disorder attendant on the *Polonaise* – the rock in the baker's window, the horse dung hurled at the shopkeeper, or the produce cart overturned in the market square. The drop in the curve in 1918 was deceptive, for these incidents at the market also became so common that many were not pursued. Another index of the problem was the conviction in 1917 of 1,256 women who had threatened violence against policemen or other public officials.

The numbers provided a glimpse into the mechanism that turned private concerns into the trigger of public protest. These concerns were immediate, concrete, and material; above all, they had to do with the supply and price of food. The concerns were also universal. They led

---

[24] Karl-Ludwig Ay, *Die Entstehung einer Revolution: Die Volksstimmung in Bayern während des Ersten Weltkrieges* (Berlin, 1968), 167.
[25] Tobin, "War and the Working Class," 287.

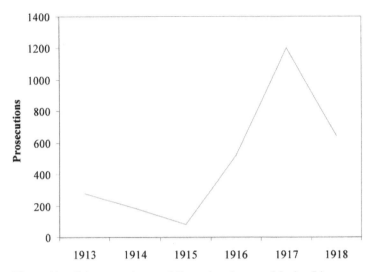

Figure 11   Crimes against public order (*source:* Moritz Liepmann, *Krieg und Kriminalität in Deutschland* [Stuttgart, Berlin, and Leipzig, 1930], 22)

large numbers of people to act together in violation of the law. They thus raised issues of public order and the authority of the state, which was massively implicated in the supply and price of food.[26] In these circumstances, the continuation of war became a public issue.

Early opposition

It was hard to oppose this war. The obstacles were as vast as the investment of moral and material resources into the slaughter. Pervasive institutional controls discouraged dissent, which was plagued, in addition, by its own conceptual ambiguities. Opposition to the war meant several different things. Basic to all forms was the belief that the war was wrong, but this proposition rested on competing representations of the conflict. One portrayed the war as a tragic mistake, for which responsibility was shared among all the great powers. This view prescribed a compromise settlement in order to bring the war to an immediate, diplomatic end. Another represented the conflict not as a tragic mistake, but instead as the result of basic internal disorders in the belligerent powers. In this view, revolutionary social and political change alone promised lasting peace.

---

[26] Klaus-Peter Müller, *Politik und Gesellschaft: Der Legitimitätsverlust des badischen Staates 1914–1918* (Stuttgart, 1988).

The popularity of the war initially overwhelmed every manner of dissent. By the time the elation began to subside, institutional safeguards were in place to make public opposition to the war exceedingly difficult. All forms of political expression fell within the broad police powers of the Deputy Commanding Generals, who could censor newspapers, read mail, confiscate pamphlets, prohibit public meetings, and imprison opponents of the war on a variety of grounds. While these controls stifled dissent for the first half of the war, they also established the framework in which protest developed during the second half of the conflict. Several truths about this process deserve emphasis. Large-scale opposition was not born in ideological maturity. It grew instead obliquely out of the privations of war. It took shape spontaneously around specific "bread-and-butter" grievances, such as prices, shortages of food and fuel, working conditions, and censorship. However (and this is a second truth), it did not spontaneously turn against either the war or the established structures of power. Before it could acquire the kind of cohesiveness, self-awareness, and political force that the word "ideology" connotes, dissent required the resources of established organizations.

Few were available. Churches of both major denominations were massively implicated in the conflict, so neither Protestant nor Catholic theology proffered a reading of the war to sustain an ideology of opposition. Marxism offered a much more plausible language of opposition, but most of the Socialist labor movement, where this ideology had been home, embraced the war effort in 1914. The central event in the gestation of effective protest was thus the fracture of the German labor movement.

The feeble history of the non-Socialist opposition bears witness to these truths. The so-called peace movement had never enjoyed much success in Germany. Its focus, the German Peace Society, comprised only a few hundred men and women in 1914, most of them middle-class progressives from the southwestern parts of Germany. They called their kind of opposition to war "pacifism"; it rested on a secular ideology of free-trade liberalism, the proposition that the nations of the world were united in a community of material and moral interest. The efforts of the pacifists to promote this principle had featured a series of international peace congresses, which preached the virtues of arms limitation and the arbitration of international disputes. Like everyone else, however, the German pacifists supported the war that broke out in 1914, for they had never questioned the right of national self-defense and they, too, were persuaded that Germany was the victim of aggression. Nevertheless, they were among the least enthusiastic about the conflict and among the first to conclude that it had been a tragic mistake, the benefits of which could not possibly justify the costs. The only remedy that they could prescribe was to urge the belligerent governments to negotiate a settlement, whose basis would be a return to the *status quo* of 1914 – a proposition that implied German renunciation of annexations in Belgium and elsewhere.

Their hapless efforts on behalf of this goal encountered the state's formidable power to muzzle dissent.[27] Pacifists were branded as defeatists, subversives, or traitors. Even in the liberal southwest, the Deputy Commanding Generals had little patience with them and invoked a full repertoire of devices to frustrate the campaign. Peace groups found their pamphlets and journals censored or confiscated, their mail watched, their meetings broken up, and their leaders shadowed or put in jail. As the membership in local peace societies dwindled further, they became little more than private debating circles. Official suppression aside, the German Peace Society rested on too narrow a social base to provide an effective foundation for opposition to the war; most of the pacifists' social peers supported the war for the duration. Attempts to establish several alternative organizations, such as the League for a New Fatherland (*Bund neues Vaterland*) and a section of the Women's League for Peace and Freedom, foundered on the same obstacles. Nor did the pacifists' efforts find support or resonance abroad, for the international networks that had linked the peace movement before the war collapsed in 1914.

The potential for organized resistance to the war appeared to be much greater among the Socialist working class. Publicly at least, on the eve of the war the Socialist labor movement represented the largest, best organized, and most determined opponent of war. The ideological roots of this opposition were Marxist; its premise was that capitalism caused wars and that the workers of the world had nothing to gain by fighting one another. The Socialist International had ritually affirmed this principle at its congresses, which continued into the last days of peace to threaten concerted action by the laboring masses to prevent the outbreak of a European war. The fact that the German Social Democratic Party thereupon endorsed the German entry into the war betrayed the power of national emotions in August 1914, as well as the erosion of anti-war sentiment, which had accompanied the growing integration of the labor movement into the social and political institutions of Imperial Germany.

Socialist affirmation of the war in 1914 reflected prevalent views among the movement's leadership, both in the Social Democratic Party and the

---

[27] Wilfried Eisenbeiss, *Die bürgerliche Friedensbewegung in Deutschland während des Ersten Weltkrieges: Organisation, Selbstverständnis und politische Praxis 1913/14–1919* (Frankfurt am Main, 1980); Ludwig Quidde, *Der deutsche Pazifismus während des Weltkrieges 1914–1918* (ed. Karl Holl, Boppard, 1979).

Socialist trade unions.[28] Most of these leaders remained supporters for the duration of the conflict, while some began to rival the nationalists in advocating German annexations as the reward for victory. To Friedrich Ebert, the general secretary of the SPD, Philipp Scheidemann, the party's parliamentary leader, and Carl Legien, the head of the Socialist unions, loyal participation in the war effort promised enormous benefits for their constituency – above all, an end to the animosity and discrimination that Socialist workers had suffered in Germany, from the shop floor to the halls of parliament. Because the government, particularly officials in the War Ministry, recognized the importance of organized labor in the management of the workforce in the war industries, labor leaders could bargain from strength to achieve a number of critical advances, including the right to organize, the establishment of arbitration boards in larger factories, and the unions' participation in administering the Auxiliary Service Law after its passage in 1916. These gains turned organized labor into an agent of mobilization, a vehicle to ensure the disciplined loyalty of the workforce. The price paid was the practical abandonment of Marxism as a conceptual guide to the war's meaning. The bulk of the labor movement henceforth became another of Germany's interest groups; and its agitation in favor of the peaceful reform of Germany's social and political institutions adjusted to the legitimacy of the war effort. As this transformation generated yet another institutional bulwark against opposition to the war, it channeled dissent against not only the state, but also the dominant institutions of the labor movement itself.

The Socialists' decision to support the war in 1914 had by no means been unanimous. Traditions of international working-class solidarity, revolutionary opposition to capitalism, and resistance to war lived on in some sectors of the German labor movement.[29] In August 1914, 14 of the 110 Social Democrats in the Reichstag had expressed opposition to the war in the party's caucus, but they bowed to party discipline and voted publicly in favor of the loans to finance the war. The next time this issue was put to a vote in the Reichstag, in December 1914, a lone Socialist, Karl

[28] Susanne Miller, *Burgfrieden und Klassenkampf: Die deutsche Sozialdemokratie im Ersten Weltkrieg* (Düsseldorf, 1974); Klaus Schönhoven (ed.), *Die Gewerkschaften in Weltkrieg und Revolution 1914–1919* (Cologne, 1985); Hans-Joachim Bieber, *Gewerkschaften in Krieg und Revolution* (2 vols., Hamburg, 1981); A. Joseph Berlau, *The German Social Democratic Party, 1914–1921* (New York, 1949); Carl E. Schorske, *German Social Democracy, 1905–1917: The Development of the Great Schism* (Cambridge, MA, 1955).

[29] David W. Morgan, *The Socialist Left and the German Revolution: A History of the German Independent Social Democratic Party, 1917–1922* (Ithaca and London, 1975); John W. Mishark, *The Road to Revolution: German Marxism and World War I, 1914–1919* (Detroit, 1967); A. J. Ryder, *The German Revolution of 1918: A Study of German Socialism in War and Revolt* (Cambridge, 1967), 1–139; Eric D. Weitz, *Creating German Communism, 1890–1990: From Popular Protests to Socialist State* (Princeton, 1997), 62–83.

Liebknecht, broke discipline and publicly opposed the war. At the end of 1915, twenty Socialists did. The importance of their action was more than symbolic, for these deputies enjoyed immunity to criticize the war in parliament; and not even the Deputy Commanding Generals could censor publication of the Reichstag's proceedings. The modest growth of parliamentary opposition accompanied the spread of anti-war sentiment in several centers of prewar labor radicalism, such as Bremen, Braunschweig, Berlin, Düsseldorf, and Leipzig, where it crystallized around the editorial staffs of Socialist newspapers – including (until it was disciplined by the party central in 1916) the national daily, *Vorwärts*.[30] Socialist opposition had to contend not only with the Deputy Commanding Generals, but also with the power of the party and trade unions, which moved against recalcitrant editors and local officials. But party discipline had its limits, and resistance survived in pockets of the labor movement, whose network of *Vereine* – including the neighborhood pubs where likeminded workers gathered – provided nascent channels of communication among dissident factory groups and party cells.

The anti-war sentiment that took root in these circles was more radical than middle-class pacifism, for it embraced a revolutionary vision of politics and society. Opposition to the war was couched here in opposition to the institutions of capitalism, whose overthrow promised lasting international peace among socialist nations. Yet Marxist opposition was itself broad enough to suggest two potentially antagonistic strategies of action. The first prescribed agitation to force an immediate end to the war, which would be the direct prelude to the thoroughgoing democratic reform of society and politics at home and the reestablishment of the Socialist International as the best guarantee of a durable peace. This approach, which was known as the "Centrist" position, corresponded to the views of most of the German Socialists who came to oppose the war, including the dissidents in the party's parliamentary group. To their left, a small group of agitators known as the Socialist "Radicals" entertained a more cataclysmic scenario. In their view, the war would continue as long as capitalist institutions survived; peace accordingly demanded a revolutionary assault on the war-making regimes – including the institutions of the labor movement that had connived with these regimes. The Socialist International, they insisted, was dead. In its stead, a new international organization of revolutionary workers was needed to complete the transition to socialism and peace. This radical position gestated primarily in Switzerland, where

---

[30] Friedhelm Boll, *Massenbewegungen in Niedersachsen 1906–1920: Eine sozialgeschichtliche Untersuchung zu den unterschiedlichen Entwicklungstypen Braunschweig und Hannover* (Bonn, 1981); Mary Nolan, *Social Democracy and Society: Working-Class Radicalism in Düsseldorf, 1890–1920* (Cambridge, 1981).

its proponents included V. I. Lenin and a small group of revolutionary exiles from other lands. In Germany its adherents initially numbered but a handful of intellectuals who stood on the fringe of the opposition – in the literal sense that its two most prominent figures, Karl Liebknecht and Rosa Luxemburg, spent much of the war in jail.[31] Nonetheless, the endless prolongation of the carnage lent cogency to their representation of the war, while they themselves attempted to provide coherence to this vision in a series of newsletters, called the "Spartacus Letters," which began in 1916 to circulate clandestinely among opposition cells in the labor movement.

During the war's first two years, varieties of opposition of every description remained scattered and powerless. Popular support for the war extended deep into the labor movement and ensured that agitation against the war found little resonance, while the Deputy Commanding Generals had no difficulty in suppressing the occasional manifestation of dissent. In this respect, the second half of the war was more dramatic. The accumulating burdens of war succeeded where agitation earlier had failed, in breeding the potential for mass unrest.

Industrial unrest: the labor movement splits

In 1916 on May Day, the traditional day of labor protest, thousands of demonstrators took to the streets in Berlin. Many of them carried placards that called for "Bread, Freedom, and Peace!" Before the police could break up the crowd, Karl Liebknecht mounted a podium and shouted, "Down with the War! Down with the government!" He was arrested. In June a military court convicted him of treason and sentenced him to four years in jail. In protest against the court's proceedings, 55,000 metalworkers from forty of Berlin's major factories went out on strike, as did sympathetic workers in Stuttgart, Bremen, Braunschweig, and Essen.

The events of May and June 1916 crowned Liebknecht as the martyr and political symbol of resistance to the war. They also represented a pivotal moment in the history of the opposition. They featured an industrial strike, which became the principal manifestation of protest during the second half of the war. This was also the most ominous form of protest, for unlike the food riot or random acts of violence, it could paralyze the war economy. In this light, the statistics of the war's last three years offered

---

[31] J. P. Nettl, *Rosa Luxemburg* (2 vols., Oxford, 1966); Annelies Laschitza and Günter Radczun, *Rosa Luxemburg: Ihr Wirken in der deutschen Arbeiterbewegung* (East Berlin, 1971); Helmut Trotnow, *Karl Liebknecht (1871–1919): A Political Biography* (Hamden, CT, 1984); Annalies Laschitza and Elke Keller, *Karl Liebknecht: Eine Biographie in Dokumenten* (East Berlin, 1982).

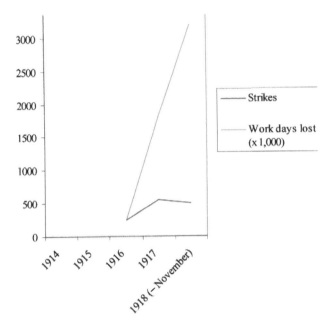

Figure 12   Industrial strikes, 1916–1918 (*source:* Gerald D. Feldman, *et al.*, "Die Massenbewegungen der Arbeiterschaft in Deutschland am Ende des Ersten Weltkrieges [1917–1920]," *Politische Vierteljahrschrift* 13 [1972], 93)

cause for alarm (see figure 12). The alarming feature of these statistics was not so much the growing frequency of strikes after 1916 as it was their size and duration, which were measured in the number of work days lost to the factories. The strikes of 1917–18 also extended a pattern laid down in the protests of 1916, insofar as they became more explicitly political. Like the workers who on May Day in 1916 had demanded "bread, freedom, and peace," strikers more routinely coupled demands for economic relief, such as higher rations, higher wages, and shorter hours, with calls for political reform and an end to the war. The very distinction between economic and political strikes now blurred, as hunger and material shortages drew the authority of the state and employers alike into question.

The open politicization of labor protest during the last years of the conflict accompanied a critical transformation in popular thinking about the war. The protesters began to question the legitimacy of the material hardships that they were being asked to bear; and they called for remedies beyond the immediate satisfaction of material wants. Their actions reflected their growing receptivity to a radical reading of the war, which traced misery to institutional injustice and the obstinacy, if not the evil designs, of Germany's leaders. The affinities between this representation of the conflict and the ideology of the Marxist opposition were transparent, as the politicization of war-weariness and hardship among the poor fed popular support for the strikes.

So did events to the east. In March 1917, the Russian capital city of Petrograd became the scene of a grand *Polonaise*. Massive bread riots, accompanied by the fraternization of soldiers and rioters, prompted the abdication of the tsar and the establishment of a provisional government of liberal and moderate socialist politicians. While the new leaders resolved to continue the war against Germany, they set plans in motion to produce a democratic constitution for their country. Insecurity lent urgency to their efforts, for the legitimacy of their new government was in dispute. In the capital, the provisional government faced a more radical organization called a soviet, a council that claimed to represent the city's workers and soldiers, in whose name it issued a public call for an immediate end to the war on the basis of "no annexations and no indemnities."

The Russian events had an electrifying impact in Germany. For one thing, they removed the Russian autocracy, the bogey that had persuaded the German Socialists to support the war in 1914. For another, the Russians furnished a model in practice of how economic issues, like bread shortages, could be exploited to bring democratic reform and – although this question remained open – an end to the war. In the event, a new wave of strikes bathed German industrial centers in specific political demands, which featured the democratization of politics in Germany and an immediate peace on the basis of no annexations. Despite efforts by the military authorities to block them with the arrest and conscription of agitators, the strikes culminated in April 1917, when the announcement of reduced bread rations drew out 300,000 strikers in Berlin, the most conspicuous of whom were metalworkers from the city's armaments factories. News of these developments brought similar actions among industrial workers in Leipzig, Braunschweig, Halle, and Magdeburg. The strikers' calls for bread, freedom, and peace now resonated to the Russian achievements, as did the formation of workers' councils in Germany to coordinate these strikes.

The appearance of these councils, which bore an uncomfortable resemblance to the soviets in Russia, advertised a remarkable feature of the strikes: they took place largely over the opposition of the union leadership.

Denied union support, the strikers devised alternative forms of organization; and their protest against the war turned as well against the established institutions of the labor movement, which were themselves implicated in the war. New institutions grew out of the organization of labor on the shop floor, as well as networks of formal and informal communication among workers at different plants – including, paradoxically, the committees that helped administer the Auxiliary Service Law.[32] A pivotal role in the movement fell to the so-called shop stewards, who, because workers elected them directly from their own ranks as factory representatives, enjoyed an authority independent of the union hierarchy. These representatives then became leading members of the strike councils, which in many cities survived the end of the strikes to become organizational rivals to the unions.

The growth of grassroots organizations of labor protest accompanied the split of the Social Democratic party. In March 1916 the majority of the Socialists in the Reichstag, who had lost patience with the indiscipline in their own ranks, voted to expel eighteen of their members who had voted against another round of war loans. The banished Socialists thereupon constituted themselves as the "Social Democratic Working Group" (*Sozialdemokratische Arbeitsgemeinschaft*), an independent caucus which remained formally within the old party. The expulsion of the dissidents nonetheless marked the beginning of the Socialist party's formal dissolution, as some local party organizations began themselves to fracture along the same ideological lines, and organizations in the more radical centers rallied to the support of the Working Group. Relations between the two factions deteriorated until April 1917 when, in the wake of the Russian upheaval, the dissidents formally founded their own party, called the Independent German Social Democratic Party (USPD).[33]

This momentous event signaled the death of working-class solidarity in Germany. The great ideal, which had energized the German labor movement almost since the moment of its birth, was a casualty of the war. Two Socialist parties, the Independents and the old party, now called the Majority Social Democratic Party (MSPD), henceforth competed for the loyalties of German workers. The parties were by now divided, however, less by the war than by the issue of how to bring it to an end. Fatigue had

---

[32] Friedhelm Boll, "Spontaneität der Basis und politische Funktion des Streiks 1914 bis 1918: Das Beispiel Braunschweig," *Archiv für Sozialgeschichte* 17 (1977), 337–66.

[33] Robert F. Wheeler, *USPD und Internationale: Sozialistsicher Internationalismus in der Zeit der Revolution* (Frankfurt am Main, 1975); Hartfrid Krause, *USPD: Zur Geschichte der Unabhängigen Sozialdemokratischen Partei Deutschlands* (Frankfurt am Main and Cologne, 1975).

spread in the ranks of the MSPD, too, most of whose leaders now favored a negotiated peace and democratic reform; they remained committed as well, however, to supporting the country's civilian and military leadership in achieving this end. The new party was not.

Atop the USPD stood a parliamentary group, which by the spring of 1917 had grown to twenty-four members. They were united foremost in their opposition to the war loans, although they also opposed the Auxiliary Service Law as an additional burden on the working class. The basis of the new party consisted of about 100 local organizations that had also broken with the mother party. These groups were concentrated in Germany's great industrial hubs, in Berlin, Saxony (particularly in Leipzig and Halle), and along the axis that extended down the Ruhr valley to the lower Rhine. The party was also strong in several other cities, such as Hamburg, Bremen, Stuttgart, and Braunschweig, which had been centers of labor militancy before the war. By 1918, the USPD numbered perhaps 100,000 adherents, many of whom were young, less-skilled male workers in the large factories. These workers had joined the labor force since the outbreak of war and were less practiced in union discipline and respect for the unions' authority.

The new party was troubled from the beginning. Opposition to the war continued to imply conflicting strategies. The "Centrist" position, which called for an immediate end to the war as the prelude to social and political reform, was still the dominant view, but the party's left wing, which was now known as the "Spartacus League" after the newsletters that had been its principal focal point, continued to advocate social and political revolution as the means to stop the war. In November 1917, after Ludendorff had packaged Lenin home to Russia from Switzerland, these German radicals found a new model in the Bolshevik revolution. As long as the war continued, however, the USPD provided accommodation for both positions and a focus for the mobilization of labor protest against the war.

The most dramatic and frightening sign of the party's importance was the massive anti-war strike that began late in January 1918.[34] This one was triggered by news of a general strike in Vienna, but it had gestated in the networks of the USPD in Germany. Its epicenter was once again the munitions and metal plants in the German capital, where some 400,000 workers struck at the end of the month. Within days the strike had spread to other industrial centers, from Kiel and Hamburg to Mannheim and Augsburg. Over 1,000,000 workers went out, demanding an end to the

[34] Stephen Bailey, "The Berlin Strike of January 1918," *Central European History* 13 (1980), 158–74.

war, democratic reform, and a catalogue of remedies for their material grievances. The leaders of the MSPD and the unions, whose authority was challenged no less than the state's, responded by joining the strike committees in hopes of regaining control of the movement. The army's swift intervention served the same purpose by other, more direct means: the soldiers arrested the strike's leaders and dispatched many of them to experience the war at the front. Although the demonstrations then dissipated after several tense days, the strike was the most defiant sign yet of the unrest that the war had generated. It represented, as one historian has noted, "an action with more revolutionary overtones than anything the modern German labor movement had known previously."[35] It revealed not only the effectiveness of the new institutions of labor protest, but also the degree to which the war and domestic reform had become linked as the issues that drove political debate throughout Germany.

War aims and constitutional change

The radicalization of the German labor movement was based on the ideological convergence of domestic and foreign-policy goals. During the last two years of the war, strikers called in the same breath for an immediate peace without annexations and for democratic reform at home. The juncture of domestic and foreign-policy questions was not the invention of the USPD, however; it had been implicit in all colorations of political thinking since the beginning of the war. Still, when the great industrial strikes drove it into the open, it became the issue on which the collapse of the *Burgfrieden* culminated.

Discussion of Germany's aims during the war was wedded to visions of what the country's political institutions would look like after the war.[36] Consensus reigned that Germans were to be rewarded after the war for their suffering. The left-wing advocates of a compromise peace – from the USPD to the middle-class Progressives – argued that the rewards were to take the form of democratization at home. Most of them agreed that this goal required abolishing the discriminatory suffrage system in Prussia and other German states, establishing responsible parliamentary government throughout Germany, and preserving the gains that organized labor had achieved during the war. An alternative vision surfaced with brutal clarity in November 1914, in the observations of Alfred Hugenberg, a member

---

[35] Morgan, *Socialist Left*, 90.
[36] Dieter Grosser, *Vom monarchischen Konstitutionalismus zur parlamentarischen Demokratie: Die Verfassungspolitik der deutschen Parteien im letzten Jahrzehnt des Kaiserreiches* (The Hague, 1970).

of the board of directors of the Krupp works and one of the most powerful industrial leaders in Germany. His subject was just these gains of
organized labor.

The consequences of the war will in themselves be unfavorable for the employers
in many ways. There can be no doubt that the capacity and willingness of the
workers returning from the front to produce will suffer considerably when they
are subordinated to factory discipline. One will probably have to count on a very
increased sense of power on the part of the workers and labor unions, which will
also find expression in increased demands on the employers and for legislation. It
would therefore be well advised, in order to avoid internal difficulties, to distract
the attention of the people and to give fantasies concerning the extension of
German territory room to play.[37]

Here Hugenberg invoked a hoary motif in German policy: the rewards
to the German people were to come not in domestic reform but instead
in massive German territorial acquisitions abroad. Annexations were to
compensate for the privations of the war, while hegemony on the European continent would fire German national pride and validate an authoritarian constitutional system that had emerged victorious from the war.
The historical verdict on democracy was to be its defeat at home and
abroad.

   Those who embraced this logic were not hard to identify. They populated the groups that had dominated politics and society in Imperial
Germany before the war. They included the country's business elites,
particularly the heavy industrialists who presided over the war economy,
the agrarian elites, the right-wing political parties, the patriotic societies,
the military leadership, and the public civilian bureaucracies which were
recruited from the *Bildungsbürgertum*. After 1916, however, the bastion
of this thinking was located in the OHL. Its most important proponent
was Ludendorff, who was well connected to these elite groups.[38] The
meaning of a "Ludendorff peace" was thus transparent. The strength
of the other side resided principally in the Reichstag, among the left-
wing parties – the USPD, MSPD, and Progressives – who represented
those sectors of German society that were enduring most of the war's
burdens.[39]

   For the first three years of the war, it was the lot of Bethmann Hollweg
to mediate between these two positions, which became more obdurate as
the war continued. His decision in the fall of 1916 to unwrap censorship

---

[37] Quoted in Feldman, *Army, Industry and Labor*, 136.
[38] Helmut Weber, *Ludendorff und die Monopole: Deutsche Kriegsziele* (East Berlin, 1966).
[39] Torsten Oppelland, *Reichstag und Aussenpolitik im Ersten Weltkrieg: Die deutschen Parteien und die Politik der USA 1914–1918* (Düsseldorf, 1995).

on discussions of war aims represented a gesture to the right; and it came at the insistence of the OHL. The manifestos that immediately emerged in public were difficult to square with the idea of a defensive war. As they enumerated in remarkable precision the annexations that would attend a German victory, they documented the consolidation of the right wing behind the position that Ludendorff now symbolized. They also encouraged the consolidation of forces on the left, which occupied the chancellor's attention, too, as it accelerated dramatically in early 1917. A month after the March revolution in Russia had brought parliamentary reform to that land, along with an offer of compromise peace in the east, the American declaration of war on Germany altered profoundly the ideological terrain on which the war was being fought. Germany, now Europe's most autocratic power, found itself in a war against the world's leading democracies.

Nowhere did the implications of these developments sit more uncomfortably than in the MSPD. Not only did events in Russia and America undercut the Socialists' argument that a German victory was necessary to defeat political reaction in Europe, but the radicalization of the labor movement at home also challenged the party for the loyalties of its own constituency. The party's leadership thus faced growing pressure from its membership to break ranks with the government and to call publicly for a compromise peace and constitutional reform. The growing turmoil on the left convinced the chancellor that some gesture towards reform was essential, and in this spirit he embraced the idea of a "new orientation" in German domestic politics. The dimensions of this new orientation were anything but clear, however; and the impediments to political change remained formidable. The most Bethmann could achieve was to persuade the Kaiser to issue a statement, the so-called "Easter Offer," which was published on the same day that the USPD was founded in April 1917. William's statement appeared to promise constitutional reform at the war's end, but it was couched in such ambiguity and evident distaste as to carry little credibility. Nor was Bethmann's own credibility above suspicion, for he simultaneously (although unbeknownst to the party leaders) endorsed the Supreme Command's demands for German annexations in France, Poland, and the Baltic lands.

When the turmoil migrated to still another camp, it brought a parliamentary crisis. Within the Catholic party, the continuation of the war had exacerbated a number of basic tensions, which reflected the social diversity of this party's constituency.[40] Vocal support for the war within the church hierarchy corresponded to the sentiments of the party's industrial

---

[40] Rudolf Morsey, *Die Deutsche Zentrumspartei 1917–1923* (Düsseldorf, 1966).

and agrarian wings. The left wing, by contrast, reflected the sentiments of the Catholic labor movement, much of which was anchored in the mining and textile centers of the northwest, where the war had inflicted enormous strains. The leader of the left wing was Matthias Erzberger, an impetuous but influential figure whose interventions had created several parliamentary sensations before the war.[41] Erzberger had been an early champion of annexations. He had nonetheless become alive to accumulating doubts about the war within his own camp when, in the spring of 1917, he learned from Austrian officials about the growing desperation of Germany's principal ally. When he then shared this news with his party colleagues in Berlin, Erzberger engineered another parliamentary sensation.

In issues of domestic politics the Catholic party had traditionally allied more easily with Conservatives to the right than with Progressives or Socialists to the left, where anti-clericalism ran deep. In the early summer of 1917, amid mounting skepticism about the success of the submarine offensive, Erzberger's revelations persuaded a majority of the Catholics in the parliament to turn left, to join with the Progressives and the MSPD in sponsoring a public resolution in favor of a compromise peace. These three parties owned a majority in the Reichstag; and on 19 July 1917, over the protests of the chancellor and the OHL, they passed the so-called "Peace Resolution." "The Reichstag strives for a peace of understanding and the permanent reconciliation of the peoples," it announced. "With such a peace, forced acquisitions of territory and political, economic, or financial oppression are inconsistent."[42] While the USPD voted against the resolution, on the grounds that it did not go far enough and demand an immediate end to the war, it went a great deal further than either Ludendorff or the civilian government wished. It was a spectacular act of parliamentary defiance. It signaled a major rift in the domestic consensus that had borne the war, and it threatened a constitutional crisis should the majority on the left refuse to vote additional war credits.

Ludendorff quickly fought back. His principal strength resided, as before, in his control of the army, his identification with Hindenburg, and – above all – in the promise of military victory, which he alone could deliver. He regarded the Reichstag's resolution with contempt and responded with a defiant act of his own. His target was the chancellor, whose caution and growing receptivity to domestic reform he disdained and whose political function he viewed, in all events, as little more than the

---

[41] Klaus Epstein, *Matthias Erzberger and the Dilemma of German Democracy* (Princeton, 1959); Wolfgang Ruge, *Matthias Erzberger: Eine politische Biographie* (East Berlin, 1976).
[42] Quoted in Arno J. Mayer, *Wilson vs. Lenin: Political Origins of the New Diplomacy* (Cleveland and New York, 1959), 133.

management of opinion in the Reichstag. The Peace Resolution was the sign of Bethmann Hollweg's terminal failure in this role, so even as the resolution made its way to the floor of the Reichstag, Ludendorff and Hindenburg threatened to resign if he were to remain in power. The chancellor now paid the price for his long history of vacillation. He had no friends left. With the support of the patriotic right, which had clamored for months for Bethmann's dismissal, Ludendorff signaled that the chancellor was an obstacle to a victorious peace; at the same time, the Reichstag's majority signaled that the same chancellor was an obstacle to a moderate peace. The Kaiser had no alternative but to replace Bethmann with a candidate more to Ludendorff's taste, a Prussian bureaucrat by the name of Georg Michaelis, who, like Ludendorff himself, cared little about his lack of support in the Reichstag. The new chancellor's response to the Peace Resolution was to explain to the assembled deputies that he would support "your" resolution "as I understand it," and that his understanding of it encompassed a peace that would "guarantee the security of Germany's borders for all time."[43]

In this spirit, the political counteroffensive broadened. Fearing the spread of the USPD's influence, the OHL undertook an intensified program of "patriotic instruction" among the troops. The homefront was likewise the object of a renewed campaign of public lectures, films, and other forms of patriotic enlightenment.[44] The purpose of the campaign both among the troops and at home was to reinvigorate the vocabulary of patriotism as the governing interpretive medium of the war. As part of the same effort, Ludendorff gave his blessing to the foundation in September 1917 of the "German Fatherland Party," an enormous new patriotic organization that was designed to mobilize popular sentiments in favor of a victorious peace – in other words, to intimidate the moderates in the Reichstag.[45] With the benefit of large subsidies from heavy industry, the open encouragement of the government and the right-wing parties, and with Alfred von Tirpitz at its helm, the Fatherland Party grew rapidly during the fall of 1917, primarily in the north and eastern parts of the land. By early 1918, it counted over 2,000 local chapters and close to 1,000,000 members; a significant portion of the local leaders were secondary-school teachers, Protestant pastors, and other local notables

---

[43] *Stenographische Berichte über die Verhandlungen des Reichstages* (19 July 1917), vol. 310, 3,570–72.

[44] Dirk Stegmann, "Die deutsche Inlandspropaganda 1917/18: Zum innenpolitischen Machtkampf zwischen OHL und ziviler Reichsleitung in der Endphase des Kaiserreiches," *Militärgeschichtliche Mitteilungen* No. 2 (1972), 75–116.

[45] Heinz Hagenlücke, *Deutsche Vaterlandspartei: Die nationale Rechte am Ende des Kaiserreiches* (Düsseldorf, 1997); Raffael Scheck, *Alfred von Tirpitz and German Right-Wing Politics, 1914–1930* (Atlantic Highlands, NJ, 1997).

who had been active in Germany's patriotic societies before the war and were fluent in the language that Ludendorff hoped to promote.

The Fatherland Party quickly provoked the establishment of a counterorganization, the "People's League for Freedom and Fatherland" (*Volksbund für Freiheit and Vaterland*), which embraced domestic reform and more moderate war aims.[46] With a membership that – on paper at least – rivaled the Fatherland Party's, this organization helped document the polarization of opinion that was the most salient feature of German politics as the war's last year began. Mass popular organizations and central political institutions now supported conflicting readings of the war and conflicting prescriptions for its termination. In the Reichstag, the proponents of a compromise peace, who were buoyed by the Papal peace note in the summer of 1917, gained in numbers and confidence. During the last two years of the war, the Reichstag's budget committee met regularly while the parliament was adjourned; and it took on the character of an executive agency for the broader body.[47] In the presence of federal ministers, it extended debate into critical matters of domestic and foreign policy. Then, in the aftermath of the Peace Resolution, the three parties that had provided the majority joined the National Liberals and established a joint committee to facilitate regular consultations among their leaders.[48] Their actions suggested the emergence of a common vision of domestic change. In October a parliamentary majority defied the government with another resolution; this one called for democratic reform of the Prussian suffrage. Its passage persuaded the OHL to sack Michaelis, who now seemed no better able than Bethmann to control the parliament. It was nonetheless a measure of the Reichstag's growing weight that Ludendorff decided to consult party leaders before he selected still another chancellor, Germany's third in four months. The choice fell this time on Georg von Hertling, a conservative Bavarian aristocrat, who, at 74, was the grand old man of the Catholic party – and a fitting symbol of the old order's exhaustion. Upon his appointment in early November, Hertling himself made significant gestures to the Reichstag majority's claims when he appeared to endorse constitutional reform and then drew several parliamentary leaders into his cabinet.

[46] Hagenlücke, *Deutsche Vaterlandspartei*, 362–71. On the divisiveness of nationalist slogans see Sven Oliver Müller, *Die Nation als Waffe und Vorstellung: Nationalismus in Deutschland und Grossbritannien im Ersten Weltkrieg* (Göttingen, 2002).

[47] Reinhard Schiffers, *Der Hauptausschuss des Deutschen Reichstags 1915–1918: Formen und Bereiche der Kooperation zwischen Parlament und Regierung* (Düsseldorf, 1979).

[48] Rudolf Morsey (ed.), *Der Interfraktionelle Ausschuss 1917/18* (Düsseldorf, 1959); Udo Bermbach, *Vorformen parlamentarischer Kabinettsbildung in Deutschland: Der Interfraktionelle Ausschuss und die Parlamentarisierung der Reichsregierung* (Cologne and Opladen, 1967).

Still, the issues were by no means decided as German politics settled uneasily into an impasse, best described perhaps as semi-parliamentarian. Throughout the early months of 1918, bitter debates on suffrage, ministerial responsibility, and other issues of constitutional reform occupied not only the Reichstag but also the state parliaments, particularly in Prussia, where the stakes were highest and the suffrage system, the keystone of the old order, was the object of growing popular protest.[49] The parliamentary debates revealed, however, that conservative forces, whose power the old suffrage system had entrenched in Prussia and elsewhere, were not prepared to abandon their privileges without a fight. It thus became clear that the resolution of the basic constitutional questions awaited the circumstances of the war's end. And Ludendorff still held trumps. Whatever their discomfort with his policies, none of the parties in the Reichstag – save the USPD – dared refuse continued funding for the war. Nor, in fact, could they refuse the blandishments of victory, once Ludendorff presented victory to them.

In the fall of 1917 the Russian armies disintegrated. The Bolshevik revolution in November then brought the end of the eastern war, in circumstances that demonstrated the full volatility of the political situation in Germany. Peace negotiations began in December – in the Polish fortress town of Brest-Litovsk – between the Central Powers and the new Bolshevik government; but the talks quickly bogged down, in large part because the Germans leadership was bent on a settlement draconian enough to appeal to the most voracious annexationist. The perception that peace might be frustrated in this fashion helped trigger the great German strikes in Berlin and elsewhere late in January.

The strikes only hardened Ludendorff's determination to extract a victor's peace in the east.[50] The impotence of the Bolshevik government eased his way, for it mandated a peace at practically any price; and so, after a brief resumption of German military action, a treaty was born in March 1918.[51] The settlement was not moderate. It consigned not only Poland and most of the Baltic lands, but also much of the Ukraine to German control in one form or another. Its proclamation mocked the idea of

---

[49] Reinhard Patemann, *Der Kampf um die preussische Wahlreform im Ersten Weltkrieg* (Düsseldorf, 1964); Hartwig Thieme, *Nationaler Liberalismus in der Krise: Die nationalliberale Fraktion des preussischen Abgeordnetenhauses 1914–1918* (Boppard, 1968).

[50] Bailey, "The Berlin Strike," 171; Winfried Baumgart, *Deutsche Ostpolitik 1918: Von Brest-Litovsk bis zum Ende des Ersten Weltkrieges* (Vienna and Munich, 1966); Peter Borowsky, *Deutsche Ukrainepolitik 1918 unter besonderer Berücksichtigung der Wirtschaftsfragen* (Lübeck and Hamburg, 1970); Oleh S. Fedyshyn, *Germany's Drive to the East and the Ukrainian Revolution, 1917–1918* (New Brunswick, NJ, 1971).

[51] John W. Wheeler-Bennett, *Brest-Litovsk: The Forgotten Peace, March 1918* (London, 1938).

a compromise, and it breathed new energy into patriotic sentiments in Germany, which echoed in scenes of popular celebration reminiscent of the summer of 1914. When the Treaty of Brest-Litovsk arrived in the Reichstag for ratification, it passed by an overwhelming majority, which included the Progressive and Catholic parties. Only the USPD voted against it. The MSPD, which was by now riddled to the point of paralysis by dissension in its ranks, could agree only to abstain.

The events of March 1918 brought temporary relief to the emerging domestic crisis. They also cast doubt on the integrity of the Reichstag's Peace Resolution and the good intentions of the parliamentary majority. Finally, they confirmed a truth that had governed German politics since the outbreak of the war. The future of Germany's domestic institutions hinged ultimately on the military outcome of the conflict. This truth blocked compromise on basic issues of domestic politics, as surely as it guaranteed that the war would continue in the west until one of the contending sides capitulated. The spectacular victory in the east seemed to vindicate Ludendorff's calculations on every score. The crisis would be resolved on the battlefield before it could culminate at home. Having won the war in the east, Ludendorff prepared to do the same in the west.

6   The war ends

Despite increasing misery on the homefront, growing unrest, the radicalization of the labor movement, and the polarization of opinion to the brink of constitutional crisis, the prospects for a German victory appeared brighter at the beginning of 1918 than they had at any time since the summer of 1914. To be sure, American entry into the war in April 1917 promised eventual relief to the Entente powers, but staggering losses among the armies of these powers in the spring and summer of 1917 threatened to end the conflict before an American army could arrive in Europe. Renewed French and British offensives in 1917 failed again to break the strategic stalemate on the western front; they also brought the French army to the verge of collapse. Events elsewhere meanwhile turned catastrophic for the Entente. To the south, the Italian army suffered a crippling defeat. In the east, the war ended amid the dissolution of the Russian armies. The domestic beneficiaries of the Russian military collapse were the Bolsheviks, who seized power in November 1917 and immediately called for an end to the war. The other beneficiaries were the Germans. The settlement that emerged at Brest-Litovsk in March 1918 left most of eastern Europe under German control. It thus promised to relieve agricultural shortages at home as it liberated German troops for service on other fronts.

The Germans won the eastern war. Victory here in 1917, and the prospect of victory to the south and west in 1918, elevated spirits on the homefront and dampened the domestic discord. Events appeared to ratify Ludendorff's leadership. They also ratified his vision of the war's conclusion and eliminated the final, frail possibility of a negotiated peace.

"Peace feelers"

Although their armies were locked in combat, the belligerent sides remained in almost constant diplomatic contact throughout the war.[1]

---

[1] David Stevenson, *The First World War and International Politics* (Oxford, 1988).

Willing intermediaries were to be found in the neutral lands, above all in Switzerland. They included businessmen who had dealings in both camps, representatives of Europe's minor royalty who had relatives in both camps, and members of the Papal diplomatic corps. Many of these contacts were the stuff of novels, stories of intrigue, shadowy go-betweens, and secret meetings among agents armed with vague promises.

The year 1917 brought a flurry of such activity.[2] Its overture came in December 1916, when, in the glow of victory over Rumania, the Central Powers offered publicly to negotiate. In its ambiguity and haughty tone, the offer married Bethmann Hollweg's hopes and Ludendorff's designs. It produced only skepticism in the allied camp. Its principal result was to ease the way towards the German decision, taken the next month, in favor of unrestricted submarine warfare. Then, however, revolution in Russia, the American entry into the war in the name of a "peace without victory," and the Reichstag's Peace Resolution all suggested new terms for a settlement short of the all-out defeat of one side or the other. The provisional Russian government explored a peace settlement with the Central Powers in the spring of 1917, even as it prepared a new offensive. In the wake of the Papal peace note in the summer, which put pressure on diplomats on both sides, there were renewed contacts between the British and German governments.[3] These "peace feelers," like the many contacts before them, came to nothing. No formula could be found to draw the warring parties together, and the diplomatic impasse remained as stubborn as the strategic stalemate. Only a decision-at-arms – the military collapse of one side – could evidently bring the war to an end.

This scenario was scripted in a sense on the first day of the war, although historiographical controversies about Germany's aims in the war have tended to obscure this point. Professor Fischer has read Bethmann Hollweg's diplomacy in the worst possible light. The German chancellor, he argues, was no less convinced an annexationist than Ludendorff and the Pan-Germans; he disdained compromise on German war aims from the start, and his repeated public declarations in favor of negotiations were but empty propaganda.[4] In response, Bethmann's defenders have pleaded the moderation of the chancellor's war aims, his genuine efforts on behalf of a negotiated peace after the fall of 1914, and the

[2] L. L. Farrar, *Divide and Conquer: German Efforts to Conclude a Separate Peace, 1914–1918* (New York, 1978); Wolfgang Steglich (ed.), *Die Friedensversuche der kriegführenden Mächte im Sommer und Herbst 1917* (Stuttgart, 1984).

[3] Wolfgang Steglich (ed.), *Der Friedensappell Papst Benedikts XV. vom 1 August 1917 und die Mittelmächte* (Stuttgart, 1970).

[4] Fischer, *Germany's Aims in the First World War.*

persistent rejection of his overtures by the French, British, and Russian governments.[5] The storm over Bethmann Hollweg has lent more weight to his views than they probably deserve. His was by no means the only – or even the most important – voice in the German government on the question of peace negotiations, particularly after the installation of the third OHL in 1916. In addition, a negotiated peace required a willingness to compromise on both sides; and as Bethmann's defenders have emphasized, the obstacles to compromise were only a little less formidable in the camp of the Entente than they were in Germany.

Whatever their public professions of good faith and willingness to negotiate, the diplomats of all the belligerent powers operated within compelling constraints, which frustrated the quest for a compromise to end the war. In the first place, the logic of coalition warfare bred cumulative commitments, which so inflated the war aims of both sides that compromise could be purchased only at an ally's expense or at the risk of the coalition's cohesion. When the Entente powers enticed Italy into the war in 1915 with the promise of Italian-speaking regions in Austria–Hungary, they tied their alliance together with an expanded program of war aims, which practically excluded a separate peace with Vienna. A separate peace between Germany and Russia – the object of much of Bethmann's diplomatic efforts in 1915 and 1916 – foundered not the least on the reluctance of the Austrians to offer concessions cut from their own territory.[6]

Calculations of timing posed another constraint. During the first two years of the war, soldiers and civilian leaders on both sides clung to the hope that military action would soon decide the issue. As long as they believed that the next offensive might bring the great strategic breakthrough, they resisted the idea of a compromise peace. Early in 1917, however, these calculations changed fundamentally. Unrestricted submarine warfare and revolution in Russia persuaded the Germans that they had the greater short-term prospects for military victory. The entry of the United States in April then convinced the western allies that they had the greater long-term prospects for military victory. On both sides, these calculations reinforced the diplomatic impasse.

In the last analysis, however, the most powerful obstacles to a compromise peace resided elsewhere. They operated on both sides, and they militated against negotiations virtually from the beginning of the war. They had to do with the representation of the war – the conviction, universally

[5] Ritter, *Sword and Scepter*, vol. III.
[6] Wilhelm Ernst Winterhager, *Mission für den Frieden: Europäische Mächtepolitik und dänische Friedensvermittlung im Ersten Weltkrieg, vom August 1914 bis zum italienischen Kriegseintritt Mai 1915* (Stuttgart, 1984).

shared, that the object of the fighting was to repel foreign aggression. The vast human and material sacrifices, which began to accumulate in the first weeks of the conflict, were thereupon debited morally, in Germany and elsewhere, to the malevolence of the enemy. A negotiated peace could neither balance the moral account nor vindicate the sacrifice. Compromise required an altogether different representation of the war – as a miscalculation. No government anywhere could have survived this terrible confession.

This logic worked with special force in Berlin. In Germany, the domestic impact of a compromise peace would have claimed more than the fall of a government. By the last two years of the war, the debates on war aims and domestic political reform had defined the price of a compromise peace as the end of a semi-authoritarian constitutional system, in whose name Germany had – at least in the eyes of its leaders – entered and prosecuted the war. The decision to pursue a compromise peace thus lay in the hands of the German leadership, the political representatives of classes whose power and privilege would have been sacrificed in compromise (but validated in victory). The logic of political suicide appealed to few of these men – least of all to Ludendorff, whose views in the end counted the most.

The force with which the vectors of power in Berlin militated against compromise was evident in Richard von Kühlmann's brief tenure in the Foreign Office. Kühlmann's appointment as Foreign Secretary came in August 1917 as part of a German diplomatic offensive. His predecessor was Arthur Zimmermann, a man of remarkably little subtlety even for a German diplomat; the famous Zimmermann telegram, which had dangled territory in Texas, Arizona, and New Mexico as the bait for a German–Mexican alliance, helped bring the United States into the war. Kühlmann, on the other hand, had spent much of his early career in the German embassy in London, where he acquired a reputation as a moderate. He was in office when, in November 1917, the Bolshevik government sued for peace. He hoped on this occasion to appeal to the left in Germany and even to split the western allies by negotiating a peace that comported, in appearance at least, with the renunciation of annexations contained in Reichstag's Peace Resolution. He accordingly cultivated pro-German groups in the Baltic provinces and the Ukraine, in hopes of turning these lands into German clients. By these means, he advocated a more subtle kind of German imperial rule in the east – what David Stevenson has called "expansion under a cloak of self-determination."[7]

---

[7] Stevenson, *The First World War*, 199; *cf.* Wolfgang Steglich, *Die Friedenspolitik der Mittelmächte 1917/18* (Stuttgart, 1964).

Even the appearance of moderation, however, was distasteful to the men who really ruled in Berlin. Early in 1918 the OHL interceded with the Kaiser to demand German military occupation of much of the Baltic lands and the creation of the *Grenzstreifen* in western Poland, which was not calculated to generate much Polish sympathy for the German cause. Kühlmann's warnings about the ill will that the OHL's policies would sow in eastern Europe went unheeded. Hindenburg and Ludendorff suffered his presence a little longer, until he announced in the Reichstag that military force alone could not bring the war to an end.

Kühlmann's dismissal in July 1918 expelled the last breath of compromise from the German diplomacy of this war. Hindenburg and Ludendorff calculated that the outcome would rest exclusively on the force of arms. They also reasoned that the decision had to come in 1918, before the arrival of American armies in Europe could tip the balance irretrievably to the western powers. In their calculations about the timing and manner of the war's end, they were right.

The enduring face of warfare

The determination of the OHL to force the issue by military means threw into high relief the vital connection between homefront and battlefront. That Germans at home were undersupplied, undernourished, unhappy, and cold was of utmost relevance to the trenches. Military power was in fact an index of conditions on the homefront. Manifold shortages and discontent on the homefront affected industrial productivity in many ways – from production bottlenecks to the stamina and morale of the workforce; and these deficiencies translated directly into the fighting strength of Germany's armies, most immediately via the supply of materials without which soldiers could not remain effective in the field – weapons, munitions, rations, and reserves of able-bodied men to replace the millions who had fallen casualty.

No one was more alive to this connection than Ludendorff himself. He had provided the energy behind the Hindenburg Program, the wholesale readjustments in the organization of war production that began on the homefront in the fall of 1916. He had also concluded in the fall of 1916 that the state of production was insufficient to support a major German offensive in the foreseeable future. German armies had withstood the monster battles of 1916, but at a cost of 1,500,000 casualties. The Entente powers had suffered more, but the ratios of strength at the beginning of 1917 nevertheless gave the German high command reason to pause, for they reflected basic inequalities of material and human resources between the two sides (see table 5).

Table 5 *Material and human resources, 1917*

	Central Powers	Entente
Actives and reserves	10,610,000	17,312,000
Field artillery	14,730	19,465
Heavy artillery	9,130	11,476
Machine guns	20,042	67,276
Airplanes	1,500	3,163

Source: Fritz Klein, *et al.*, *Deutschland im Ersten Weltkrieg* (3 vols., Berlin, 1968–69), vol. II, 53

The Hindenburg Program represented a desperate response to these massive disadvantages. It was based on the calculation that Germany could compensate in determination and productive efficiencies for what the country lacked in resources.

Implicit in the Hindenburg Program was also a German commitment to defensive warfare in the west in 1917. The emphasis in German military planning shifted accordingly in late 1916 to the consolidation and strengthening of positions already held and to the rebuilding of German armies in anticipation of a great offensive, whose timing slid towards 1918.[8] German forces in the field meanwhile adjusted and tightened their defenses all along the western front. In the center, they built a forbidding new set of concrete and steel defenses to the rear of their frontlines. The so-called Hindenburg or Siegfried Line stretched like a chain of subterranean colonies seventy miles east of Arras; it comprised three parallel lines, situated far enough apart to escape simultaneous fire from French artillery. In March 1917 the German army staged a general withdrawal to these new positions, leaving the evacuated area sterilized of human beings, animals, crops, and buildings.

Adjustments in tactical training accompanied the repositioning. The analogue of the limited strategic withdrawal was a new emphasis on "indepth" defensive tactics, which featured retreats in the face of superior enemy firepower to more defensible positions. In the hope of relieving the futility of massed infantry assaults, German troops now received instruction in small-group, "storm-troop" tactics of infiltration and envelopment, whose object was to probe enemy lines and to direct troop concentrations to weak points.[9] Artillery training was also adjusted to stress

[8] See Rod Paschall, *The Defeat of Imperial Germany, 1917–1918* (New York, 1989).
[9] Bruce Gudmundsson, *Stormtroop Tactics: Innovation in the German Army, 1914–1918* (New York, 1989).

short, intense bombardment as the prelude to infantry attack, and then the use of rolling barrages to provide close support for the advance of the footsoldiers.[10]

Military events on the western front in 1917 demonstrated the wisdom of these adjustments. The campaigns recalled the action of 1915 (see map 9). The armies of the western powers again took the offensive, but their operations suggested that despite the availability of armored vehicles, which had first seen action at the Somme in 1916, the British and French were adjusting with more difficulty than the Germans to the tactical imperatives of land warfare. The massive offensives that the western powers launched along the western front began again with protracted artillery bombardments; these were again the prelude to assaults by the footsoldiers, who were again arrayed largely in linear formations. The British initiated the action in April 1917 in the west, near the town of Arras, in a sector that faced the western end of the Hindenburg Line. The shelling of the German positions continued around the clock for eight days. In part because of effective air support and the presence of tanks in the main assault, the British initially made significant gains until the deep German defenses smothered the momentum of the attack. In six weeks of fierce fighting the British lost 142,000 casualties.

A simultaneous French offensive to the southeast, in the Champagne district, was designed to exploit the Germans' duress around Arras. The hilly terrain that Robert Nivelle, the commander of the French army, had selected as the site of the attack was, however, laced with rivers and ill suited for offensive action. Much of the artillery bombardment, with which the French occupied the first nine days of the offensive, fell onto empty landscape that the Germans had, unbeknownst to the French generals, earlier evacuated. When the French footsoldiers then encountered the German positions, which were anchored in the heights known as the Chemin des Dames, the results were familiar. Seven weeks of French infantry attacks purchased insignificant advances at a price of 250,000 casualties.

This exercise in futility, which was known as the "Nivelle Offensive," then produced the gravest crisis that the French army suffered during the war. In the summer of 1917, forty-five French divisions mutinied in the face of orders to continue the attack on German lines. That the crisis did not result in the disintegration of the French army was due to several fortunate circumstances, not the least of which was German ignorance of the scope of the unrest. Nivelle was replaced at the head of the French

[10] David Zabecki, *Steel Wind: Colonel Georg Bruchmüller and the Birth of Modern Artillery* (Westport, CT, 1994).

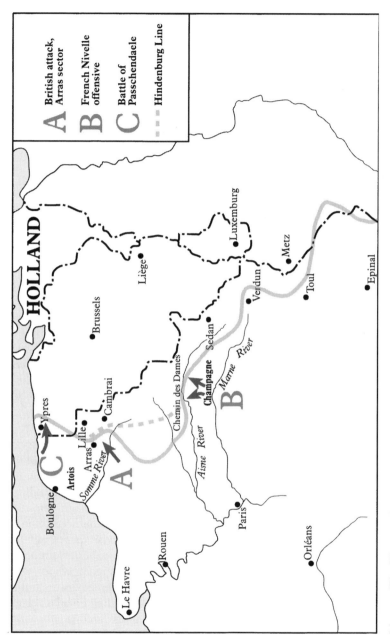

Map 9   The Western Front, 1917

army by Philippe Pétain, the hero of the French defense of Verdun, who contained the crisis with draconian discipline in selected instances, as well as a general program of tactical reform and improvements in the feeding and furloughing of the troops. The crisis nonetheless assured that the French would undertake no additional offensives in 1917.

The role of attacker fell accordingly again to the British. In July 1917 they again assaulted German positions, this time in Flanders, where they hoped to break through to the channel coast and capture the ports from which German submarines were preying on allied shipping. In action reminiscent of the Somme, the Battle of Passchendaele, as the British came to call the offensive, continued for five months until it stalled of exhaustion in the mud. The costs were once again out of all proportion to the negligible strategic gains. The British lost 324,000 casualties.

The efforts of the Entente powers to relieve the stalemate in the west thus not only failed; they also brought the French armies to the brink of collapse. Meanwhile, events on the eastern front demonstrated what might well have happened in France. The allied plans called for a Russian offensive in the spring of 1917, to coincide with the British attack at Arras and the French offensive in the Champagne. The leader of the provisional Russian government, Alexander Kerensky, undertook this commitment despite doubts about its political wisdom. Its military feasibility was even more problematic, for indications were rife that the Russian army was on the verge of disintegration. When the so-called Kerensky Offensive finally began in July, it recalled the action of the previous year on the eastern front (see map 10). The Russians again attacked in the south, into Galicia, against positions held primarily by Austrians; and they again made significant initial gains against dispirited resistance. Again, however, the Russian offensive halted as soon as German reinforcements arrived from the north. The ensuing German counterattack in the south and to the north, in the Baltic, not only erased the Russian gains but also signaled the end of the Russian army as a military institution. Discipline collapsed amid retreat; Russian footsoldiers deserted their units in millions and marched east, where many of them joined the urban uprisings that brought the Bolsheviks to power and the war with Germany to an end.

The Central Powers enjoyed additional good fortune in the fall of 1917. After two years of stalemate warfare in the Alps, the southern front broke. In October, German and Austrian armies overran Italian positions along the Isonzo River near the town of Caporetto. The wholesale disintegration of a defeated and dispirited army loomed again, as Italian defenses crumbled along the entire front. Before the lines finally stabilized in exhaustion along the Piave River, 200 miles to the west, the Italians had lost over 600,000 men to capture or desertion; and they had endured territorial losses on a scale unknown on the western front.

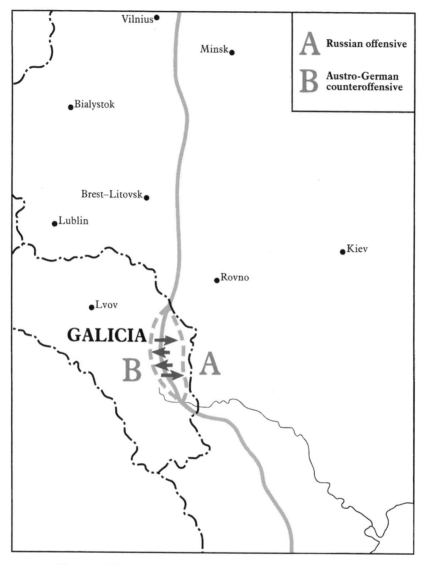

Map 10   The Kerensky Offensive, 1917

The Ludendorff Offensive

The course of events to the south and east buoyed German spirits at the close of the year and raised the prospects for a general end to the war in 1918. Victory in the east appeared to offer the Germans a brief moment of strategic opportunity in the west, which would expire upon the arrival – anticipated in late 1918 – of significant numbers of American troops in Europe. By March 1918, when the eastern peace treaty was signed with the new Soviet government, the Germans had moved thirty-three divisions, more than 500,000 soldiers, from the east and south to the western front. Against French and British armies that had suffered frightfully in the action of the previous year, Ludendorff planned one last battle. A great offensive, to which the Hindenburg Program had been gauged, would break through the allied defenses, paralyze their forces, and compel them to sue for peace.

Ludendorff's vision was the product of his wishful thinking. It bore little relation to the foundations of military power. The German armies had suffered almost as many casualties in 1917 in the western theater as they had during the dreadful year before.[11] In spite of the arrival of the reinforcements from the east early in 1918, German active forces in the west numbered – at about 4,000,000 men – only about 80 percent of the allied armies, which were also better supplied and provisioned. German inferiority reflected basic limits in the country's demographic resources, as well as the demands of the Hindenburg Program, which claimed close to 1,000,000 male workers of draft age; it was also due to the punitive character of eastern settlement, which required leaving another 1,000,000 troops in the east, in order to occupy the areas brought under German control. Throughout the last year of the war, despite efforts to comb warriors ever older and younger out of civilian life, German strategic designs were thus frustrated by a mounting crisis of manpower.

Other statistics from early 1918 also foretold the fancy of Ludendorff's plan (see table 6). It is worth pausing at these figures, for they testify to the industrial forces that in the end decided the war. That the Germans managed to deploy in the west even three-quarters as many artillery pieces as the allies did was tribute to exertions forced by the Hindenburg Program at home. So was the number of German airplanes, and these machines spared the Germans from having to concede immediate supremacy in a dimension of warfare that had – via the airplane's role in reconnaissance, artillery-spotting, and trench-raiding – become essential to troop movements on the ground. Conversely, the vast German inferiority in trucks reflected the limits of homefront exertions; and it spoke to massive strategic disadvantages faced by the German army, which continued – to a far greater extent than the western allies – to rely on horse-drawn wagons for the transport of supplies beyond railheads. To appreciate the weight of this liability in a strategic offensive, the German generals needed only to ponder the failure of the Schlieffen Plan.

---

[11] Reichsarchiv, *Der Weltkrieg*, vol. XIV, 68.

Table 6 *Material resources, early 1918*

	Germany (Western forces)	Western Allies
Machine guns (per infantry division)	324	1,084
Artillery	c.14,000	c.18,500
Airplanes	c.3,670	c.4,500
Trucks	23,000	c.100,000
Tanks	10	800

Source: Fritz Klein, *et al., Deutschland im Ersten Weltkrieg* (3 vols., Berlin, 1968–69), vol. III, 230–31, 314

The tanks represented a special problem. The ten in the German army had all been captured. The low regard in which the German high command held these machines was not without foundation. The early allied tanks were slow, short-ranged, prone to break down, and vulnerable to land mines and artillery fire, particularly as the British and French commanders employed them singly or in small groups to support infantry attacks. Nor did the Germans reconsider this judgment of the tanks in the light of action in November 1917, when – to the surprise of everyone involved – more concentrated formations of British tanks penetrated the Hindenburg Line near the town of Cambrai. This attack, too, soon dissipated amid confusion and mechanical breakdowns; and the Germans recaptured most of the ground they had lost. However, even had they read much significance into this battle, the Germans could not have produced tanks in significant numbers, for their industry was already strained to capacity in fashioning other machines of war.

These grave disadvantages notwithstanding, Ludendorff and his advisors began at the end of 1917 to plan the ultimate offensive in the west. To call the result of their deliberations a "military absurdity" is perhaps an exaggeration, but the plan did in truth disdain material constraints; and it foresaw a remarkable scenario.[12] Its premise was that a breakthrough in a sector where the Germans enjoyed local superiority would occasion the collapse of the allied armies. The disintegration of Russian and Italian forces the previous year figured in Ludendorff's reasoning, but his thinking reflected more clearly the burdens of the western stalemate, which was rooted in tactical obstacles to offensive operations. Ludendorff's plan also bore a curious resemblance to Schlieffen's, for both soldiers foresaw the wholesale collapse of enemy forces in the wake of a single apocalyptic

---

[12] Correlli Barnett, *The Swordbearers: Supreme Command in the First World War* (Bloomington and London, 1975), 282.

operation. Schlieffen was open to the charge that he had paid insuffi-cient attention to tactical difficulties that attended his extravagant vision. Ludendorff's problem lay elsewhere. As he had been throughout the war, he was again preoccupied with the tactics of breakthrough – to the extent that the term "strategy" seems foreign to his thinking, which harbored no coherent concept of how to exploit local success more broadly. As one of his commanders noted, Ludendorff reduced strategy in this fashion to a question of "we'll see what happens then."[13] This approach had at least the virtue of concealing a deeper problem: whether the Germans any longer commanded the resources to exploit tactical success on a strategic scale at all.

The so-called Ludendorff Offensive occupied the entire spring of 1918 (see map 11). In four consecutive assaults, the German armies revisited many of the most dreadful sites of this war, but their experience made clear that they lacked the strength and mobility to fulfill the goals that their leader had set for them. The pattern of action was common to all phases of the offensive. German attacks exploited local superiority, surprise, and tactical finesse to bring significant initial gains, before exhaustion, inade-quate supplies, allied reserves, and the difficulties of operating in this war-disfigured terrain frustrated hopes of the great breakthrough. "Operation Michael," the first and most hopeful of these assaults, commenced on 21 March at the junction of the British and French armies along the Somme River. German advances of up to fifty miles along a sector of eighty miles were the greatest achieved by either side since 1914, but the momentum collapsed after three weeks of desperate fighting, as the allied armies in the sector, reinforced and now under the unified command of the French marshal, Ferdinand Foch, assembled defenses that the Germans found impenetrable. The second German blow, "Operation Georgette," struck at British lines in Flanders, south of Ypres. It was originally planned as a complement to the attack in the Somme sector, but the demands of the first operation retarded preparations for the second. The delay robbed the two operations of their articulation and permitted the timely rein-forcement of British defenses in Flanders, where the German offensive dissipated after less than a week.

The breakdown of the first two assaults failed to deter Ludendorff. Instead, his attentions turned towards French positions to the east, where he reassembled his tired forces in May for another blow. "Operation Blücher" began on 27 May and swept quickly forward over the Chemin des Dames towards the Marne River, which German troops saw on

---

[13] Cited in Fritz Klein, *et al., Deutschland im Ersten Weltkrieg*, vol. III, 236.

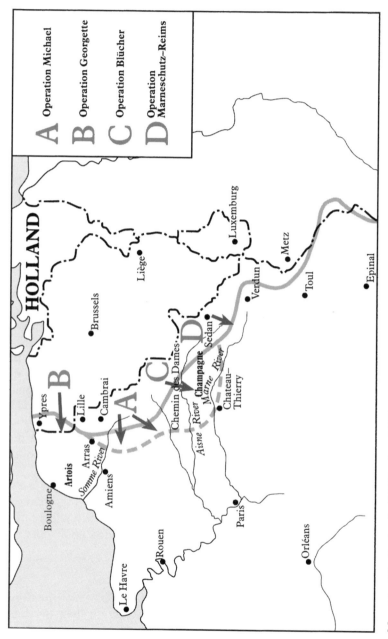

Map 11   The Ludendorff Offensive, 1918

30 May for the first time since September 1914. And here again the German offensive stalled. A final attack towards the east, called "Operation Marneschutz–Reims," for which Ludendorff mobilized every available unit, carried German troops at great cost a short distance across the Marne, but it quickly broke down in the face of French artillery and armored counterattack.

During the spring of 1918, the allied cause appeared to be in jeopardy, as the Germans advanced again within three days' march of Paris. To the informed eye, however, the German offensive represented instead a last, desperate gamble. The material resources on which it was based conformed in no way to either the fears of the allies or the objectives of its own command. It could not purchase the breakthrough. The fatal failing of the campaign was thus, given the strategic context of this war, to have brought only "ordinary victories."[14] When, in mid-July, the attack stalled, the Germans' position was far weaker than it had been in March, despite the dramatic territorial gains that their offensive had registered in the meantime.

Tactical success harbored negative strategic consequences. The extent of the German lines grew by eighty miles between March and July, as German positions forfeited the compact integrity that had made them so formidable in defense in 1917. The irregular protrusions, or "salients," that now described the German lines were more than aesthetic flaws; they were also vulnerable to two-pronged counterattack. The German situation was made all the more perilous by the huge losses that the offensive had extracted in men and equipment. German casualties in the spring numbered almost 500,000 men.[15] The units that remained in place after multiple deployments were decimated, exhausted, dispirited, and in no position to resume offensive action. Particularly high were the losses of horses, junior officers, and so-called "mobile divisions," the units that had spearheaded the offensives and were known for their discipline and initiative.

Ludendorff's last offensive failed to win the war for Germany. It also fatally undermined the capacities of his armies to defend themselves in the positions to which they had advanced – at a time when allied forces were at last accumulating the advantage that had eluded Ludendorff.

The end

In August 1917, in the German naval port of Wilhelmshaven on the North Sea, some 400 unhappy sailors defied their officers, left their warships,

[14] *Ibid.*, 260.   [15] Reichsarchiv, *Der Weltkrieg*, vol. XIV, 300–464.

and spent several hours milling about the town's taverns. Then, the same evening, they returned to their ships. Their action constituted the famous German "naval mutiny," the most serious case of organized indiscipline in the German armed forces during the war. In response, the navy's leadership ordered the imprisonment of seventy-five of the sailors and the execution of two of them. The savage reaction was out of all proportion to the severity of the sailor's disobedience, which grew out of grievances specific to the German navy during this conflict – the frustration and boredom of the sailors, who had seen little action and were compensated with poor rations and the arrogance of their officers. But the reaction of the naval leadership to the episode reflected broader concerns.[16] Anti-war literature had been found in Kiel, another major naval base, and the navy's leaders believed that several of the mutineers had ties to the USPD. Anxieties were mounting in Berlin about the integrity of the country's fighting forces. However gratifying it was from a strategic perspective, the dissolution of the Russian army in 1917 offered disquieting lessons about the vulnerability of unhappy warriors to political subversion in the name of peace. The founding of the USPD and the great industrial strikes of the spring of 1917 boded the spread of the same corrosive forces in Germany.

No such mutiny occurred in the German army. Here conditions were more resistant to organized indiscipline. There was no German analogue to the French army mutinies of 1917. While military courts stood watch, discipline appeared to hold in the German trenches, where the common experience of combat bound men and junior officers, as it deflected resentments rearward, towards the homefront and officers in staff or administrative positions. The army's leadership was nonetheless vigilant for signs of incipient unrest or resistance, particularly after the collapse of the Russian armies. The intensification of "patriotic instruction" in the German army was a response to growing turmoil on the homefront, and it was calculated to provide inoculation against the spread of the "Russian spirit" of defeatism and revolution among the troops.

A number of episodes suggested that concerns about this "spirit" were well founded, for it provided a political idiom in which to channel the myriad mundane frustrations that accumulated in the ranks during the last years of the conflict. Complaints about officers' privileges turned towards the unequal distribution of power in both the army and at home.[17] Officers noted with alarm the circulation of USPD pamphlets and flyers among German units on the eastern front in the fall of 1917, as well as

[16] Wilhelm Deist, "Die Unruhen in der Marine 1917/18," in Deist, *Militär*, 165–84.
[17] Wolfgang Kruse, "Krieg und Klassenheer: Zur Revolutionierung der deutschen Armee im Ersten Weltkrieg," *Geschichte und Gesellschaft* 22 (1996), 530–61.

isolated instances of fraternization between Russian and German troops at the end of the year. A more alarming sign was the disappearance of significant numbers of soldiers (as many as 10 percent, according to some estimates) in the winter of 1917–18, during their transportation from the eastern to the western front.[18] The army's own practice of punishing the leaders of industrial strikes with service at the front seemed almost calculated to fan unrest there, particularly after the great munitions strikes of January 1918 yielded a rich harvest of discontent. Strikers sent to the front represented "less a reinforcement of the troops," complained a staff officer in the spring of 1918, "than a poison."[19]

Despite signs of trouble, the discipline and cohesion of German combat forces remained high during the offensives of the spring of 1918. These operations were animated in the belief, spawned by the high command and communicated systematically to the troops, that success would bring the war to a victorious conclusion. The failure of the offensive to achieve this object had catastrophic results. It not only placed the German armies in precarious positions, in lightly fortified trenches where they could only with difficulty be supplied over war-torn terrain; it also left them exhausted and demoralized. Frustration thus dismantled much of the moral scaffolding on which discipline and cohesion had survived in the ranks.

Allied counteroffensives began against these vulnerable troops on 18 July 1918 (see map 12). The French army struck first against the half-fashioned German defenses in the Marne salient. In a week of furious combat, often called the Second Battle of the Marne, the French exploited numerical superiority and their own tactical innovations to push the Germans back across the river. Short artillery barrages were now the prelude to French infantry attacks that were spearheaded by formations of tanks. Late in July the Germans were compelled to withdraw, as they had in September 1914, to more secure positions near the Aisne River. Even with the modified tactics, however, the dynamics of combat dealt disproportionate losses to the attackers. The action on the Marne cost the German army 25,000 men; it cost the French nearly four times as many. Now, though, the mathematics worked entirely to the disadvantage of the Germans, for their antagonists could far better afford the price. One phase of the campaign drove this point home with particular force. As part of the allied offensive on the salient, American troops saw their first major action of the war against German positions at the Marne River.

---

[18] Wilhelm Deist, "Der militärische Zusammenbruch des Kaiserreichs: Zur Realität der 'Dolchstosslegende,'" in Deist, *Militär*, 219.

[19] Kruse, "Krieg und Klassenheer," 556–7.

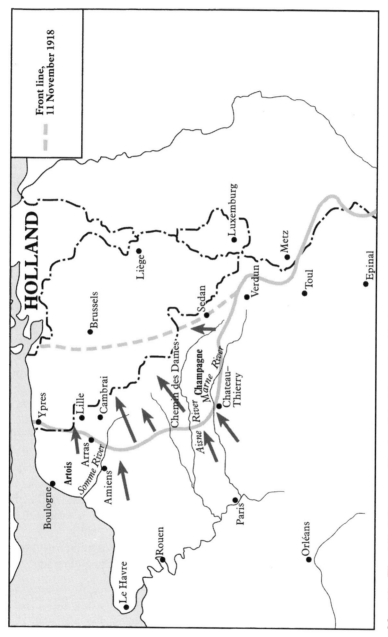

Front line,
11 November 1918

HOLLAND

Boulogne

Le Havre

Rouen

Ypres

Artois

Arras

Amiens

Somme River

Lille

Cambrai

Brussels

Liège

Chemin des Dames

Aisne River

Champagne

Marne River

Chateau–
Thierry

Paris

Orléans

Luxemburg

Sedan

Verdun

Metz

Toul

Epinal

Map 12   The Allied Counteroffensive, July–November 1918

Around the town of Chateau-Thierry, in an attack that laid bare their inexperience, the Americans lost 35,000 casualties. But even as they did so, an additional 150,000 American soldiers were arriving in France.

The next blow against the German lines arrived to the west, in the Somme sector. On 8 August British troops attacked badly outnumbered German positions to the south of that river, near Amiens. With the close support of artillery and airplanes, over 400 tanks led the assault here, too. Although the British advance stalled after two days, the action on this sector enjoys a special notoriety. Ludendorff called 8 August "the black day of the German army." The significance of the attack lay less in the bare patch of territory that the Germans abandoned than in the number of the troops they lost – or rather in the character of the losses. In two days of fighting, 20,000 Germans were killed or wounded, while 30,000 surrendered, in the clearest signal to date of the erosion of morale in the German army. Ludendorff's comment spoke as well, however, to the state of his own morale. The collapse of his indomitable confidence began now to register in erratic failures of judgment and orders for counterattacks that stood no hope of success.

As the allied attacks gathered momentum on several sectors throughout August and September, the German army began to dissolve. The wholesale surrender of German troops during this action provided one index to the erosion of the will to continue. Another was the number of German troops who contrived to escape combat in a hopeless cause, whether by surrendering, disappearing rearwards, or by feigning light injury or sickness. The fact that influenza swept the German trenches in the summer of 1918 provided a degree of credibility to many of these instances, but the evasive practices themselves reached epidemic proportions. In light of estimates that between 750,000 and 1,000,000 soldiers avoided battle in this manner, the historian Wilhelm Deist has spoken of a "covert military strike" in the German army during the last months of the war.[20] That the Germans were able in these circumstances to avoid collapse and to stage a coherent retreat was itself a remarkable feat, although it also bespoke the limited range of the allied tanks and the logistical difficulties that the allied command faced in supporting a war of movement over difficult terrain.

Nonetheless, by October 1918 German forces were in full retreat homeward. So were their allies. At the end of September, the Bulgarians, who

---

[20] Deist, "Verdeckter Militärstreik im Kriegsjahr 1918?" in Wolfram Wette (ed.), *Der Krieg des kleinen Mannes: Eine Militärgeschichte von unten* (Munich and Zurich, 1992), 146–67; Deist, "Der militärische Zusammenbruch," 211–34. See also Benjamin Ziemann, "Fahnenflucht im deutschen Heer 1914–1918," *Militärgeschichtliche Mitteilungen* 55 (1996), 93–130.

had born the brunt of an allied attack northward from Macedonia into Serbia, sued for peace. Then, in late October, the southern front collapsed. When Italian armies, reinforced by British and French troops, broke through Austrian lines along the Piave River, the armies of the Habsburg monarchy dissolved into their component ethnic units and withdrew in disarray from the war. By October 1918 the military outcome of the Great War was no longer in doubt. Germany lost.

Still, crucial issues remained to be resolved. These had to do with the specific circumstances of the war's end, and their resolution had momentous implications for the future arrangement of politics in Germany. During the last six weeks of the conflict, the burden of making the fundamental decisions shifted, in Germany and elsewhere, from the soldiers to statesmen and political leaders. Much of their agenda emerged, however, in the shadow of late maneuvers by the German military leadership.

It is not certain when Ludendorff finally admitted to himself that the plight of his armies was hopeless – that the campaign of 1919, if it were to be fought, would be played out on German soil. In all events, he kept this conclusion a secret from the emperor and the civilian leadership until 29 September, when he precipitously announced to them that the war was lost and that the government was to negotiate an immediate armistice. This shocking news set into motion processes that not only brought the military action to a halt, but also transformed the face of German politics.

The German leaders had concluded that the most attractive avenue to an armistice led through the American president, Woodrow Wilson, whose "Fourteen Points" had given an idealistic ring to public statements of American war aims and suggested the possibility of a lenient peace. On 3 October 1918, the first of several German notes thus ventured out to explore peace terms in Washington. In these circumstances, however, far-reaching constitutional changes also became unavoidable in Germany. The impending defeat of the German armies robbed the defenders of German authoritarianism of their last prop. Moreover, it was transparent to all that democratic reform at home would encourage the likelihood of leniency from Wilson, the champion of a "world safe for democracy."[21]

Accordingly, at the insistence of both the OHL and his civilian advisors, the emperor announced a series of constitutional changes that presented the democratic reformers in Germany with virtually everything they wanted. Hertling ceded the chancellorship to the liberal prince Max

[21] Leo Haupts, *Deutsche Friedenspolitik 1918–1919: Eine Alternative zur Machtpolitik des Ersten Weltkrieges* (Düsseldorf, 1976); Klaus Schwabe, *Deutsche Revolution und Wilson-Friede: Die amerikanische und deutsche Friedensstrategie zwischen Ideologie und Machtpolitik* (Düsseldorf, 1971).

of Baden, whose new government rested on the support of a parliamentary majority of Catholics, Progressives, and the MSPD. An imperial
proclamation then inscribed responsible cabinet government into the federal constitution, placed foreign and military policy in the purview of
parliamentary control, and democratized the Prussian suffrage. Simultaneous negotiations between the trade unions and leading employers'
associations formalized the gains made by organized labor during the
war, including the eight-hour day, the legal right to bargain collectively,
and the establishment of arbitration committees in the larger industries.
Finally, on 9 November 1918, two days before the armistice was signed,
William II, the symbol supreme of German militarism, abdicated the
throne at the insistence of his own military advisors.

The perverse irony of these developments would be worth savoring
were it not for their fatal long-term consequences. Constitutional reform
in Germany was the by-product of a military decision to seek an end to
the war. The father of German democracy was Erich Ludendorff. In the
desperation of the war's last weeks, he and his political allies determined
to save as much of the old order as possible – by conceding as much to
their opponents as necessary. They succeeded to a remarkable degree.
Their "revolution from above" resolved basic constitutional issues to the
satisfaction of most of the Social Democrats, before social turmoil at
the end of the war presented the specter of a German revolution on the
Russian model of the previous year. When, on the eve of the armistice,
the leaders of the MSPD took over the reigns of power and confronted
this danger, they were resolved above all to preserve the constitutional
gains with which they had now been presented. In the name of stability,
they resisted more thoroughgoing changes in the social infrastructure of
German politics, the socialization of industry, or the purges of the military
and civilian bureaucracies. As a consequence, men whose political loyalties were affixed to the Imperial regime survived in positions of political
and social power to exacerbate the ordeal of the new republican regime.

Ludendorff himself was not one of these survivors. Two weeks before
the armistice, he fled into exile. But his legacy lived on in many ways.
Arguably the most fateful of these derived from his victory in the last
campaign, the object of which was to frame the memory of the war.

The "stab in the back"

Late in July 1916, as battle raged at Verdun, on the Somme, and on
the eastern front, an "Ernest Appeal from the Front" appeared in newspapers throughout Germany. "Are Germans on the homefront still the
people they were at the war's beginning," read the inquiry: "or have

everyday concerns again taken over? German People! Do not jeopardize the great cause, the lives and future of every German, with your petty discontents."[22] By the middle of the war, this motif was already a common marker of the growing tensions between the home and fighting fronts; and it continued to surface regularly among the troops. During the summer of 1918, several weeks before he shared his bleak prognosis about the war with the civilians, Ludendorff himself invoked the motif when he complained to his staff that the German offensive had stalled because the homefront had withheld adequate supplies and reserves.

This reasoning appealed powerfully to the German military leadership on the eve of defeat; and in the circumstances in which the impending conclusion of the war became more widely known, the same reasoning found broad popular resonance. Ludendorff's actions during the final stages of the conflict were designed to shape the final representation of the war. He was well equipped to do so, for the army's monopoly of information survived almost to the end. News of the initial successes of the Ludendorff Offensive had encouraged the belief on the homefront that a victorious end to the war was near. The official reports from the front continued to speak the language of optimism until late September. Then the tone shifted suddenly and radically. Ludendorff's insistence at just this moment that power be served to the civilians grew out of the same attempt to steer popular thinking about impending defeat. In the scenario that he scripted for them, the new leaders' most pressing and immediate responsibility was to sue for peace. To the civilians, not the soldiers, thus fell the unenviable role of presiding over the precipitous termination of the war, an eventuality for which the German public at home was utterly unprepared.

The war ended amid extraordinary popular confusion in Germany and a host of unanswered questions. Ludendorff and his allies had answers to these questions, and they were eager to share their views. The chief element in their brief was that the German armies had not lost the war. Instead, the soldiers remained in the field, valiant and in good order, until the homefront collapsed in the fall of 1918 amid a bitter harvest of subversion and agitation by pacifists, socialists, slackers, and Jews. Hindenburg himself lent semi-official credence, as well as an enduring label, to this reading of the war's end when, in 1919, he testified to a parliamentary committee of investigation that "*die deutsche Armee ist von hinten erdolcht worden*" – "the German army was stabbed in the back."[23]

---

[22] "Ein ernster Aufruf aus dem Felde," *Die Volkswacht* (Freiburg im Breisgau), 21 July 1916.

[23] Andreas Dorpalen, *Hindenburg and the Weimar Republic* (Princeton, 1964), 51–52.

By the time Hindenburg offered this guide to the war's conclusion, prominent officers and right-wing political leaders had begun a campaign to cultivate the legend that the victorious army was stabbed in the back by treacherous forces on the homefront. Hindenburg probably believed what he said, while others embraced his views with more cynicism. All of the proponents of the *Dolchstoss* could capitalize on general ignorance and fleeting impressions, which seemed at first glance to lend some credibility to the legend. The retreat of the German army did take place in reasonably good order, at least until it reached the German frontier. The Socialists, some of whose leaders were Jews, did come to power at the war's end. The civilian government, with Erzberger in the lead, did sign the armistice agreement, whose provisions were far harsher than Ludendorff had hoped. The leaders of the new republican government unwittingly connived in the legend when they referred publicly to the return home of Germany's undefeated troops.

The "stab in the back" played on central features of the relationship between the homefront and the fighting front – the tensions between the two theaters of war, the homefront's exhaustion, which no one denied, and the inextricable link between productivity at home and the performance of the troops in the field. The myth also spoke to themes that had informed the "spirit of 1914," insofar as the collapse of the great community of national resolve could be traced now to the machinations of elements who had never really belonged to it. The reasons for the subsequent vitality of the legend must be sought as well, however, in the unsettled politics of memory during the Weimar era.[24]

In all events, the *Dolchstoss* was a shameless exercise in evasion. It was calculated to deflect blame for defeat away from the parties who were responsible for it. Prominent in this group stood the army's leadership, whose decisions had been based on fantastic beliefs about the endurance of civilians and soldiers alike. The arrogant miscalculation of the soldiers – what one is tempted to call the *Frontstoss* or "stab from the front" – was a decisive factor in 1918, when the Ludendorff Offensive failed. Their miscalculation had also been decisive in 1917, when the submarine offensive failed, and in 1916, when the Verdun offensive and Hindenburg Program intensified the ordeal of the army and the homefront – and in 1914, when the failure of the Schlieffen Plan dashed hopes for the only kind of war that the Germans could expect to win.

[24] Bessel, *Germany after the First World War*, especially 254–84.

Epilogue: A great war

George Kennan fashioned an indelible label for the First World War when he called it *"the* great seminal catastrophe of this century."[1] It is a fitting characterization. This great conflict destroyed the old European order and let loose political storms that required another world war to calm them. Ideological divisions spawned in the First World War hovered over the political geography of Europe until 1989. In the many European lands that were locked in combat, the Great War demolished millions of lives, squandered untold riches, and left few phases of human existence untouched for the worse.

However broadly the effort is cast, describing the repercussions of this terrible war in a single European land is an exercise in disproportion, which can only plead for pardon on the grounds that a more comprehensive history would require a much different – and much longer – book. In deference to the war's more comprehensive impact, the question nonetheless insists on at least a summary hearing: was the German experience of this war different or special in any significant way? The question itself is complex. It invokes issues of comparative costs, privation, and suffering, as well as military performance; and its implications reach well beyond the four years in which the battles raged. The following brief remarks accordingly suggest some general terms in which the German experience of the Great War might be set into two analytical contexts. The one pertains to the experience of war in other belligerent countries, the other to a broader chronological span of German history, during which the war's bitter legacy played out.

The general patterns of mobilizing for war were similar everywhere.[2] From Great Britain to Russia, economies and societies improvised to

---

[1] George F. Kennan, *The Decline of Bismarck's European Order: Franco-Russian Relations, 1875–1890* (Princeton, 1979), 3 (his emphasis).

[2] F. P. Chambers, *The War Behind the War, 1914–1918: A History of the Political and Civilian Fronts* (New York, 1939); John Williams, *The Other Battleground: The Homefronts – Britain, France and Germany, 1914–1918* (Chicago, 1972); Gerd Hardach, *The First World*

accommodate the voracious appetites of industrial warfare. No belligerent country was exempt from the sorts of upheavals that defined the
German experience of war. Armies initially claimed millions of men
from field and factory, until the prolongation of combat revealed that
some kinds of factories were no less essential to the war than were the
armies themselves. This truth then dictated the rapid reorganization of
economies and societies under the state's bureaucratic auspices, the ruthless redirection of human and material resources into manufacturing and
operating the tools of war. While the attendant dislocations offered opportunities to some categories of workers, like women, the disruptions were
general. They bore with special force on the food supply, which became
an early object of commercial warfare, even as agriculture relinquished
its manpower and animals to the armies and its fertilizers to the makers
of munitions. Anxiety about food became a staple feature of war on the
homefront, like fear for the physical safety of loved ones. So did inflation,
the issue of unbridled military demand, irrepressible public expenditures,
and the reluctance of public authorities to tax already beleaguered populaces. At home, these tribulations were calculated to breed exhaustion,
discontent, and protest, which accumulated foremost in groups, like the
labor movement, whose grievances and disaffections antedated the war.
The battlefront offered its own tribulations, which bred their own characteristic modes of discontent and protest. But armies in the field were
intimately bound to the societies that succored them from home. The
battlefield was the ultimate measure of the homefront's ordeal, for the
combat strength of field armies registered faithfully the strains of mobilization at home. The war eventuated in the collapse of armies at the front
and the collapse of governments at home. The empires of the Romanovs,
Habsburgs, and Osmanlis thus joined the empire of the Hohenzollerns
as crown witnesses to another axiom of this war, that revolution at home
was the price of a great power's military defeat on the field of battle.

The strains of industrial war challenged everywhere the moral and
material bonds that held states and societies together. Some belligerents,
however, were better organized than others to withstand the ordeal. The
war placed a premium on the capacity of belligerent states to generate
and channel resources to military ends. This capacity in turn correlated
with a variety of circumstances that social scientists and historians have
analyzed broadly in metaphors of "development" or "modernization."
Whatever it is called, the process suggests several propositions. Waging

War, 1914–1918 (Berkeley and Los Angeles, 1977). See now the collection of essays
edited by John Horne, *State, Society and Mobilization in Europe during the First World War*
(Cambridge, 1997).

protracted industrial war required – one is tempted to say by definition – an established and well-articulated industrial base to supply huge quantities of essential military materials, chiefly metals and chemicals. Mobilizing production rapidly for war far exceeded the capacities of the market alone; it required an administrative apparatus with the competence and power to redirect human and material resources for military use – as well as to manage agricultural shortages. This vast administrative undertaking overtaxed the limits of bureaucratic compulsion; it demanded, as John Horne has recently argued, a "balance of coercion and persuasion."[3] The effectiveness of mobilization depended to a large degree on the assent and cooperation of the populaces with whose aid – and in whose name – the war was being prosecuted. Durable popular support for war in turn correlated with some significant degree of civic integration, a general acceptance of the state's legitimacy, and a sense of common moral obligation among a society's constituent groups, whether or not civic obligation corresponded to institutionalized participation in government.

Martial virtues belonged somewhere in this catalogue. In its principal theaters, however, the First World War offered little reward for the virtues that had distinguished soldiers of earlier eras. Strategic virtuosity, operational flare, cavalry charges, and other battlefield heroics did not decide this war. The potentially heroic moment passed early, and unfulfilled, in the fall of 1914. The skills that the war thereafter demanded of soldiers were organizational; and they pertained as much to questions of industrial management as they did to the movement of troops and supplies. Whether military officers oversaw railroad schedules, manpower allocations, labor relations, or the supply of fertilizer, they became central figures in the management of civilian economic affairs. Civil–military relations often revolved therefore, in Germany and elsewhere, as much around disputes over war contracts as strategic priorities.

Some statistics speak to the common strains of war, as well as to the differing capacities of the belligerent states to manage the ordeal (see table 7). These figures require caution. They cannot be precise. Most of them reflect the work of scholars in the immediate aftermath of the conflict, and, given the formidable difficulties of collecting the statistics of war, the numbers were in most cases based on educated guesses. The figures for Russia are particularly misleading, for most of them exclude losses and costs incurred in the war's immediate aftermath of revolution and civil war. If these broader costs are figured in,

---

[3] John Horne, "Remobilizing for 'Total War': France and Britain, 1917–1918," in *ibid.*, 195.

Table 7 *Some costs of the war*

	United Kingdom[1]	France[2]	Germany[3]	Austria-Hungary[3]	Russia (−1917)[4]
Population, 1910–11[5]	40,460,000	39,192,000	64,296,000	51,356,000	160,700,000
Male population, 1910–11[5]	19,638,000	19,254,000	32,040,000	25,374,000	78,790,000
Men mobilized	6,211,427	8,660,000[6]	13,250,000	8,000,000	13,700,000
Percentage of male population mobilized	31.6	45.0	41.4	31.5	17.4
Military casualties	2,437,964	3,100,000	6,193,058	6,400,000	5,409,000
Dead	744,702	1,400,000	2,044,900	1,100,000	1,660,000
Wounded	1,693,262	1,700,000	4,148,158	5,300,000	3,749,000
Casualties per 1,000 prewar male population	124	161	193	252	69
Civilian deaths due to war[7]	292,000	500,000	624,000	2,320,000	5,050,000
Birth deficits[8]	1,788,000	3,074,000	5,436,000	5,063,000	26,000,000[9]
Monetary costs					
Direct	$44,029,011,868	$25,812,782,800	$40,150,000,000	$20,622,960,600	$24,383,950,000
Cost per head	$1,088	$659	$624	$402	$152
Loss of life: capitalized value[10]	$3,083,066,280	$4,060,000,000	$6,911,762,000	$2,992,000,000	$3,353,500,000
Property losses	$1,750,000,000	$10,000,000,000	$1,750,000,000	$1,250,000,000	$1,250,000,000

[1] Francis W. Hirst, *The Consequences of the War to Great Britain* (London, 1934)

[2] Charles Gide and William Oualid, *Le bilan de la guerre pour la France* (Paris, n.d.)

[3] Leo Grebler and Wilhelm Winkler, *The Cost of the World War to Germany and to Austria–Hungary* (New Haven, 1940)

[4] Stanislaus Kohn and Alexander F. Meyendorff, *The Cost of the War to Russia* (New Haven, 1932)

[5] B. R. Mitchell, *European Historical Statistics, 1750–1970* (New York, 1978), 4–8

[6] Includes colonial troops

[7] Horst Mendershausen, *The Economics of War* (New York, 1941), 307

[8] Derek H. Aldcroft, *From Versailles to Wall Street, 1919–1929* (Berkeley and Los Angeles, 1977), 15

[9] Includes period of revolution and civil war

[10] Calculated from figures in Ernest L. Bogart, *Direct and Indirect Costs of the Great World War* (New York, 1919)

Russian civilian and military losses probably exceeded those of all the rest of Europe combined. The money costs are figured in 1914 US dollars – when $440 purchased a Ford "Runabout" (when a gallon of gas cost a dime), $4 purchased a pair of shoes, $5 a pair of young men's trousers, and $12 a bicycle.[4] Total US federal expenditures in 1914 comprised $726,000,000.

Several of these numbers are of particular interest, for they suggest what might be called an east–west gradient in organizational effectiveness. France and Germany mobilized significantly larger proportions of their male populations for military service than did Russia or Austria–Hungary. The low British figure reflects the delay of conscription in that country until the end of 1916. Ratios of direct costs to population suggest that Britain, France, and Germany also mobilized material wealth more effectively than did the two eastern monarchies, where staggering numbers of civilian casualties betrayed as well the mismanagement of the domestic food supply – and the fact that enemy blockades isolated both lands from overseas supplies.

The Russian and Austro-Hungarian monarchies were by virtually every conventional index the least "developed" of the major powers. Their many weaknesses ought to have recommended a conciliatory foreign policy in 1914, for they rendered both empires, despite their large armies, unequal to the pressures of the war that erupted that summer. In both lands, the sinews of industrial development and political legitimacy were alike fragile. Russia's industrial resources were abundant but largely untapped.[5] A meager railway system, which staggered under the challenge of Imperial Russia's vast distances, throttled the movement of industrial raw materials to the manufacturing centers, food to the cities, and troops, weapons, and supplies to the front. The tsar stood atop the most autocratic political system in Europe. His officials regarded all signs of civic initiative with suspicion and hence subverted the advice and cooperation offered to them in a rush of patriotism by the feeble Duma, business organizations, the local administrative councils (*zemstvos*), and a host of voluntary organizations like the Red Cross. Industrial mobilization thus proceeded with little coordination among public and private agencies. Oversight of the war effort remained centralized in principle, where it was ultimately hostage to court favorites and a corps of bureaucrats, both military and civilian, most of whom were neither practiced nor trained in the skills now demanded

---

[4] Scott Derks (ed.), *The Value of a Dollar: Prices and Incomes in the United States, 1860–1989* (Detroit, 1994), 143.
[5] W. Bruce Lincoln, *Passage through Armageddon: The Russians in War and Revolution, 1914–1918* (New York and Oxford, 1994); M. T. Florinsky, *The End of the Russian Empire* (New York, 1961).

of them, and whose incompetence was rivaled only by their corruption. Mismanagement of the economy rivaled that of the army. The results surfaced in paralyzing shortages of basic goods on the homefront and in the grotesque deficiencies in modern weapons, munitions, and supplies that plagued Russian footsoldiers in their encounters with the armies of Imperial Germany. Opposition built quickly in the industrial centers, particularly in Petrograd and Moscow, which were home to enormous concentrations of hungry and maltreated munitions workers. Resistance built as well among the troops, as repeated operational misadventures and incompetent leadership eroded the stolid residual loyalties to the monarchy that for three years had furnished the primary prop of discipline in this peasant army.

To judge by the performance of its soldiers in the field against the Russian army, the Habsburg monarchy was even less prepared to wage an extended industrial war.[6] Material backwardness was not as crippling a handicap as in Russia, for the integrated foundations of an industrial economy had been laid in Bohemia, western Hungary, and the environs of Vienna. The problem lay rather in the precarious state of ethnic relations in the Dual Monarchy, the intensification of national passions that had threatened the legitimacy of the Imperial constitution even before the war broke out. The war's great paradox was that mobilization required administrative centralization, which, because Germans and Magyars presided over it, could only exacerbate resentments among the other, subordinate ethnic groups that were the objects of its heavy hand. Mobilization bred a sprawling, hybrid bureaucratic colossus of civilians and soldiers, which was more efficient and less corrupt than in Russia (and less efficient and more corrupt than in Germany). During the first three years of the war, the army was the dominant force in the mobilization of the homefront. Military administration descended onto broad swaths of territory that abutted the many fronts on which Austrian troops were fighting. The army's role in the management of the war-related industries was more direct than in Germany; and it extended to the militarization of factories in the core areas of production. If this arrangement kept the soldiers in the field better equipped than their Russian antagonists, it could not relieve a more comprehensive torment. The breakdown of the food supply, both at home and in the field, followed upon the allied blockade, the inadequacy of the Austrian railway system, and one of the monarchy's basic constitutional features – the autonomy of its Hungarian half, which survived in significant degrees, even amid the mobilization, to constrict

---

[6] Robert J. Wegs, *Die österreichische Kriegswirtschaft 1914–1918* (Vienna, 1979); Josef Redlich, *Österreichs Regierung und Verwaltung im Weltkriege* (Vienna, 1925).

the movement of grains to the Austrian half. Misery in the Habsburg lands was thus defined by hunger, as well as by the nearly uninterrupted calamities that failures of staff and command inflicted on Austrian armies on the eastern front. Opposition to the war rapidly accumulated. It found expression primarily in ethnic unrest at home and within the army, where it debilitated military performance. The unreliability of Czech units was manifest early in the contest; and by the last two years of the war, the high command had grounds for anxiety over the loyalty of many others, including contingents of Poles, Ruthenians, Serbs, Rumanians, and Italians. The pressures of war, which had swelled in the monarchy's ethnic fissures, thus hastened the collapse of both the army and the Habsburg state in 1918.

The two eastern European monarchies collapsed in the wake of defeat; France and Great Britain survived the ordeal of the war. The fact that these two western European lands were home to much broader and more centralized parliamentary regimes, with traditions of civilian control over the military, was more than incidental to this outcome. The strains of industrial mobilization nourished domestic strife here, too, which surfaced foremost in industrial strikes and other manifestations of labor unrest, particularly during the final two years of the war. Domestic discord was more serious in France, where it peaked in 1917; but neither the mutinies in the army nor the spread of defeatist sentiment on the left destroyed the military and political foundations of the war effort. In both Britain and France, compulsory arbitration tribunals helped mollify labor, while governments could rely on extended networks of voluntary associations, from political parties to teachers' organizations, to stoke the popular consensus in support of the war during the darkest periods in 1917 and early 1918. Thus in 1917, as revolution arrived in Russia and a new Austrian emperor desperately sought a way out of the war, the two western powers engineered a "remobilization" of their energies under the leadership of two powerful civilian politicians, Georges Clemenceau and David Lloyd George.[7]

French mobilization was the most thorough among the major belligerents.[8] The country comprised the smallest population, and it ceded the bulk of its industrial resources to German occupation during the first

---

[7] John Horne, "Remobilizing for 'Total War': France and Britain, 1917–1918," in Horne, *State, Society and Mobilization*, 195–211.

[8] Leonard V. Smith, Stéphane Audoin-Rouzeau, and Annette Becker, *France and the Great War, 1914–1918* (Cambridge, 2003). Patrick Fridenson (ed.), *The French Home Front, 1914–1918* (Providence and Oxford, 1992); Jean-Jacques Becker, *The Great War and the French People* (Leamington Spa, 1985); John F. Godfrey, *Capitalism at War: Industrial Policy and Bureaucracy in France, 1914–1918* (New York and Leamington Spa, 1987).

weeks of the war. These were grave burdens in an industrial war, and they required, in compensation, the ruthless conscription of manpower into the army and industry. The French industrial effort reassembled in the interior; its ownership and management remained in the hands of the industrialists, but its planning took place in central civilian public agencies, which evolved in 1917 into a Ministry of Armaments. To this extent, the industrial mobilization in France, the melding of private enterprise and public direction, resembled the process in Germany and elsewhere, except that the first French Minister of Armaments was a Socialist. That France became the Entente's principal manufacturing source of weapons testified to the effectiveness of this arrangement, as well as to the availability of industrial raw materials from abroad.

The British mobilization required the greatest degree of innovation and improvisation.[9] The most basic institutions were absent at the outset, for Great Britain was unique among the European powers in lacking a conscript army and an attendant military bureaucracy. The British economy in 1914 was also unique in its freedom from public intervention. Paradoxically, these failings were initially a liability but ultimately advantageous in the long war that eventuated, for while mobilization required basic and painful ruptures with established practices, it was relatively unencumbered by bureaucratic tradition or jurisdictional conflicts in either the military or economic realms. The institutions that emerged were hence geared better to the new mandates of industrial war. The process culminated in the creation of a Ministry of Munitions, which imposed centralized direction on business and labor, and a mass army, which was fed initially by volunteers and then, beginning in 1916, by conscripts. Along with the Royal Navy, these institutions shielded the country's civilian populace from the worst material privations, and they enabled the British army to bear the brunt of the military effort against Germany during the last year and a half of the war.

While the dynamics and broad institutional contours of mobilization were similar in all the major belligerent states, each case displayed characteristic features, which corresponded to the unique political, social, and cultural circumstances in which it was set. In Germany, the setting was governed by massive bureaucratic intervention, the dominant place of the army in politics and society, and the endurance of basic domestic conflicts. That these aspects of German mobilization produced baleful consequences is easy to demonstrate, but so is the fact that feckless

---

[9] Llewellyn Woodward, *Great Britain and the War of 1914–1918* (London, 1967); J. M. Bourne, *Britain and the Great War, 1914–1918* (London, 1989).

bureaucratic intrusions, powerful soldiers, and domestic conflict were prominent features of mobilization elsewhere. Did they result in the failure of mobilization in Germany?

Did mobilization in Germany fail? If the criteria of success are marked out in November 1918, the question begs a positive answer. In this light, the exhaustion of the German homefront was pivotal. It can be traced to basic administrative failures – above all, to those that confounded management of the food supply – and to the collapse of domestic consensus on the legitimacy of the war, which the soldiers and their civilian allies insisted on prosecuting to the limit for aggressive and uncompromising ends at home and abroad. Several problems attend this logic, including the question whether the renunciation of aggressive war aims would have resulted in a compromise peace. A more basic question arises from the observations of a distinguished authority on international history. "With no considerable assistance from her allies," writes Professor Northedge, Germany "had held the rest of the world at bay, had beaten Russia, had driven France, the military colossus of Europe for more than two centuries, to the end of her tether, and in 1917, had come within an ace of starving Britain into surrender."[10] Whether France was a military colossus any longer or whether Britain came within an ace of starving are not at issue. By Northedge's criteria, the German mobilization was no failure. It was effective.[11] It sustained a remarkable military feat, a comprehensive national exertion that for more than four years defied material odds to hold at bay a far superior coalition of enemies.

This reasoning is compelling. It invites comparisons away from mobilization, the organization of resources, to these resources themselves – and their limits. Here the numbers speak an unambiguous language (see table 8). These statistics relate only to the major powers. They anticipate neither the German occupation of Belgium and the French industrial north, nor the changes in the cast of characters in 1917, when the Russians departed and the Americans entered the war (nor do they account for the resources of the British empire). They reveal nonetheless that in the categories most pertinent to an extended industrial war – those that translated directly into producing soldiers and deadly machines – the opposing sides were dramatically unequal. The figures also suggest that the fateful

---

[10] F. S. Northedge, *The Troubled Giant: Britain among the Great Powers* (London, 1966), 623; *cf.* Paul Kennedy, *The Rise and Fall of the Great Powers: Economic Change and Military Conflict from 1500 to 2000* (New York, 1987), 268–69.

[11] See Paul Kennedy, "Military Effectiveness in the First World War," in Allan R. Millett and Williamson Murray (eds.), *Military Effectiveness* (4 vols., Boston, 1988–89), vol. I, 329–50.

Table 8 *Material resources, 1913*

	Germany	Austria–Hungary	Central Powers	France	Russia	Britain	Entente	USA	Entente and USA
Population (in millions)	66.9	52.1	**119.0**	39.7	175.1	44.4	**259.2**	97.3	**356.5**
Iron and steel production (millions of tons)	17.6	2.6	**20.2**	4.6	4.8	7.7	**17.1**	31.8	**48.9**
Percent of world manufacturing output	14.8	4.4	**19.2**	6.1	8.2	13.6	**27.9**	32.0	**59.9**

Source: Paul Kennedy, *Rise and Fall of the Great Powers: Economic Change and Military Conflict from 1500 to 2000* (New York, 1987), 199–202, 258–71

moments of the war came at the first hour, when the British intervened in the continental conflict, and then in early 1917, when the United States formally joined the coalition arrayed against the Central Powers. The British intervention was pivotal. Apart from ensuring the commitment of British troops and material resources to the coalition, it turned the commercial balance to the decisive disadvantage of the Central Powers, which were, for all intents and purposes, denied access to overseas trade for the duration of the war. The western powers, by contrast, henceforth enjoyed privileged access to the resources of the world's most formidable industrial power. Agricultural imports from America likewise spared the western powers from food shortages in the degree that plagued the Central Powers. The German decision to risk war with the United States in 1917 rested in part on the (accurate) perception that the American economy was already underwriting the Entente's war effort; but the same decision sealed the eventual defeat of the Central Powers, for it led to the acceleration and expansion of the American commitment of financial, material, and human resources to the war against Germany. However skillful the organization and management of their military resources, the Germans could not, as Paul Kennedy has emphasized, contend with "this massive disadvantage in sheer economic muscle, and the considerable disadvantage in the size of total mobilized forces."[12]

The terrible costs of defying this disadvantage visited Germans in a multitude of guises during the four and a half years of the war. They also bequeathed a paralyzing legacy to the republican regime that emerged in the war's aftermath.[13] Indeed, the most fateful consequences of the Great War lay in the manner Germans dealt with its lingering costs – and its memory.

The political institutions of Imperial Germany collapsed in the fall of 1918, along with the army. Into this institutional chaos, which was compounded by the return of millions of veterans from the front, trod the German Social Democrats, who had hoped that the end of the war and the disappearance of authoritarianism would ease the way to democracy and social peace in Germany. From the instant when its representatives signed the armistice on 11 November 1918, however, the successor regime was saddled with the dreadful burdens of the war. The restoration of civic order was purchased eventually at the high price of civil war, during which the wartime schism in the German labor movement was

---

[12] Kennedy, *Rise and Fall of the Great Powers*, 273.
[13] For good introductions see Bessel, *Germany after the First World War*; Detlev J. K. Peukert, *The Weimar Republic: The Crisis of Classical Modernity* (New York, 1989); Hans Mommsen, *The Rise and Fall of Weimar Democracy* (Chapel Hill, NC, 1996).

sealed in blood and the permanent alienation of a significant part of the working class from the new republic. The Treaty of Versailles, the formal instrument of international peace, was thereupon communicated to the Germans. Beyond the territorial and financial tributes it imposed, it inflicted a crippling symbolic blow to the parliamentary republic, whose constitution was announced at virtually the same moment in the summer of 1919. The treaty married the republic with national humiliation; and it mocked the argument that the war had brought political benefits. It also discouraged sober analysis of Germany's defeat. Paradoxically, in leaving the foundations of German power largely intact, it kept alive nationalist visions of a Germany unvanquished militarily and still destined for dominance in Europe.

The treaty also marked out formally the dimensions of the war's material costs. The payment of these vast sums importuned the republic's agenda for the next fourteen years. The enormous domestic debt, which had accumulated during four years of public borrowing, evaporated amid the spectacular inflation of the early twenties. The systematic dilution of the currency with paper drove the logic of wartime finance to a grotesque climax; but it also brought the financial obliteration of much of the German middle class, whose savings had financed the war. The peace settlement set the Germans' international debt at $33 billion in reparations, a sum that putatively corresponded to the costs of war born by the victorious allies. The justice, wisdom, and feasibility of these payments remain to this day a subject of controversy. Reparations did nothing, in all events, to promote a stable German recovery from the war. They helped instead to pervert patterns of public and private investment in that land; and they encouraged German reliance on an international capital market that was itself distorted by the massive transfers of financial resources that political decisions had made necessary. The Great Depression, which paralyzed the German economy in 1929, was thus due in no small degree to the war, for the collapse of the international capital market in the wake of the Wall Street crash resulted immediately in the collapse of domestic investment in Germany.

The economic crises that punctuated the brief life of the first German republic were legacies of war. The conflicts that flourished in this climate of crisis were themselves long-standing features of life in Imperial Germany, which the privations and resentments of war had exacerbated – so much so that the war appeared at times not to have ended on the German home front in 1918. The war's outcome bred pervasive recriminations, in which few groups, however unfairly, were spared blame: workers and Catholics for their indifferent loyalties, farmers and businessmen for their greed, urban dwellers for their importunity, public officials for their incompetence. In these circumstances, the search for a durable political consensus – much less one in favor of the republic – was fatally impaired. In assigning Germany's former ethnic minorities to France, Denmark, and the new Polish state, the Versailles settlement did less to resolve this order of conflict than to translate it into an issue of bitter foreign-policy debate. The Weimar Constitution provided for a much more centralized state, but it did not put an end to regional conflict, which surfaced in a series of violent episode, like the Beer-Hall putsch in Munich, in which separatism played a leading role. Regional conflict also registered in continued strife between urban and rural Germany, which was aggravated in the worldwide collapse of agricultural prices. Confessional discord persisted, too, although its focus shifted to anxieties among Protestants and Catholics alike about the secular policies of the Social Democrats, who now held office at all levels of government. These Social Democratic policies were oriented in general towards an ambitious program of public welfare and peaceful resolution of industrial disputes. They failed to bring social peace, in part because social grievances had been gravely exacerbated, while their principal *locus* migrated during the war away from the main body of organized labor. It settled instead in the militant periphery of the labor movement, whose political voice, the German Communist party, had emerged out of the USPD. The grievances were also rife in those sectors of the German lower-middle classes that the war and the succeeding turmoil had most jeopardized. When the Depression then added mass unemployment to the litany of grief, it so swelled the ranks of those who were disaffected that one could more easily count those who were not disaffected.

The mobilization of discontent on the radical right was inconceivable absent the war. For one thing, Hitler himself and many of his lieutenants were veterans of the conflict; and their ideas found resonance among the multitudes of ex-warriors who, like many other categories of people, were casualties of economic crisis. National Socialism, the eclectic amalgam of these ideas, was vitally indebted to the war. In its very name, National Socialism recalled slogans that were current during the war. By way of the stab-in-the-back legend, it transformed the wartime discourse of the German right into a pernicious explanation of the postwar crisis, as well as an effective program of political action. It reduced the multiple dimensions of domestic conflict in Germany to a single, biological denominator, which it defined as a conspiracy of Jews and their allies, the "November criminals," who had subverted the war effort in order to seize power in the republican regime that followed. As antidotes, National Socialism promised to have done with this regime, to revitalize the "spirit of 1914," and to achieve the great goal of German hegemony on the

European continent, which had eluded the country's rulers during the war.

The reasons for the broad appeal of this vision, which in 1933 was inscribed into the program of a new dictatorial government, lie well beyond the scope of this essay. As an historical analysis of the German experience during Great War, however, the vision was a monument of perversity and intellectual folly. As it occluded the real reasons for Germany's defeat in one world war, it laid the foundations for another.

DDR-Geschichtswissenschaft," in Jürgen Rohwer (ed.), *Neue Forschungen zum Ersten Weltkrieg: Literaturberichte und Bibliographien von 30 Mitgliedstaaten der "Commission internationale d'histoire militaire comparée"* (Koblenz, 1985), 91–97. Two recent bibliographical articles provide an excellent overview of the newer literature: Michael Epkenhans, "Neuere Forschungen zur Geschichte des Ersten Weltkrieges," *Archiv für Sozialgeschichte* 38 (1998), 458–87; Christoph Nonn, "Oh what a Lovely War? German Common People and the First World War," *German History* 18 (2000), 97–111.

The richest, most comprehensive account of Germany in the First World War is still the three-volume survey edited under the direction of Fritz Klein, *Deutschland im Ersten Weltkrieg* (3 vols., East Berlin, 1968–69). The work displays both the strengths and weaknesses of German Marxist-Leninist scholarship. While it follows the military history of the war in detail, it emphasizes the economic and social dimensions of the conflict. Its principal theme, however, is the pre-history of the GDR, the emergence of the German Communist party out of radical opposition to a war undertaken in the interests of monopoly capitalism. The other general surveys tend to be much more narrowly riveted to military affairs and high politics. This proposition applies alike to Peter Graf Kielmansegg, *Deutschland und der Erste Weltkrieg* (Frankfurt am Main, 1968); Hans Herzfeld, *Der Erste Weltkrieg* (Munich, 1968); Karl Dietrich Erdmann, *Der erste Weltkrieg* (Munich, 1980); Günther Mai, *Das Ende des Kaiserreichs: Politik und Kriegführung im Ersten Weltkrieg* (Munich, 1987); and Holger Herwig, *The First World War: Germany and Austria-Hungary, 1914–1918* (London, 1997), which has the virtue of including the Habsburg monarchy in the account. Laurence V. Moyer, *Victory Must Be Ours: Germany in the Great War, 1914–1918* (New York, 1995), treats the homefront more centrally, but it lacks a conceptual framework robust enough to control the rich material that it collects. The essays in Wolfgang Michalka (ed.), *Der Erste Weltkrieg: Wirkung, Wahrnehmung, Analyse* (Munich and Zurich, 1994), contain a wealth of information on diverse phases of the conflict. The collected essays of Imanuel Geiss, *Das Deutsche Reich und der Erste Weltkrieg* (Munich and Zurich, 1985), provide a provocative and readable introduction to a number of the issues that dominated the historiography of the war in the 1960s and 1970s.

Important volumes have appeared in the last several years. The essays in Niall Ferguson's *The Pity of War: Explaining World War I* (New York, 1999) have assaulted much of the conventional thinking about the war, including the wisdom of British intervention. Many of the author's contentions have provoked a furious response, however, and the book should be read with care. The essays in the volume edited by Bruno Thoss and Hans-Erich Volkmann, *Erster Weltkrieg / Zweiter Weltkrieg*

(Paderborn, 2002), perform a great service in seeking to compare the two world wars of the last century. Wolfgang Mommsen has provided a concise and readable account in his contribution to the new Gebhardt series, *Die Urkatastrophe Deutschlands: Der Erste Weltkrieg 1914–1918* (Stuttgart, 2002), while the German case figures prominently in the essays assembled in Roger Chickering and Stig Foerster (eds.), *Great War, Total War: Combat and Mobilization on the Western Front, 1914–1918* (Cambridge, 2000). The *Enzyklopädie Erster Weltkrieg / Encyclopedia of the First World War* (Paderborn and Zurich, 2003), which Gerhard Hirschfeld, Gerd Krumeich, and Irina Renz have edited, promises to be a standard reference for a long time.

Introductions to new trends in the cultural history of World War I can be found in several other valuable collections of essays. They include Gerhard Hirschfeld et al. (eds.), *"Keiner fühlt sich hier mehr als Mensch . . ."*: *Erlebnis und Wirkung des Ersten Weltkrieges* (Frankfurt am Main, 1996); and Wolfgang Kruse (ed.), *Eine Welt von Feinden: Der Grosse Krieg 1914–1918* (Frankfurt am Main, 1997). Gerhard Hirschfeld et al. (eds.), *Kriegserfahrungen: Studien zur Sozial- und Mentalitätsgeschichte des Ersten Weltkriegs* (Essen, 1997), belongs in the same genre, and it contains a number of good local studies.

MILITARY AFFAIRS

Most of the surveys cited above offer reliable introductions to the military dimension of the war. The most complete examination of operations, logistics, and military planning for all theaters in which German **land forces** participated is the Reichsarchiv's exhaustive official history, *Der Weltkrieg 1914 bis 1918* (14 vols., Berlin, 1925–44). Analyses of tactics and the effort to find effective tactical reform can be found in Bruce Gudmundsson, *Stormtroop Tactics: Innovation in the German Army, 1914–1918* (New York, 1989); Hans Linnenkohl, *Vom Einzelschuss zur Feuerwalze: Der Wettlauf zwischen Technik und Taktik im Ersten Weltkrieg* (Koblenz, 1990); Timothy Lupfer, *The Dynamics of Doctrine: The Changes in German Tactical Doctrine during the First World War* (Fort Leavenworth, 1981); G. C. Wynne, *If Germany Attacks: The Battle in Depth in the West* (Westport, CT, 1976); and David Zabecki, *Steel Wind: Colonel Georg Bruchmüller and the Birth of Modern Artillery* (Westport, CT, 1994). For the action of German armies on the eastern front there is Norman Stone's *The Eastern Front, 1914–1917* (London, 1975), and Gunther E. Rothenberg, *The Army of Francis Joseph* (West Lafayette, IN, 1976). Lance Farrar provides a provocative multi-dimensional interpretation of the first phase of the war in *The Short-War Illusion: German Policy, Strategy, and Domestic*

Affairs, August–December 1914 (Santa Barbara and Oxford, 1973). For a narrower military analysis of the war's last phase in the west, see Rod Paschall, *The Defeat of Imperial Germany, 1917–1918* (Chapel Hill, NC, 1989); and Barrie Pitt, *1918: The Last Act* (New York, 1963).

There is a rich literature on **individual battles**, much of it in English. The best accounts are both readable and sensitive to historical context. Alistaire Horne, *The Price of Glory: Verdun 1916* (New York, 1962), and Dennis Showalter, *Tannenberg: Clash of Empires* (Hamden, CT, 1991), are models. Accessible histories of German action in other major battles include Sebastian Haffner and Wolfgang Venohr, *Das Wunder an der Marne: Rekonstruktion der Entscheidungsschlacht des Ersten Weltkrieges* (Bergisch Gladbach, 1982); Wolfgang Paul, *Entscheidung im September: Das Wunder an der Marne* (Esslingen, 1974); Robert B. Asprey, *The First Battle of the Marne* (New York, 1962); Karl Unruh, *Langemarck: Legende und Wirklichkeit* (Koblenz, 1986); German Werth, *Verdun: Die Schlacht und der Mythos* (Bergisch Gladbach, 1979); Bryan Cooper, *The Battle of Cambrai* (New York, 1968); and Gregory Blaxland, *Amiens: 1918* (London, 1968).

The **German Commanders** have suffered a mixed fate at the hands of their biographers. The most fortunate has been Erich von Falkenhayn, the subject of Holger Afflerbach's splendid scholarly biography, *Falkenhayn: Politisches Denken und Handeln im Kaiserreich* (Munich, 1996), which stands in a class by itself. The biographies of other leading German military figures tend to be shallow, although Annika Mombauer has now written a scholarly study of the man who led the German armies into battle in 1914: *Helmuth von Moltke and the Origins of the First World War* (Cambridge, 2001). The demise of the Weimar Republic has been the focus for much of the biographical interest in Hindenburg. The best studies of his wartime career are dated: John W. Wheeler-Bennett's *Hindenburg: The Wooden Titan* (London, 1936); and Walter Goerlitz, *Hindenburg: Ein Lebensbild* (Bonn, 1953). Others include the biography by the East German scholar, Wolfgang Ruge, *Hindenburg: Porträt eines Militaristen* (East Berlin, 1977); Rudolf Olden, *Hindenburg: Oder der Geist der preussischen Armee* (Hildesheim, 1982); and Werner Maser, *Hindenburg: Eine politische Biographie* (Rastatt, 1989). The absence of a scholarly biography of Ludendorff is lamentable, for this titan of the war was as interesting a figure as he was important. He, along with the younger Moltke, is the subject of a stimulating portrait in Correlli Barnett's *The Sword-Bearers: Supreme Command in the First World War* (Bloomington and London, 1963). Ludendorff is also the subject of several popular military biographies: D. J. Goodspeed, *Ludendorff: Genius of World War I* (Boston, 1966); Roger Parkinson, *Tormented Warrior: Ludendorff and the Supreme*

Command (London, 1978); and Wolfgang Venohr, *Ludendorff: Legende und Wirklichkeit* (Berlin, 1993), which serves the legend better than the reality. I myself have analyzed Ludendorff's retrospective efforts to make sense of the German defeat in "Sore Loser: Ludendorff's Total War," in Roger Chickering and Stig Foerster (eds.), *The Shadows of Total War: Europe, East Asia, and the United States, 1919–1939* (Cambridge, 2003), 151–78. Hindenburg and Ludendorff have been featured together in several popular studies: Trevor N. Dupuy, *The Military Lives of Hindenburg and Ludendorff of Imperial Germany* (New York, 1970); Robert B. Asprey, *The German High Command at War: Hindenburg and Ludendorff and the First World War* (London, 1991). On Groener there is the biography by his daughter, Dorothea Groener-Geyer, *General Groener, Soldat und Staatsmann* (Frankfurt am Main, 1954).

On the **German navy** in the First World War there is also a massive official history: *Der Krieg zur See 1914–1918* (23 vols., Berlin, 1920–66). A better place to start is Paul G. Halpern's fine study, *A Naval History of World War I* (Annapolis, 1994). Holger H. Herwig, *"Luxury" Fleet: The Imperial German Navy, 1888–1918* (London and Atlantic Highlands, NJ, 1987) is strong on technical details. On the Germans at Jutland, see V. E. Tarrant, *Jutland: The German Perspective: A New View of the Great Battle, 31 May 1916* (London, 1995). Problems of naval policy, particularly with respect to submarine warfare, are treated in Bernd Stegemann, *Die deutsche Marinepolitik 1916–1918* (Berlin, 1970). On the unrest in the navy in 1917, see Daniel Horn, *The German Naval Mutinies of World War I* (New Brunswick, NJ, 1969); and Wilhelm Deist, "Die Unruhen in der Marine 1917/18," in his *Militär, Staat und Gesellschaft: Studien zur preussisch-deutschen Militärgeschichte* (Munich, 1991), 153–64.

Events in the **air war** are traced in John H. Morrow, Jr., *German Air Power in World War I* (Lincoln, 1982); and Peter Kilduff, *Germany's First Air Force, 1914–1918* (London, 1991).

MOBILIZATION OF THE ECONOMY

The social and economic history of the Great War was the subject of the comprehensive, multinational studies that the Carnegie Endowment for International Peace sponsored in the 1920s. Many of the works that made up the German series are still indispensable. The volume by Otto Goebel, *Deutsche Rohstoffwirtschaft im Weltkrieg* (Stuttgart, Berlin, and Leipzig, 1930), deals with the administration of industrial raw materials and the Hindenburg Program. **Industrial mobilization**, particularly the links among state, economy, and military, has inspired several more recent analyses. The most balanced is Friedrich Zunkel, *Industrie*

und Staatssozialismus: Der Kampf um die Wirtschaftsordnung in Deutsch-
land 1914–1918 (Düsseldorf, 1974), while several East German studies emphasize the significance of this link as a factor in the crisis of
German capitalism: Alfred Schröter, *Krieg-Staat-Monopol 1914 bis 1918:*
Die Zusammenhänge von imperialistischer Kriegswirtschaft, Militarisierung
der Volkswirtschaft und staatsmonopolitischem Kapitalismus in Deutschland
während des ersten Weltkrieges (East Berlin, 1965); and Helmuth Weber,
Ludendorff und die Monopole: Deutsche Kriegspolitik (East Berlin, 1966).
Hermann Schäfer, *Regionale Wirtschaftspolitik in der Kriegswirtschaft:*
Staat, Industrie und Verbände während des Ersten Weltkrieges in Baden
(Stuttgart, 1983), provides an excellent guide to the bureaucratic maze
that mobilization spawned in the federal state of Baden, while Hans
Gotthard Ehlert, *Die wirtschaftliche Zentralbehörde des Deutschen Reiches*
1914 bis 1919: Das Problem der "Gemeinwirtschaft" in Krieg und Frieden
(Wiesbaden, 1982), presents a more general institutional map. On the
role of Walther Rathenau in industrial mobilization there are many
studies, among them: Lothar Burchhardt, "Walther Rathenau und die
Anfänge der deutschen Rohstoffbewirtschaftung im ersten Weltkrieg,"
Tradition: Zeitschrift für Firmengeschichte und Unternehmerbiographie 15
(1970), 169–96; Gerhard Hecker, *Walther Rathenau und sein Verhältnis zu*
Militär und Krieg (Boppard, 1983); David Graham Williamson, "Walther
Rathenau and the KRA, August 1914 – March 1915," *Zeitschrift für*
Unternehmensgeschichte 23 (1978), 118–36.

The problems of **agriculture and the food supply** were first analyzed thoroughly in two volumes of the Carnegie series: Friedrich
Aereboe, *Der Einfluss des Kriegs auf die landwirtschaftliche Produktion in*
Deutschland (Stuttgart, Berlin, and Leipzig, 1927); and August Skalweit,
Die deutsche Kriegsernährungswirtschaft (Stuttgart, Berlin, and Leipzig,
1927). Anne Roerkohl's exhaustive studies of the food supply are fundamental: *Hungerblockade und Heimatfront: Die kommunale Lebensmittelver-*
sorgung in Westfalen während des Ersten Weltkrieges (Stuttgart, 1991); and
"Die Lebensmittelversorgung während des Ersten Weltkrieges im Span-
nungsfeld kommunaler und staatlicher Massnahmen," in Hans-Jürgen
Teuteberg (ed.), *Durchbruch zum modernen Massenkonsum: Lebensmit-*
telmärkte und Lebensmittelqualität im Städtewachstum des Industriezeitalters
(Münster, 1987), 309–70. Armin Triebel examines food consumption
in "Variations in Patterns of Consumption in Germany in the Period
of the First World War," in Richard Wall and Jay Winter (eds.),
The Upheaval of War: Family, Work and Welfare in Europe, 1914–1918
(Cambridge, 1988), 159–96. George L. Yaney, *The World of the Manager:*
Food Administration in Berlin during World War I (New York, 1994),
analyzes the problem of food shortages in the light of the managerial

challenge. On the impact of the blockade on the German food supply, see C. Paul Vincent, *The Politics of Hunger: The Allied Blockade of Germany, 1915–1919* (Athens, OH, 1985); Marion C. Siney, *The Allied Blockade of Germany, 1914–1916* (Ann Arbor, MI, 1957); and the pertinent essays in Avner Offer, *The First World War: An Agrarian Interpretation* (Oxford, 1989). Several recent studies deal with the German peasantry during the war, although their emphasis falls on agrarian politics: Robert Moeller, *German Peasants and Agrarian Politics, 1914–1924: The Rhineland and Westphalia* (Chapel Hill, NC, 1986); Moeller, "Dimensions of Social Conflict in the Great War: The View from the German Countryside," *Central European History* 14 (1981), 142–68; Martin Schumacher, *Land und Politik: Eine Untersuchung über politische Parteien und agrarische Interessen 1914–1923* (Düsseldorf, 1978); Jens Flemming, *Landwirtschaftliche Interessen und Demokratie: Ländliche Gesellschaft, Agrarverbände und Staat 1890–1925* (Bonn, 1978).

Gerald Feldman's *Army, Industry and Labor in Germany, 1914–1918* (Princeton, 1966), remains the basic study of **labor relations** in Germany during the war. The older volume in the Carnegie series, Paul Umbreit and Charlotte Lorenz, *Der Krieg und die Arbeitsverhältnisse* (Stuttgart, Berlin, and Leipzig, 1928) contains a lot of information about trade unions (and women's labor), but it has now been largely superseded. Robert Armeson deals with the difficulties of labor recruitment in *Total Warfare and Compulsory Labor: A Study of the Military-Industrial Complex in Germany during World War I* (The Hague, 1964). Günter Mai has provided an important regional survey, *Kriegswirtschaft und Arbeiterbewegung in Württemberg 1914–1918* (Stuttgart, 1983), as well as a valuable anthology of essays: Günter Mai (ed.), *Arbeiterschaft in Deutschland 1914–1918: Studien zu Arbeitskampf und Arbeitsmarkt im Ersten Weltkrieg* (Düsseldorf, 1985).

Feldman has also now published the standard work on German **war finances and inflation**, *The Great Disorder: Politics, Economics, and Society in the German Inflation, 1914–1924* (New York and Oxford, 1993). It supersedes the older East German studies of this problem: Ruth Andexel, *Imperialismus, Staatsfinanzen, Rüstung, Krieg: Probleme der Rüstungsfinanzierung des deutschen Imperialismus* (East Berlin, 1968); and Kurt Gossweiler, *Grossbanken, Industriemonopole, Staat, Ökonomie und Politik des staatsmonopolischen Kapitalismus* (East Berlin, 1983). Manfred Zeidler provides an overview in "Die deutsche Kriegsfinanzierung 1914 bis 1918 und ihre Folgen," in Wolfgang Michalka (ed.), *Der Erste Weltkrieg: Wirkung, Wahrnehmung, Analyse* (Munich and Zurich, 1994), 415–33. Martin Geyer's cultural history of the inflation in postwar Munich contains an introductory section on the war: *Verkehrte Welt:*

Revolution, Inflation, und Moderne – München 1914–1924 (Göttingen, 1998).

SOCIAL HISTORY OF THE WAR

The Carnegie series offers important studies on several phases of the war's social history. The essays in the volume edited by F. Bumm, *Deutschlands Gesundheitsverhältnisse unter dem Einfluss des Weltkrieges* (Stuttgart, Berlin, and Leipzig, 1928), document the impact of malnutrition and other shortages on public health. Moritz Liepmann, *Krieg und Kriminalität in Deutschland* (Stuttgart, Berlin, and Leipzig, 1930) documents the erosion of the legal order, while the essays of Otto Baumgarten and his team of scholars, *Geistige und sittliche Wirkungen des Krieges in Deutschland* (Stuttgart, Berlin, and Leipzig, 1927), examine the breakdown of the moral order. The massive study overseen by Jay Winter and Robert Louis, *Capital Cities at War: Paris, London, Berlin 1914–1919* (Cambridge, 1997), stands in many respects as the heir of the Carnegie Studies, and it contains a wealth of information about the German capital.

Several broader studies trace the effect of war on the evolution of German **social policy**: Ludwig Preller, *Sozialpolitik in der Weimarer Republik* (Stuttgart, 1949), which contains an extended prologue on the war; Rolf Landwehr, "Funktionswandel der Fürsorge vom Ersten Weltkrieg bis zum Ende der Weimarer Republik," in Rolf Landwehr and Rüdiger Baron (eds.), *Geschichte der Sozialarbeit: Hauptlinien ihrer Entwicklung im 19. und 20. Jahrhundert* (Weinheim and Basel, 1983), 73–138; Christof Sachsse and Florian Tenstedt, *Geschichte der Armenfürsorge in Deutschland* (2 vols., Stuttgart, 1988); and Christof Sachsse, *Mütterlichkeit als Beruf: Sozialarbeit, Sozialreform und Frauenbewegung, 1871–1929* (Frankfurt, 1986). Robert Weldon Whalen's fascinating study, *Bitter Wounds: German Victims of the Great War, 1914–1939* (Ithaca, 1984), treats, among other things, efforts to provide public assistance to injured soldiers during the war; so does Ewald Frie, "Vorbild oder Spiegelbild? Kriegsbeschädigtenfürsorge in Deutschland 1914–1919," in Wolfgang Michalka (ed.), *Der Erste Weltkrieg: Wirkung, Wahrnehmung, Analyse* (Munich and Zurich, 1994), 563–80. Deborah Cohen's book analyzes the mobilization of injured veterans after the war, but it contains useful information about developments during the war: *The War Come Home: Disabled Veterans in Britain and Germany, 1914–1939* (Berkeley and Los Angeles, 2001). Although it, too, is concerned primarily with the war's aftermath, Richard Bessel's *Germany after the First World War* (Oxford, 1993), offers a compact survey of the war's social history.

The **front experience** has been the subject of a large literature, but the German counterpart of Paul Fussell's intriguing essay on the English case, *The Great War and Modern Memory* (London, 1975), remains to be written. Like Whalen's *Bitter Wounds*, Erich Leed's offering in this genre, *No Man's Land: Combat and Identity in World War I* (Cambridge and New York, 1979), adduces material from the German trenches. In his *Der grosse Krieg der Sprachen: Untersuchungen zur historischen Semantik in Deutschland und England zur Zeit des Ersten Weltkriegs* (Essen, 2000), Aribert Reimann has sought to link several dimensions of the war by means of the metaphors that organized experience on the battlefront and the homefronts in Germany and England. Although his goals are more modest, Benjamin Ziemann has documented convincingly the complexity of the forces that bound the home front and fighting front: *Front und Heimat: Ländliche Kriegserfahrungen im südlichen Bayern 1914–1923* (Essen, 1997). The confusion and panic of the battlefield are documented in a gripping analysis by John Horne and Alan Kramer of German actions in Belgium and northern France during the first weeks of the war, *German Atrocities, 1914: A History of Denial* (New Haven and London, 2001). Paul Lerner's superb study of war neurosis, *Hysterical Men: War, Psychiatry, and the Politics of Trauma in Germany, 1890–1930* (Ithaca, 2003), illuminates another problematic dimension of the battlefield experience.

The attention of German scholars has turned recently, with excellent results, to trench newspapers and the *Feldpostbrief* as source material. In addition to the work of Reimann and Ziemann, see Bernd Ulrich, "Feldpostbriefe im Ersten Weltkrieg – Bedeutung und Zensur," in Peter Knoch (ed.), *Kriegsalltag: Die Rekonstruktion des Kriegsalltags als Aufgabe der historischen Forschung und der Friedenserziehung* (Stuttgart, 1989), 40–83; Ulrich, "Feldpostbriefe des Ersten Weltkrieges – Möglichkeiten und Grenzen einer alltagsgeschichtlichen Quelle," *Militärgeschichtliche Mitteilungen* 53 (1994), 73–84; and Anne Lipp, "Friedenssehnsucht und Duchhaltebereitschaft: Wahrnehmungen und Erfahrungen deutscher Soldaten im Ersten Weltkrieg," *Archiv für Sozialgeschichte* 36 (1996), 279–92. Bernd Ulrich and Benjamin Ziemann (eds.), *Frontalltag im Ersten Weltkrieg: Wahn und Wirklichkeit* (Frankfurt am Main, 1994), contains documents of everyday life in the frontlines. The deterioration of morale among the troops is analyzed in Wilhelm Deist, "Der militärische Zusammenbruch des Kaiserreichs: Zur Realität der 'Dolchstosslegende,'" in Deist, *Militär, Staat und Gesellschaft: Studien zur preussisch-deutschen Militärgeschichte* (Munich, 1991), 211–34; Deist, "Verdeckter Militärstreik im Kriegsjahr 1918?" in Wolfram Wette (ed.), *Der Krieg des kleinen Mannes: Eine Militärgeschichte von unten* (Munich and Zurich, 1992), 146–67; Wolfgang Kruse, "Krieg und Klassenheer: Zur Revolutionierung der deutschen Armee im Ersten Weltkrieg," *Geschichte und Gesellschaft* 22 (1996), 530–61; Benjamin Ziemann, "Fahnenflucht im deutschen Heer 1914–1918," *Militärgeschichtliche Mitteilungen* 55

(1996), 93–130; and Christoph Jahr, *Gewöhnliche Soldaten: Desertion und Deserteure im deutschen und britischen Heer 1914–1918* (Göttingen, 1998).

Much of the East German scholarship has focused on the experience of **class** in war, particularly among industrial workers. Jürgen Kocka's book, *Klassengesellschaft im Krieg. Deutsche Sozialgeschichte 1914–1918* (Göttingen, 1973) (translated into English as *Facing Total War: German Society, 1914–1918* [Cambridge, MA, 1984]), has defined the basic issues that have dominated these discussions outside Marxist-Leninist circles. Additional material can be found in the essays by Rudolf Meerwarth, Adolf Günther, and Waldemar Zimmermann in *Die Einwirkung des Krieges auf Bevölkerungsbewegung, Einkommen und Lebenshaltung in Deutschland* (Stuttgart, Berlin, and Leipzig, 1932), which appeared in the Carnegie series.

A number of studies have examined the impact of the war on **women and gender relations**. The older ones tended to evaluate the experience on women positively, as the prelude to political emancipation: Ursula von Gersdorff, *Frauen im Kriegsdienst 1914–1945* (Stuttgart, 1969); and Stefan Baujohr, *Die Hälfte der Fabrik: Geschichte der Frauenarbeit in Deutschland 1914–1945* (Marburg, 1979). More recent work, especially that of Ute Daniel, has thrown doubt on this view and introduced more nuance into the study of gender (and class) relations in war: Ute Daniel, *Arbeiterfrauen in der Kriegsgesellschaft: Beruf, Familie und Politik im Ersten Weltkrieg* (Göttingen, 1989). This book is now available in English as *The War from Within: German Working-Class Women in the First World War* (New York and Oxford, 1997); so is a précis, "Women's Work in Industry and Family: Germany, 1914–1918," in Richard Wall and Jay Winter (eds.), *The Upheaval of War: Family, Work and Welfare in Europe, 1914–1918* (Cambridge, 1988), 267–96. The plight of soldiers' wives in this war (and the next) is the theme of Birthe Kundrus, *Kriegerfrauen, Familienpolitik und Geschlechterverhältnisse im Ersten und Zweiten Weltkrieg* (Hamburg, 1995). The work of Lutz Sauerteig has illuminated the problems of venereal disease. In addition to his book, *Krankheit, Sexualität, Gesellschaft: Geschlechtskrankheiten und Gesundheitspolitik in Deutschland im 19. und frühen 20. Jahrhundert* (Stuttgart, 1999), he has presented his findings about the war in English, as "Sex, Medicine and Morality during the First World War," in Roger Cooter et al. (eds.), *War, Medicine and Modernity* (Phoenix Mill, 1998), 167–88. The complex connection between gender and political activism is explored in Belinda J. Davis, *Home Fires Burning: Food, Politics, and Everyday Life in World War I Berlin* (Chapel Hill, NC, 2000). Karen Hagemann, who has written extensively on the subject of war and gender relations, has joined Stefanie Schüler-Springorum in editing a valuable series of essays that deal centrally with the First World War:

Home/Front: The Military, War, and Gender in Twentieth-Century Germany (New York and Oxford, 2002). A classic on the subject of gender relations remains Magnus Hirschfeld et al., *The Sexual History of the World War* (New York, 1934).

For the effects of the war on Germany's **youth**, the Carnegie studies still offer the principal resource. The pertinent material is to be found in the essay of Wilhelm Flitner, "Der Krieg und die Jugend" in the volume of Otto Baumgarten, *Geistige und sittliche Wirkungen des Krieges in Deutschland* (Stuttgart, Berlin, and Leipzig, 1927). Edward Ross Dickinson, *The Politics of German Child Welfare from the Empire to the Federal Republic* (Cambridge, MA, 1996), examines the evolution of this phase of social policy during the war. See also the pertinent chapter in Robert Wohl's stimulating study, *The Generation of 1914* (Cambridge, 1979).

CULTURAL THEMES

Many authors have analyzed the impact of war on **the arts**. Wolfgang Mommsen's massive history of Imperial Germany contains a lucid survey: *Bürgerstolz und Weltmachtstreben 1890–1918* (Berlin, 1995), 828–92. An English summary is available in Mommsen, "German Artists, Writers and Intellectuals and the Meaning of War, 1914–1918," in John Horne (ed.), *State, Society and Mobilization in Europe during the First World War* (Cambridge, 1997), 21–38. Several other essays provide introductions to this theme: Eckart Koester, *Literatur und Weltkriegsideologie: Positionen und Begründungszusammenhänge des publizistischen Engagements deutscher Schriftsteller im Ersten Weltkrieg* (Kronberg, 1977); Helmut Fries, "Deutsche Schriftsteller im Ersten Weltkrieg," in Wolfgang Michalka (ed.), *Der Erste Weltkrieg: Wirkung, Wahrnehmung, Analyse* (Munich and Zurich, 1994), 825–48; Scott D. Denham, *Visions of War: Ideologies and Images of War in German Literature before and after the Great War* (Berne, 1992); Martin Patrick Anthony Travers, *German Novels on the First World War and the Ideological Implications, 1918–1933* (Stuttgart, 1982); Hermann Korte, *Der Krieg in der Lyrik des Expressionismus: Studien zur Evolution eines literarischen Themas* (Bonn, 1981). Peter Jelavich's essay on German culture during the war appears in an impressive comparative volume edited by Aviel Roshwald and Richard Stites, *European Culture in the Great War: The Arts, Entertainment, and Propaganda, 1914–1918* (Cambridge, 1999). Klaus Vondung has argued for the importance of apocalyptic motifs in cultural representations of the war: *Die Apokalypse in Deutschland* (Munich, 1988); and Vondung (ed.), *Kriegserlebnis: Der Erste Weltkrieg in der literarischen Gestaltung und symbolischen Deutung der Nationen* (Göttingen, 1980). Wolfgang Natter's volume, *Literature at War,*

1914–1940: Representing the "Time of Greatness" in Germany (New Haven and London, 1999), investigates the massive institutional influences that shaped the German literary depiction of the war. Modris Eiksteins offers a provocative analysis of the war's cultural significance, in which Germany stands as a paradigmatic instance of "modernism": *Rites of Spring: The Great War and the Birth of the Modern Age* (Boston, 1989). On the role of motion pictures in the war, see Klaus Kremeier's study of UFA, which is now available in translation: *The Ufa Story: A History of Germany's Greatest Film Company, 1918–1945* (New York, 1996).

Several important studies, including Mommsen's survey, have investigated the way the war affected German **scholarship** and the men who presided over it. Klaus Schwabe has emphasized the aggressive political views of the German professoriate in *Wissenschaft und Kriegsmoral: Die deutschen Hochschullehrer und die politischen Grundfragen des Ersten Weltkrieges* (Göttingen, 1969). Sven Papcke surveys the views of scholars in several disciplines in "Dienst am Sieg: Die Sozialwissenschaften im Ersten Weltkrieg," in *Vernunft und Chaos: Essays zur sozialen Ideengeschichte* (Frankfurt am Main, 1985). Kurt Flasch's volume concentrates on the reactions of German philosophers to the war: *Die geistige Mobilmachung: Die deutschen Intellektuellen und der Erste Weltkrieg* (Berlin, 2000). Steffen Bruendel has recently examined more broadly the debates among German scholars over war aims and domestic reform in his *Volksgemeinschaft oder Volksstaat: Die "Ideen von 1914" und die Neuordnung Deutschlands im Ersten Weltkrieg* (Berlin, 2003). Two substantial works address a notorious episode in which scholars invoked their authority on behalf of German policy: Jürgen Ungern-Sternberg von Pürkel and Wolfgang von Ungern-Sternberg, *Der Aufruf an die Kulturwelt: Das Manifest der 93 und die Anfänge der Kriegspropaganda im Ersten Weltkrieg* (Stuttgart, 1996); Bernhard vom Brocke, " 'Wissenschaft und Militarismus': Der Aufruf der 93 'An die Kulturwelt!' und der Zusammenbruch der internationalen Gelehrtenrepublik im Ersten Weltkrieg," in W. M. Calder, III, et al. (eds.), *Wilamowitz nach 50 Jahren* (Darmstadt, 1985), 649–719.

The history of the German **churches and confessional relations** can still draw from the essays by Arnold Rademacher on the Catholic church and by Erich Foerster on the Protestant churches in the volume edited by Otto Baumgarten, *Geistige und sittliche Wirkungen des Krieges in Deutschland* (Stuttgart, Berlin, and Leipzig, 1927). More recent studies of German Catholicism include Heinz Hürten, "Die katholische Kirche im Ersten Weltkrieg," in Wolfgang Michalka (ed.), *Der Erste Weltkrieg: Wirkung, Wahrnehmung, Analyse* (Munich and Zurich, 1994), 725–35; Richard van Dülmen, "Der deutsche Katholizismus und der Erste Weltkrieg," *Francia* 2 (1974), 347–76; Heinrich Lutz, *Demokratie im*

Zwielicht: Der Weg der deutschen Katholiken aus dem Kaiserreich in die Republik 1914–1925 (Munich, 1963); and Heinrich Missalla, *"Gott mit uns": Die deutsche katholische Kriegspredigt 1914–1918* (Munich, 1968). On the Protestant churches, see Kurt Meier, "Evangelische Kirche und Erster Weltkrieg," in Wolfgang Michalka (ed.), *Der Erste Weltkrieg: Wirkung, Wahrnehmung, Analyse* (Munich and Zurich, 1994), 691–724; Karl Hammer, "Der deutsche Protestantismus und der Erste Weltkrieg," *Francia* 2 (1974), 398–414; Günter Brakelmann, *Protestantische Kriegstheologie im Ersten Weltkrieg: Reinhold Seeberg als Theologe des deutschen Imperialismus* (Bielefeld, 1974); Wilhelm Pressel, *Die Kriegspredigt 1914–1918 in der evangelischen Kirche Deutschlands* (Göttingen, 1967). On Germany's Jews during the war, see Christard Hoffmann, "Between Integration and Rejection: The Jewish Community in Germany, 1914–1918," in John Horne (ed.), *State, Society and Mobilization in Europe during the First World War* (Cambridge, 1997), 89–104; Christian Picht, "Zwischen Vaterland und Volk: Das deutsche Judentum im Ersten Weltkrieg," in Wolfgang Michalka (ed.), *Der Erste Weltkrieg: Wirkung, Wahrnehmung, Analyse* (Munich and Zurich, 1994), 736–55; Werner E. Mosse (ed.), *Deutsches Judentum in Krieg und Revolution 1914–1923* (Tübingen, 1971); and Egmont Zechlin, *Die deutsche Politik und die Juden im Ersten Weltkrieg* (Göttingen, 1969). Much of this work has now been superseded by Ulrich Sieg, *Jüdische Intellektuelle im Ersten Weltkrieg: Kriegserfahrungen, weltanschauliche Debatten und kulturelle Neuentwürfe* (Berlin, 2001), whose scope is broader than the title implies.

WAR AIMS AND INTERNATIONAL RELATIONS

This aspect of the war has inspired almost as much interest as the military dimension. David Stevenson's masterful survey, *The First World War and International Politics* (Oxford, 1988), provides an introduction to the **diplomacy of the war**. The older work by Arno Mayer, *Wilson vs. Lenin: The Political Origins of the New Diplomacy, 1917–1918* (New Haven, 1959), offers a provocative conceptual framework, while John W. Wheeler-Bennett's *Brest-Litovsk: The Forgotten Peace, March 1918* (London, 1938) remains the best introduction to this topic. See also Werner Hahlweg (ed.), *Der Friede von Brest-Litovsk: Ein unveröffentlichter Band aus dem Werk des Untersuchungsausschusses der Deutschen Verfassunggebenden Nationalversammlung und des Deutschen Reichstages* (Düsseldorf, 1971).

Germany's relations with its **allies** (or erstwhile allies) are treated in Gary W. Shanafelt, *The Secret Enemy: Austria-Hungary and the German Alliance, 1914–1918* (New York, 1985); Ulrich Trumpener, *Germany* *and the Ottoman Empire, 1914–1918* (Princeton, 1968); Frank G. Weber, *Eagles on the Crescent: Germany, Austria-Hungary, and the Turkish Alliance, 1914–1918* (Ithaca, 1970); Wolfgang-Uwe Friedrich, *Bulgarien und die Mächte 1913–1915: Ein Beitrag zur Weltkriegs- und Imperialismusgeschichte* (Stuttgart, 1985); and Alberto Monticone, *Deutschland und die Neutralität Italiens 1914–1915* (Wiesbaden, 1982).

The question of **German war aims** has dominated the literature on wartime foreign policy, particularly after Fritz Fischer's provocation in *Griff nach der Weltmacht: Die Kriegszielpolitik des kaiserlichen Deutschland 1914–1918* (Düsseldorf, 1961) (translated into English as *Germany's Aims in the First World War* [New York, 1967]). On the controversy, see John A. Moses, *The Politics of Illusion: The Fischer Controversy in German Historiography* (New York, 1975). The collection of essays edited by Ernst W. Graf von Lynar, *Deutsche Kriegsziele 1914–1918* (Darmstadt, 1964), provides an introduction to the major issues originally at stake. Several older studies are still relevant to the debate: Hans Gatzke, *Germany's Drive to the West (Drang nach Westen): A Study of Germany's Western War Aims during the First World War* (Baltimore, 1950); Henry Cord Meyer, *Mitteleuropa in German Thought and Action, 1815–1945* (The Hague, 1955). In the wake of Fischer's book, a number of dissertations and other studies appeared – some by Fischer's students – on the planning and execution of German war aims. Prominent among these are: Imanuel Geiss, *Der polnische Grenzstreifen 1914–1918: Ein Beitrag zur deutschen Kriegszielpolitik im Ersten Weltkrieg* (Lübeck and Hamburg, 1960); Peter Borowsky, *Deutsche Ukrainepolitik 1918: Unter besonderer Berücksichtigung der Wirtschaftsfragen* (Lübeck and Hamburg, 1970); Karl-Heinz Janssen, *Macht und Verblendung: Kriegszielpolitik der deutschen Bundesstaaten 1914/18* (Göttingen, 1963); Hans-Erich Volkmann, *Die deutsche Baltikumpolitik zwischen Brest-Litovsk und Compiègne: Ein Beitrag zur "Kriegszieldiskussion"* (Cologne, 1970); Winfried Baumgart, *Deutsche Ostpolitik 1918: Von Brest-Litovsk bis zum Ende des Ersten Weltkrieges* (Vienna and Munich, 1966); and Oleh S. Fedyshyn, *Germany's Drive to the East and the Ukrainian Revolution, 1917–1918* (New Brunswick, NJ, 1971). On the peripheries of German war aims, see Martin Kröger, "Revolution als Programm: Ziele und Realität deutscher Orientpolitik im Ersten Weltkrieg," in Wolfgang Michalka (ed.), *Der Erste Weltkrieg: Wirkung, Wahrnehmung, Analyse* (Munich and Zurich, 1994), 366–91, and Thomas Hughes, "The German Mission to Afghanistan 1915–1916," *German Studies Review* 25 (2002), 447–76.

The effort to parry the charges of Fischer and other critics has focused on German efforts to secure a **negotiated peace** with one or more of the Entente powers. In a series of massive documentary collections, disciples of Gerhard Ritter have argued the case that these efforts were genuine: Wolfgang Steglich (ed.), *Die Friedenspolitik der Mittelmächte 1917/18* (Stuttgart, 1964); Steglich (ed.), *Die Friedensversuche der kriegführenden Mächte im Sommer und Herbst 1917* (Stuttgart, 1984); Steglich (ed.), *Der Friedensappell Papst Benedikts XV vom 1. August 1917 und die Mittelmächte* (Stuttgart, 1970); and Wilhelm Ernst Winterhager (ed.), *Mission für den Frieden: Europäische Mächtepolitik und dänische Friedensvermittlung im Ersten Weltkrieg, vom August 1914 bis zum italienischen Kriegseintritt Mai 1915* (Stuttgart, 1984). More critical is the documentary collection of André Scherer and Jacques Grunewald (eds.), *L'Allemagne et les problèmes de la paix pendant la première guerre mondiale: Documents extraits des archives de l'Office allemand des affaires étrangères* (3 vols., Paris, 1966–76). See also K. E. Birnbaum, *Peace Moves and U-Boat Warfare: A Study of Imperial Germany's Policy towards the United States, April 18, 1916 – January 9, 1917* (Uppsala, 1958); L. L. Farrar, *Divide and Conquer: German Efforts to Conclude a Separate Peace, 1914–1918* (New York, 1978).

Questions of foreign policy and war aims are difficult to disentangle from the history of **German-occupied Europe**. The older study of Ludwig von Köhler in the Carnegie series analyzes the administration of Belgium: *Die Staatsverwaltung der besetzten Gebiete: Belgien* (Stuttgart, Berlin, and Leipzig, 1927). Frank Wende, *Die belgische Frage in der deutschen Politik des Ersten Weltkrieges* (Hamburg, 1969), looks as well at debates over the issue in Germany, while Brigitte Hattke, *Hugo Stinnes und die drei deutsch-belgischen Gesellschaften von 1916* (Stuttgart, 1990), examines the modes of economic exploitation. On German policy in Poland and the Baltic lands, there is a large literature. An excellent place to start is the fascinating study by Vejas Liulevicius, *War Land on the Eastern Front; Culture, National Identity and German Occupation in World War I* (Cambridge, 2000). See also, in addition to Geiss' study on the "border strip": Werner Basler, *Deutsche Annexionspolitik in Polen und im Baltikum 1914–1918* (East Berlin, 1962); Martin Broszat, *Zweihundert Jahre deutsche Polenpolitik* (Munich, 1963); Werner Conze, *Polnische Nation und deutsche Politik im ersten Weltkrieg* (Graz and Cologne, 1958); and the chapters in Egmont Zechlin's book, *Die deutsche Politik und die Juden im Ersten Weltkrieg* (Göttingen, 1969), that deal with German policy towards the eastern European Jews.

The body of scholarship on the middle-class German **peace movement** during the war is much less extensive. It features Karl Holl's edition of Ludwig Quidde's memoir, *Der deutsche Pazifismus während des Weltkrieges 1914–1918* (Boppard, 1979); Wilfried Eisenbeiss, *Die bürgerliche Friedensbewegung in Deutschland während des Ersten Weltkrieges: Organisation, Selbstverständnis und politische Praxis 1913/14–1919*

(Frankfurt am Main, 1980); and James Shand, "Doves among the Eagles: German Pacifists and Their Government during World War I," *Journal of Contemporary History* 10 (1975), 95–108. F. L. Carsten incorporates the pacifists' efforts into a much broader narrative context in *War against War: British and German Radical Movements in the First World War* (Berkeley and Los Angeles, 1982).

DOMESTIC POLITICS

The polarization of German politics during the war has also received considerable attention. The starting point is the so-called "**spirit of 1914**," the mood of elation that allegedly gripped Germans of all stations at the beginning of the war. This phenomenon has inspired a large literature in the last several years. The pioneer was Jeffrey Verhey, whose dissertation has now been published in English as *The Spirit of 1914: Militarism, Myth and Mobilization in Germany* (Cambridge, 2000). Other important contributions to this discussion include Thomas Raithel, *Das "Wunder" der inneren Einheit: Studien zur deutschen und französischen Öffentlichkeit bei Beginn des Ersten Weltkrieges* (Bonn, 1996), which ventures a comparison with the popular mood in France; and the case-study by Christian Geinitz, *Kriegsfurcht und Kampfbereitschaft: Das Augusterlebnis in Freiburg: Eine Studie zum Kriegsbeginn 1914* (Essen, 1998). A good survey of the problem is in Wolfgang Kruse, "Die Kriegsbegeisterung im Deutschen Reich zu Beginn des Ersten Weltkrieges: Entstehungszusammenhänge, Grenzen und ideologische Strukturen," in Marcel van der Linden and Gottfried Mergner (eds.), *Kriegsbegeisterung und mentale Kriegsvorbereitung: Interdisziplinäre Studien* (Berlin, 1991), 73–87.

The breakdown of the consensus in favor of the war has attracted the attention of Marxist scholars, who have analyzed it in anticipation of the revolution that followed the end of the war. The classic statement of this view is Arthur Rosenberg, *The Birth of the German Republic* (London, 1931). Western scholars have preferred to speak of a collapse of legitimacy. See, for example, Klaus-Peter Müller, *Politik und Gesellschaft im Krieg: Der Legitimätsverlust des badischen Staates 1914–1918* (Stuttgart, 1988). Matthew Stibbe, *German Anglophobia and the Great War, 1914–1918* (Cambridge, 2001), treats efforts to avert this process and to turn the counter-symbol of Great Britain into the basis of popular unity in favor of the war. However, the recent study by Sven Oliver Müller, *Die Nation als Waffe und Vorstellung: Nationalismus in Deutschland und Grossbritannien im Ersten Weltkrieg* (Göttingen, 2002), emphasizes the limits of nationalism as an ideology of integration in both Germany and Britain.

On the **constitutional and administrative aspects** of German domestic politics, one begins with the work of Wilhelm Deist, whose *Militär und Innenpolitik im Weltkrieg 1914–1918* (2 vols., Düsseldorf, 1970) documents the activities of the Deputy Commanding Generals. A masterful analysis of the problem precedes the documents, and it has been reprinted, along with a number of Deist's other major essays on the war, as "Voraussetzungen innenpolitischen Handelns des Militärs im Ersten Weltkrieg," in *Militär, Staat und Gesellschaft: Studien zur preussisch-deutschen Militärgeschichte* (Munich, 1991), 103–52. On the broader problem of civil–military relations during the war, the classic study is Gerhard Ritter's *Staatskunst und Kriegshandwerk: Das Problem des "Militarismus" in Deutschland* (4 vols., Munich, 1954–68) (translated into English as *Sword and Scepter: The Problem of Militarism in Germany* [3 vols., Coral Gables, FL, 1969–73]). Karl-Heinz Janssen studies civil–military relations through two key figures in the confrontation: *Der Kanzler und der General: Die Führungskrise um Bethmann Hollweg und Falkenhayn (1914–1916)* (Göttingen, 1967). Martin Kitchen examines the last two years of the war in *The Silent Dictatorship: The Politics of the German High Command under Hindenburg and Ludendorff, 1916–18* (New York, 1976), as does Dirk Stegmann, "Die deutsche Inlandspropaganda 1917/18: Zum innenpolitischen Machtkampf zwischen OHL und ziviler Reichsleitung in der Endphase des Kaiserreiches," *Militärgeschichtliche Mitteilungen* No. 2 (1972), 75–116. Several works examine the problem of **censorship and the press**. The recent study by David Welch, *Germany, Propaganda and Total War, 1914–1918. The Sins of Omission* (New Brunswick, 2000), offers a good guide to the pertinent literature, but it contains many errors and should be read with care; Heinz-Dietrich Fischer (ed.), *Pressekonzentration und Zensurpraxis im Ersten Weltkrieg: Texte und Quellen* (Berlin, 1973); Kurt Koszyk, *Deutsche Pressepolitik im Ersten Weltkrieg* (Düsseldorf, 1968); Wilhelm Deist, "Zensur und Propaganda in Deutschland während des Ersten Weltkrieges," in Deist, *Militär, Staat und Gesellschaft: Studien zur preussisch-deutschen Militärgeschichte* (Munich, 1991), 153–64; Wolfgang J. Mommsen, "Die Regierung Bethmann Hollweg und die öffentliche Meinung 1914–1917," *Vierteljahrshefte für Zeitgeschichte* 17 (1969), 117–55; and Gary Stark, "All Quiet on the Home Front: Popular Entertainments, Censorship and Civilian Morale in Germany, 1914–1918," in Frans Coetzee and Marilyn Shevin-Coetzee (eds.), *Authority, Identity and the Social History of the Great War* (Providence, RI, and Oxford, 1995), 57–80. Karl Lange, *Marneschlacht und deutsche Öffentlichkeit 1914–1939: Eine verdrängte Niederlage und ihre Folgen* (Düsseldorf, 1974), deals with the management of the press in a single notable incident.

A number of leading German political figures have been the subjects of **biographies**. The search for the "real" Bethmann Hollweg has spawned a small industry, to which Klaus Hildebrand, *Bethmann Hollweg – Der Kanzler ohne Eigenschaften? Urteile der Geschichtsschreibung* (Düsseldorf, 1970), offers preliminary guidance. The chancellor's biographies include Eberhard von Vietsch, *Bethmann Hollweg: Staatsmann zwischen Macht und Ethos* (Boppard, 1969); Willibald Gutsche, *Aufstieg und Fall eines kaiserlichen Reichskanzlers: Theobald von Bethmann Hollweg 1850–1921: Ein politisches Lebensbild* (East Berlin, 1971); Konrad H. Jarausch, *The Enigmatic Chancellor: Bethmann Hollweg and the Hubris of Imperial Germany* (New Haven and London, 1973); Günter Wollstein, *Theobald von Bethmann Hollweg: Letzter Erbe Bismarcks, Erstes Opfer der Dolchstosslegende* (Göttingen and Cologne, 1990). Jost Dülffer has brought out a critical edition of Bethmann Hollweg's *Betrachtungen zum Weltkriege* (Essen, 1989). The Kaiser, too, has recently attracted the renewed interest of the biographers. John Röhl's massive biographical enterprise is eventually to reach the war. Other authors already have: Willibald Gutsche, *Wilhelm II: Der letzte Kaiser des Deutschen Reiches* (Berlin, 1991); Lamar Cecil, *William II: Emperor and Exile, 1900–1941* (Chapel Hill, NC, 1996). Christopher Clark, *Kaiser Wilhelm II* (Essex, 2000), 225–45, provides an excellent introduction. On Erzberger, the best book remains Klaus Epstein, *Matthias Erzberger and the Dilemma of German Democracy* (Princeton, 1959); but see also Wolfgang Ruge, *Matthias Erzberger: Eine politische Biographie* (East Berlin, 1976). John Williamson provides a good study of the Treasury Secretary, *Karl Helfferich, 1872–1924: Economist, Financier, Politician* (Princeton, 1971).

On the major **political parties and pressure groups** there are a number of standard works, including Rudolf Morsey, *Die deutsche Zentrumspartei 1917 bis 1923* (Düsseldorf, 1966); Hartwig Thieme, *Nationaler Liberalismus in der Krise: Die nationalliberale Fraktion des preussischen Abgeordnetenhauses 1914–1918* (Boppard, 1968). On the ambivalence of the major parties towards democratic institutions, see Reinhard Patemann, *Der Kampf um die preussische Wahlreform im Ersten Weltkrieg* (Düsseldorf, 1964); Dieter Grosser, *Vom monarchischen Konstitutionalismus zur parlamentarisichen Demokratie: Die Verfassungspolitik der deutschen Parteien im letzten Jahrzehnt des Kaiserreiches* (The Hague, 1970); Marcus Wanque, *Demokratisches Denken im Krieg: Die deutsche Debatte im Ersten Weltkrieg* (Berlin, 2000); Torsten Oppeland, *Reichstag und Aussenpolitik im Ersten Weltkrieg: Die deutschen Parteien und die Politik der USA 1914–1918* (Düsseldorf, 1995), has recently charted this ambivalence through the lens of attitudes towards the United States. The halting emergence of a durable coalition among the parties on the left is the subject of several works: Rudolf Morsey (ed.), *Der Interfraktionelle Ausschuss 1917/18* (Düsseldorf, 1959); Udo Bermbach, *Vorformen parlamentarischer Kabinettsbildung in Deutschland: Der Interfraktionelle Ausschuss und die Parlamentarisierung der Reichsregierung* (Cologne and Opladen, 1967); Reinhard Schiffers, *Der Hauptausschuss des Deutschen Reichstags, 1915–1918: Formen und Bereiche der Kooperation zwischen Parlament und Regierung* (Düsseldorf, 1979). Manfred Rauh's *Die Parlamentarisierung des Deutschen Reiches* (Düsseldorf, 1977) offers an optimistic analysis of these parliamentary trends. On the Fatherland Party see Heinz Hagenlücke, *Deutsche Vaterlandspartei: Die nationale Rechte am Ende des Kaiserreiches* (Düsseldorf, 1997); Raffael Scheck, *Alfred von Tirpitz and German Right-Wing Politics, 1914–1930* (Atlantic Highlands, NJ, 1997), offers a view of the restless politics of the German right during the war.

The political history of the **labor movement** has also been the subject of numerous works, many of which deal principally with the revolution at the end of the war. The foremost study of the Social Democratic party during the war is Susanne Miller, *Burgfrieden und Klassenkampf: Die deutsche Sozialdemokratie im Ersten Weltkrieg* (Düsseldorf, 1974). Wolfgang Kruse, *Krieg und nationale Integration: Eine Neuinterpretation des sozialdemokratischen Burgfriedensschlusses 1914/15* (Essen, 1993), has more recently analyzed the hard calculations that recommended the Socialists' support for the war. There are also a number of good older works in English: Carl E. Schorske, *German Social Democracy, 1905–1917: The Development of the Great Schism* (Cambridge, MA, 1955); A. Joseph Berlau, *The German Social Democratic Party, 1914–1921* (New York, 1949); John W. Mishark, *The Road to Revolution: German Marxism and World War I, 1914–1919* (Detroit, 1967). Introductions to the history of the trade unions during the war can be found in Hans-Joachim Bieber, *Gewerkschaften in Krieg und Revolution* (2 vols., Hamburg, 1981); and Klaus Schönhoven (ed.), *Die Gewerkschaften in Weltkrieg und Revolution 1914–1919* (Cologne, 1985). A number of local studies address the factors that promoted (or retarded) the radicalization of the labor movement. These studies include Friedhelm Boll, "Spontaneität der Basis und politische Funktion des Streiks 1914 bis 1918: Das Beispiel Braunschweig," *Archiv für Sozialgeschichte* 17 (1977), 337–66; Boll, *Massenbewegungen in Niedersachsen 1906–1920: Eine sozialgeschichtliche Untersuchung zu den unterschiedlichen Entwicklungstypen Braunschweig und Hannover* (Bonn, 1981); Elizabeth H. Tobin, "War and the Working Class: The Case of Düsseldorf 1914–1918," *Central European History* 17 (1985), 257–99; Mary Nolan, *Social Democracy and Society: Working-Class Radicalism in Düsseldorf, 1890–1920* (Cambridge, 1981); and Volker Ullrich, *Die Hamburger Arbeiterbewegung vom Vorabend des Ersten Weltkrieges bis* *zur Revolution 1918/19* (Hamburg, 1976). See, in addition, the survey of working-class unrest by Gerald D. Feldman, Eberhard Kolb, and Reinhard Rürup, "Die Massenbewegungen der Arbeiterschaft in Deutschland am Ende des Ersten Weltkrieges (1917–1920)," *Politische Vierteljahrschrift* 13 (1972), 84–105.

The emergence of **political opposition** within the labor movement was a moment of truth in the German Democratic Republic, whose scholars were intensely concerned with the history of this phenomenon. In addition to the general East German surveys of the war, in which it functions as the principal plot line, see Heinz Wohlgemuth, *Die Entstehung der Kommunistischen Partei Deutschlands 1914 bis 1918* (Berlin, 1978). A good survey of the literature on the Independent Social Democratic party, as well as an excellent history of the party itself, is to be found in David Morgan, *The Socialist Left and the German Revolution: A History of the German Independent Social Democratic Party, 1917–1922* (Ithaca and London, 1975). Robert Wheeler's *USPD und Internationale: Sozialistischer Internationalismus in der Zeit der Revolution* (Frankfurt, 1975) remains an indispensable account of this phenomenon. Other studies include Hartfrid Krause's political survey, *USPD: Zur Geschichte der Unabhängigen Sozialdemokratischen Partei Deutschlands* (Frankfurt am Main and Cologne, 1975); A. J. Ryder, *The German Revolution of 1918: A Study of German Socialism in War and Revolt* (Cambridge, 1967), 1–139; and Eric D. Weitz's survey, *Creating German Communism, 1890–1990: From Popular Protests to Socialist State* (Princeton, 1997), 62–83. Rosa Luxemburg has been the subject of several biographies, the best of which is J. P. Nettl, *Rosa Luxemburg* (2 vols., Oxford, 1966); but see also Paul Fröhlich's classic, *Rosa Luxemburg: Her Life and Work* (New York and London, 1972); and the East German study by Annelies Laschitza and Günter Radczun, *Rosa Luxemburg: Ihr Wirken in der deutschen Arbeiterbewegung* (Berlin, 1971). On Karl Liebknecht there is Helmut Trotnow, *Karl Liebknecht (1871–1919): A Political Biography* (Hamden, CT, 1984); and Annalies Laschitza and Elke Keller, *Karl Liebknecht: Eine Biographie in Dokumenten* (Berlin, 1982).

Index

NEW APPROACHES TO EUROPEAN HISTORY

11 EDWARD MUIR
Ritual in Early Modern Europe
0 521 40169 0 hardback
0 521 40967 5 paperback

12 R. PO-CHIA HSIA
The World of Catholic Renewal 1540–1770
0 521 44041 6 hardback
0 521 44596 5 paperback

13 ROGER CHICKERING
Imperial Germany and the Great War, 1914–1918
see below (number 27)

14 W. R. WARD
Christianity under the Ancien Régime, 1648–1789
0 521 55361 X hardback
0 521 55672 4 paperback

15 SIMON DIXON
The Modernisation of Russia 1676–1825
0 521 37100 7 hardback
0 521 37961 X paperback

16 MARY LINDEMANN
Medicine and Society in Early Modern Europe
0 521 41254 4 hardback
0 521 42354 6 paperback

17 DONALD QUATAERT
The Ottoman Empire, 1700–1922
0 521 63328 1 hardback
0 521 63360 5 paperback

18 REX A. WADE
The Russian Revolution, 1917
0 521 41548 9 hardback
0 521 42565 4 paperback

19 JAMES R. FARR
Artisans in Europe, 1300–1914
0 521 41888 7 hardback
0 521 42934 X paperback

20 MERRY E. WIESNER
Women and Gender in Early Modern Europe Second edition
0 521 77105 6 harback
0 521 77822 0 paperback